Jawaharlal Nehru

JAWAHARLAL NEHRU

Dr. C.P. Raj
Dr. Ved Prakash

AMIGA PRESS. INC
Delhi -110051

AMIGA PRESS. INC
H.O :- 28-A, Indra Park, Chander Nagar
Delhi :- 110051 (India)
Tel :- 011-22504028, +91-98736-57000
Email :- amigapress@gmail.com
amigaeditorial@gmail.com
Website :- www.amigapress@co.in

This edition is published by Amiga Press.Inc

ISBN : 978-93-84533-25-0

First Published 2018

PRINTED : THOMSON PRESS INDIA

Preface

Pandit Jawaharlal Nehru (November 14,1889–May 27, 1964) was a major political leader of the Congress Party, a pivotal figure in the Indian independence movement and the first Prime Minister of independent India. Nehru's greatest contribution to India in the importance that he had given to science, technology and industrialisation without which progress was impossible. He was fighting alongside the main currents of socio-cultural life in the country. He was opposed to traditions and superstitions.

In the 1920s, Nehru was elected president of the All India Trade Unions Congress. He and Subhash Chandra Bose had become the most prominent youth leaders, and both demanded outright political independence of India. In 1927, he became a member of the League against Imperialism created in Brussels. Nehru criticised the Nehru Report prepared by his father in 1928, which called for dominion status for India within the British Empire. The radicalism of Nehru and Bose would provoke intense debates during the 1928 Congress session in Guwahati. Arguing that India would deliver an ultimatum to the British and prepare for mass struggle, Nehru and Bose won the hearts of many young Indians. To resolve the issue, Gandhi said that the British would be given two years to grant India dominion status. If they did not, the Indian National Congress (INC) would launch a national struggle for full political independence. Nehru and Bose succeeded in reducing the statutory deadline to one year.

Prime Minister Nehru led the Congress to major election victories in 1957 and 1962. The Parliament passed extensive reforms that increased the legal rights of women in Hindu society, and further legislated against caste discrimination and untouchability. Nehru advocated a strong initiative to enroll India's children to complete primary education, and thousands of schools, colleges and institutions of advanced learning, such as the Indian Institutes of Technology were founded across the nation. Nehru advocated a socialist model for the economy of India—no taxation for Indian farmers, minimum wage and benefits for blue-collar workers, and the nationalization of heavy industries such as steel, aviation, shipping, electricity and mining. An extensive public works and industrialization campaign resulted in the construction of major dams, irrigation canals, roads, thermal and hydroelectric power stations.

Nehru's foreign policy was the inspiration of the Non-Aligned Movement, of which India was a co-founder. Nehru maintained friendly relations with both the United States and the Soviet Union, and encouraged the People's Republic of China to join the global community of nations. In 1956, when the Suez Canal Company was seized by the Egyptian government, an international conference voted 18-4 to take action against Egypt. India was one of the 4 backers of Egypt, along with Indonesia, Sri Lanka, and the USSR.

India had controversially opposed the partition of Palestine and the 1956 invasion of the Sinai by Israel, Britain and France, but did not oppose the Chinese occupation of Tibet and the suppression of a pro-democracy movement in Hungary by the Soviet Union. Although Nehru disavowed nuclear ambitions for India, Canada and France aided India in the development of nuclear power stations for electricity. India also negotiated an agreement in 1960 with Pakistan on the just use of the waters of seven rivers shared by the countries.

Nehru has asked us to understand the spirit of his writing and not merely find the meanings.

—*Editor*

Contents

1

Biography

Pandit Jawaharlal Nehru (November 14,1889–May 27, 1964) was a major political leader of the Congress Party, a pivotal figure in the Indian independence movement and the first Prime Minister of independent India. He was also a key figure in international politics in the post-war period (in which he was considered the leader of third world interests) and patriarch of the Nehru-Gandhi family, one of the most influential forces in Indian politics. He is popularly referred to as Panditji (*Scholar*) and Pandit Nehru.

The son of the wealthy Indian barrister and politician Motilal Nehru, Nehru became a leader of the left-wing of the Indian National Congress at a remarkably young age. Rising to Congress President under the mentorship of Mahatma Gandhi, Nehru was a charismatic, radical leader, advocating complete independence from the British Empire, and was eventually recognised as Gandhi's political heir. A life-long liberal intellectually, Nehru was also an advocate for Fabian socialism and the public sector as the means by which long-standing challenges of economic development could be addressed.

Serving as Congress President, Nehru raised the flag of independent India in New Delhi on August 15, 1947, and served as Prime Minister. His daughter Indira and grandson Rajiv would both also serve as Prime Minister and President of the Indian National Congress, as would Rajiv's wife Sonia. His long tenure was instrumental in shaping the traditions and structures of independent India.

CHILDHOOD AND FAMILY OF JAWAHARLAL NEHRU

Jawaharlal Nehru, the first Prime Minister of India, had a strong and influential lineage. Born on the 14th of November, 1889 at Allahabad, Jawaharlal Nehru was the eldest child of Motilal Nehru and Swarup Rani. His family was from Kashimiri heritage and belonged to a high Hindu caste. They were Saraswat Brahmins, who were revered greatly in Allahabad in those days. Originally part of the Kashmiri Pandit community, the Nehrus had to shift to what was called United Provinces. But the family gelled well with the people there and Motilal Nehru, Jawaharlal's father, started practicing law in Allahabad. He was also a highly influential man, both socially as well as politically. He was a learned scholar too. He excelled in several languages that included Persian, Urdu, Arabic, English and many more.

Jawaharlal Nehru and his entire family lived in a large house called 'Anand Bhawan' in Allahabad. The house is still there. Motilal Nehru was a successful man, who was also well known in the society. He was a barrister by profession and won several accolades for his legal works from different spheres. All these brought him lot of name and fame. As a result, he could give his children the best of everything in life. Jawaharlal Nehru was his only son, while he also had two beautiful daughters named Vijaya Lakshmi Pandit and Krishna Pandit. No discrimination was made between the son and daughters in the family. All of them were provided quality education and privileges. All the children were brought amidst immense luxury and comfort. With a swimming pool and a tennis court in the house premises, Jawaharlal Nehru led a lavish life.

Motilal Nehru never compromised on the education and other facilities that are required to make a happy upbringing for children. He emphasized on English and western education for his children. Jawaharlal Nehru received his initial education at home under an English governess. Hindi and Sanskrit were also taught to the children at the Nehru House. Training was also provided to converse in English fluently. Apart from formal education, various English mannerisms and customs were also taught to Jawaharlal Nehru in his childhood days. The dresses that were adorned by the Nehru family also reflected English style. After some formal education at home, Jawaharlal Nehru also went to a local convent school in Allahabad. At the age of fifteen, he went to England to study at Harrow.

The illustrious family of the Nehrus had a deep impact on the life and childhood of Jawaharlal Nehru. At home, his mother practiced several staunch Hindu customs and even tried to influence young Nehru by them. But she was not much successful in it. Motilal was not a very strong follower of religion, but he was not an absolute atheist too. Motilal Nehru was concerned about very minute details regarding his son. He corresponded with his son, even when he was abroad and enquired about every small detail regarding his stay, studies and all the other curricular activities. Even after coming back from abroad, Jawaharlal Nehru began a firm and solid career with the help of his father. He attained instant fame and glory in his profession and made himself and his family proud.

Motilal Nehru was an active member of the Indian National Congress, which had also influenced and helped in shaping the political life of Jawaharlal

Nehru. Motilal Nehru shared extremely good and cordial relation with the British officials. He had a strong belief on British justice and British promises. Several incidents have been sited when Motilal Nehru had been in support of the British officers. His home was also open to various British officers. British officers also respected him and his family and welcomed them to their homes. As a result of this intermingling, Jawaharlal Nehru and his two sisters also got opportunities to have a glimpse of British lifestyle. Some of the British officers could also fluently speak Urdu and Hindi.

Motilal Nehru was a stylish man and he loved to live life luxuriously. He was a follower of beauty and beautiful things. He had the passion of collecting various beautiful articles from various parts of India as well as from foreign countries. He had made a huge collection of artifacts that were considered as masterpieces and rare articles. One of the most important facts that were seen in the family of Jawaharlal Nehru was that, there were no class restrictions or class distinctions. People of all castes and religions were accepted and welcomed in 'Anand Bhawan'. There were many servants in the Nehru household, who belonged to different castes and religions. The doors of 'Anand Bhawan' remained open for all people irrespective of differences in caste and religion.

Another important part of the family of Jawaharlal Nehru was the active participation of his two sisters, Vijaya Lakshmi Pandit and Krishna Pandit in various matters of the family as well as in politics. They supported him and he had a great influence on their lives. Vijaya Lakshmi Pandit mentioned in one of her lectures about the childhood they had spent together. She also emphasized on the influence that Jawaharlal Nehru had on her political career and personal life.

Jawaharlal Nehru did not have a blissful married life. He was married at a young age in the year 1916. When he was at Harrow, Motilal Nehru and his wife decided to find a perfect match for Jawaharlal Nehru. They started their search and found Kamala Kaul, a girl from a middle-class Kashmiri Brahmin family in 1912. She was a thirteen year old girl, well-educated at home and knew Hindu and Urdu. They waited till 1916, when Kamala attained the age of seventeen years. Kamala was finally married to Jawaharlal Nehru in February, 1916.

The initial years of marriage were not very happy for Kamala as Nehru was then basking in glory and paid little importance to the home front. Kamala Nehru was a strong woman and she endured all this without any protest. She also had to endure several blunt remarks from her husband's relatives regarding her inferior social origins. But she did not retaliate to any of these. She began to involve herself in the Indian freedom struggle and even went to the prison. This event also helped her to come closer to her husband. Jawaharlal Nehru and Kamala Nehru also had a beautiful daughter in 1917, who was called Indira Priyadarshini Gandhi. Kamala Nehru also gave birth to a pre-matured baby boy, who died in 1924. After that she underwent a miscarriage after three years.

Kamala Nehru could not bear this trauma and fell seriously ill. She was diagnosed of tuberculosis and underwent treatment in various hospitals in the country as well as abroad. It was during this time that Jawaharlal Nehru realized his love and passion for her. He used to visit her regularly and even took her abroad for treatment. They also spent few days in Switzerland. Finally she breathed her last in 1936. To summarize, it has been observed that childhood of Jawaharlal Nehru had a great influence on the later life of this great Indian personality. Though he was brought up amidst immense luxury and glory, it did not restrict him from mingling with general masses and feeling their pulse. His family also had a great influence on his social and political career.

EARLY LIFE

Jawaharlal Nehru was born in the city of Allahabad, situated along the banks of the Ganges River (now in the state of Uttar Pradesh). He was the eldest child of Swarup Rani, the wife of wealthy barrister Motilal Nehru. The Nehru family descended from Kashmiri heritage and belonged to the Saraswat Brahmin caste of Hindus. Training as a lawyer, Motilal had moved to Allahabad and developed a successful practise and had become active in India's largest political party, the Indian National Congress. Nehru and his sisters — Vijaya Lakshmi and Krishna — lived in a large mansion called Anand Bhavan and were raised with English customs, mannerisms and dress. While learning Hindi and Sanskrit, the Nehru children would be trained to converse fluently and regularly in English.

After being tutored at home and attending some of the most modern schools in India, Nehru travelled to England at the age of 15 to attend Harrow. Nicknamed "Joe" while there, he proceeded to study natural sciences at Trinity College, Cambridge before choosing to train as a barrister at the Inner Temple in London.

Frequenting the theatres, museums and opera houses of London, he would spend his vacations travelling across Europe. Observers later described him as an elegant, charming young intellectual and socialite. Nehru also actively participated in the political activities of the Indian student community, growing increasingly attracted to socialism and liberalism, which were beginning to influence the politics and economies of Europe.

Upon his return to India, Nehru's marriage was arranged with Kamala Kaul. Married on February 8, 1916, Nehru was 27 and his bride was 17 years old, at the time. The first few years of their marriage were hampered by the cultural gulf between the anglicized Nehru and Kamala, who observed Hindu traditions and focused on family affairs. The following year Kamala gave birth to their only child, their daughter Indira Priyadarshini. Having made few attempts to establish himself in a legal practise, Nehru was immediately attracted to Indian political life, which at the time was emerging from divisions over World War I. The moderate and extremist factions of the Congress had reunited in its 1916 session in Lucknow, and Indian politicians had demanded *Home Rule* and dominion status for India. Joining the Congress under the patronage of his father, Nehru grew increasingly disillusioned with the liberal and anglicized nature of Congress politicians, which included his father. Although frequently hailed as a future leader of the Congress and India, Nehru's political rise did not begin until the arrival of Mahatma Gandhi on India's political arena.

Young Leader

Nehru was very strongly attracted to Gandhi's philosophy and leadership. Gandhi had led a successful rebellion on behalf of indentured Indian workers while a lawyer in South Africa. Upon his return to India, Gandhi organised the peasants and farmers of Champaran and Kheda in successful rebellions against oppressive tax policies levied by the British. Gandhi espoused what he termed as *satyagraha* — mass civil disobedience governed by *ahimsa*, or complete non-violence. A forceful exponent of Indian self-reliance, Gandhi's success electrified Indians, who had been divided in their approach to contesting British rule. Having met Gandhi and learning his ideas, Nehru assisted him during the Champaran agitation.

Following Gandhi's example, Nehru and his family abandoned their Western-style clothes, possessions and wealthy lifestyle. Wearing clothes spun out of *khadi*, Nehru emerged as one of the most energetic supporters of Gandhi. Under Gandhi's influence, Nehru began studying the *Bhagavad Gita* and practiced yoga throughout his life.

He would increasingly look to Gandhi for advice and guidance in his personal life, and would spend a lot of time travelling and living with Gandhi. Nehru travelled across India delivering political speeches aimed at recruiting India's masses, especially its youth into the agitation launched in 1919 against the Rowlatt Acts and the Khilafat struggle. He spoke passionately and forcefully to encourage Hindu-Muslim unity, spread education and self-reliance and the need to eradicate social evils such as untouchability, poverty, ignorance and unemployment. Emerging as a key orator and prominent organiser, Nehru became one of the most popular political leaders in northern India, especially with the people of the United Provinces, Bihar and the Central Provinces. His youth and passion for social justice and equality attracted India's Muslims, women and other minorities.

Nehru's role grew especially important following the arrest of senior leaders such as Gandhi and his father, and he was also imprisoned along with his mother and sisters for many months. Alarmed by growing violence in the conduct of mass agitations, Gandhi suspended the struggle after the killing of 22 state policemen by a mob at Chauri Chaura on February 4, 1922. This sudden move disillusioned some, including Nehru's father Motilal, who joined the newly formed Swaraj Party in 1923. However, Nehru remained loyal to Gandhi and publicly supported him.

A lull in nationalist activities enabled Nehru to turn his attention to social causes and local government. In 1924, he was elected president of the municipal corporation of Allahabad, serving as the city's chief executive for two years. Nehru launched ambitious schemes to promote education, sanitation, expand water and electricity supply and reduce unemployment — his ideas and experience proved valuable to him when he would assume charge of India's government in 1947. Achieving some success, Nehru was dissatisfied and angered by the obstruction of British officials and corruption amongst civil servants. He resigned from his position within two years.

In the early part of the decade, his marriage and family life had suffered owing to the constant activity on his part and that of his father. Although facing domestic pressures and tensions in the absence of her husband, Kamala would increasingly travel with Nehru, address public meetings and seek to sponsor and encourage nationalist activities in her hometown. In the late 1920s, the initial marital gulf between the two disappeared and the couple grew closer to each other and their daughter. In 1926 Nehru took his wife and daughter to Europe so that Kamala could receive special medical care. The family travelled and lived in England, Switzerland, France and Germany. Continuing his political work, Nehru was deeply impressed by the rising currents of radical socialism in Europe, and delivered fervent speeches in condemnation of imperialism. On a visit to the Soviet Union, Nehru was favourably impressed by the command economy, but grew critical of Stalin's totalitarianism.

Congress President

In the 1920s, Nehru was elected president of the All India Trade Unions Congress. He and Subhash Chandra Bose had become the most prominent youth leaders, and both demanded outright political independence of India. In 1927, he became a member of the League against Imperialism created in Brussels. Nehru criticised the Nehru Report prepared by his father in 1928, which called for dominion status for India within the British Empire. The radicalism of Nehru and Bose would provoke intense debates during the 1928 Congress session in Guwahati. Arguing that India would deliver an ultimatum to the British and prepare for mass struggle, Nehru and Bose won the hearts of many young Indians. To resolve the issue, Gandhi said that the British would be given two years to grant India dominion status. If they did not, the Indian National Congress (INC) would launch a national struggle for full political independence. Nehru and Bose succeeded in reducing the statutory deadline to one year.

The failure of talks with the British caused the December 1929 session in Lahore to be held in an atmosphere charged with anti-Empire sentiment. Preparing for the declaration of independence, the AICC elected Jawaharlal Nehru as Congress President at the encouragement of Gandhi. Nehru himself recalled that he was sensible of the fact that it was considered somewhat surprising:

> *"I have seldom felt quite so annoyed and humiliated... It is not that I was not sensible of the honour... But I did not come to it by the main entrance or even the side entrance: I appeared suddenly from a trap door and bewildered the audience into acceptance."*

On December 31, 1929 President Nehru hoisted the flag of independence before a massive public gathering along the banks of the Ravi River. The Congress would promulgate the *Purna Swaraj* (*Complete Independence*) declaration on January 26, 1930. With the launching of the Salt Satyagraha in 1930, Nehru travelled across Gujarat and other parts of the country participating and encouraging in the mass rebellion against the salt tax. Despite his father's death in 1931, Nehru and his family remained at the forefront of the struggle. Arrested with his wife and sisters, Nehru was imprisoned for all but four months between 1931 and 1935. During that same period, however, his popularity grew enormously. According to John Gunther, Nehru was both "distrustful of it, while simultaneously unable to control being somewhat " exhilarated and impressed".

His family quickly chastened him with raillery; his wife and sisters, and even his small daughter, began to call him in the home the names he was given by the crowd. They would say, "Oh Jewel of India, what time is it?" or "Oh Embodiment of Sacrifice, please pass the bread."

Nehru was released by the British and he traveled with his family once again to Europe in 1935, where his ailing wife Kamala would remain bedridden. Torn between the freedom struggle and tending to his wife, Nehru would travel back and forth between India and Europe. Kamala Nehru died on February 28, 1936. Deeply saddened, Nehru nevertheless continued to maintain a hectic schedule. In her memory, he wore a fresh rose on his coat for the rest of his life.

His popularity continued to grow, and his personal discomfort with that popularity rose with it. In the November, 1937 issue of the Calcutta-based journal *Modern Review*, an article entitled 'The Rashtrapati' severely criticized him. The anonymous author acknowledged Nehru's initiative and innate drive but also pointed out glaring streaks of autocracy, saying that his character was marked by "intolerance of others and a certain contempt for the weak and inefficient". The author, who signed himself "*Chanakya*", added that Nehru's conceit was "already formidable", and worried that soon "Jawaharlal might fancy himself as a Caesar". It was not suspected at the time that *Chanakya* was Nehru himself. This publication is a significantly important example of autocritique.

Nehru had been re-elected Indian National Congress(INC) President in 1936, and had presided over its session in Lucknow. Here he participated in a fierce debate with Gandhi, Patel and other Congress leaders over the adoption of socialism as the official goal of the party. Younger socialists such as Jaya Prakash Narayan, Mridula Sarabhai, Narendra Dev and Asoka Mehta began to see Nehru as leader of Congress socialists. Under their pressure, the Congress passed the *Avadi Resolution* proclaiming socialism as the model for India's future government. Nehru was re-elected the following year, and oversaw the Congress national campaign for the 1937 elections. Largely leaving political organisation work to others, Nehru travelled the length and breadth of the country, exhorting the masses on behalf of the Congress, which would win an outright majority in the central and most of the provincial legislatures. Although he did not contest elections himself, Nehru was seen by the national media as the leader of the Congress.

Maulana Azad and Nehru

At the outbreak of World War II, the Assemblies were informed that the Viceroy had unilaterally declared war on the Axis on behalf of India, without consulting the people's representatives. Outraged at the viceroy's arbitrary decision, all elected Congressmen resigned from their offices at the instigation of Subhash Bose and Nehru. But even as Bose would call for an outright revolt and would proceed to seek the aid of Nazi Germany and Japan, Nehru remained sympathetic to the British cause. He joined Maulana Azad, Chakravarthi Rajagopalachari and Patel in offering Congress support for the war effort in return for a commitment from the British to grant independence after the war.

In doing so, Nehru broke ranks with Gandhi, who had resisted in supporting war and remained suspicious of the British. The failure of negotiations and Britain's refusal to concede independence outraged the nationalist movement. Gandhi and Patel called for an all-out rebellion, a demand that was opposed by Rajagopalachari and resisted by Nehru and Azad. After intensive debates and heated discussions, the Congress leaders called for the British to *Quit India* — to transfer power to Indian hands immediately or face a mass rebellion.

Despite his skepticism, Nehru travelled the country to exhort India's masses into rebellion. He was arrested with the entire Congress Working Committee on August 9, 1942 and transported to a maximum security prison at a fort in Ahmednagar. Here he remained incarcerated with his colleagues till June 1945. His daughter Indira and her husband Feroze Gandhi were also imprisoned for a few months. Nehru's first grandchild, Rajiv Gandhi was born in 1944.

After his release from prison at the end of the Second World War, Nehru immediately resumed his political work and toured through India preparing grounds for the elections that had been promised for 1946. In October 1945, with the decisions to carry on with the INA trials announced, Nehru was instrumental in announcing the formation of the INA Defence Committee for the defence of the officers of the Indian National Army who faced court Martial in Delhi. Nehru chaired the INA Defence Committee and the legal defence team, while at the same time carrying on with his political work.

EDUCATION OF JAWAHARLAL NEHRU

Jawaharlal Nehru was the first Prime Minister of India. He was also a major persona in the Indian Independence movement. The early education of Jawaharlal Nehru played a major role in his political views and economic policies.

Jawaharlal Nehru was the son of Motilal Nehru. Motilal Nehru was a wealthy barrister by profession. He practiced English law in the colonial Indian courts. The family belonged to the educated genteel class. It was also to a large extent anglicized. Jawaharlal Nehru received primary education under the guidance of an English governess. Young Jawaharlal was taught to converse in English from an early age. He also learnt the appropriate customs of the British Raj.

Motilal Nehru wanted his son to get a proper English education. He wished his son to qualify for and serve the Indian Civil Services or I.C.S. He sent his son Jawaharlal to Harrow, the elite Public school in England. Jawaharlal Nehru was to spend the next six years of his life by studying at the hallowed portals of Harrow and Cambridge.

The young Jawaharlal did not enjoy his schooling at Harrow. He found the school syllabus stifling and the standard of residency conditions unbearable. All students of the school were forced to condition themselves to the daily specter of bathing and washing themselves in cold water. After completing school, Nehru took the University of Cambridge entrance examinations in 1907. The same year, he got admission into the University.

Jawaharlal Nehru studied natural sciences at Cambridge University. His chosen subjects were physics, chemistry and geology. Jawaharlal Nehru was weak in mathematics. For this reason, Physics was later substituted by botany.

The tripos subjects taken up at Cambridge University were not voluntarily chosen by Nehru. He studied the three natural science subjects with only one aim, to pass the Indian Civil Services examination. Nevertheless, Jawaharlal Nehru enjoyed his stay at Cambridge. The liberal atmosphere of the University encouraged him to do a host of non-academic activities. Jawaharlal Nehru passed the final Cambridge degree examinations successfully, where he stood second.

Jawaharlal Nehru joined the Inner Temple for his legal studies in October 1910. This decision, again, was not taken due to Nehru's fascination with the law. The event merely marked a career move as charted by his barrister father Motilal Nehru. Jawaharlal Nehru passed the Bar final examination in 1912. After clearing the examination, he was called to the bar later that year.

Nehru's education years at England fostered in him the Indian nationalist movement.

He believed that the colonial English administration wilfully discriminated against Indians. This thinking was further fuelled by the abrasive attitude of the British Imperial order against Indians. Jawaharlal was attracted by the socialism of the British Fabians. The forte of equality in socialism acted as a magnet for the impressionable Jawaharlal Nehru.

Jawaharlal Nehru was very much influenced by the socialist and liberal political atmosphere prevalent in Europe in those days. The 1900s heralded the culmination of the Western Age of Enlightenment. The atmosphere of liberalism prevalent in that era emphasized the importance of the rights of the individual. It also emphasized on the rights of the equality of opportunity. This liberal viewpoint came to prominence during Nehru's later years. His British sojourn also instilled in him a secular ethos that was far ahead of his time. This moral uprightness would help him to dream of a new India that would accommodate citizens of all religions.

London was a hotbed of political movements in the early part of the 20th century. The student Jawaharlal Nehru liked to visit the cultural attractions of the capital city of the British Empire. He frequented the museums, opera houses and the theatres of London. Nehru was influenced by the deep social cauldron of pre-World War I London. Socialism was one of the prominent influences affecting the English political class at that time.

The early education of Jawaharlal Nehru influenced him in his later life. The influence was clearly visible on the economic policies adopted by the Indian state after its independence in 1947. Nehru clearly favoured a more socialist approach when compared to other South Asian economies. The first Prime Minister was clearly thinking about his heady educational period in London when he promulgated the socialist ideology that influenced Indian government of the 1950's. The economy was treated with a mixed control. The Indian government was in control of the primary industries like electricity, mining and heavy engineering workshops.

The socialist leaning of Jawaharlal Nehru was apparent in the land redistribution programme announced by the Indian government in the middle of the 20th century. The rural sector was given importance. Nehru correctly thought that since the majority of the Indian population lived in its villages, the rural sector should also get a lion's share of the country's economic resources. Dams were built. Canals were dug. The British education of Nehru is starkly visible in the promotion of fertilizers to increase the crop yield of the land.

The British education of Jawaharlal Nehru is also displayed in the Prime Minister's quest for independent energy sufficiency. Nehru actively promoted the acquiring and development of Nuclear Energy. Hydro-electric power projects were also enthusiastically taken. The License Raj was also his creation.

The License Raj was a unique byproduct of Nehru's combined Social-Liberal philosophy. The License Raj was started with the view to help the Indian industrial sector. The intention led to limited success. Indian industries soon became unprofitable and became globally uncompetitive. The failure of the License Raj led to its gradual scrapping by successive Indian governments from the 1980's.

Jawaharlal Nehru was the epitome of a resurgent India in the middle of the 20th century. He had the best of worlds, a privileged British education and an Indian upbringing. His study at the Harrow School helped him to get a firm grounding of the British cultural ethos. This was further cemented by his attendance at the Trinity College in the University of Cambridge. His stint as a Barrister at the Inner Temple in London helped to hone his already sharp negotiation skills at the bar. This legal training would help him to negotiate the treacherous minefield of pre-independence British politics from 1910 to 1947.

Chronological Proceedings Influencing Nehru's Thought

An attempt has been made to present the formative influences on Nehru's thought, his political ideas in the achievement of social goals. In assessing the multidimensional personality of a leader, his contribution to history, society, politics, Indian state, and his role as the Prime Minister should be seen in the light of the total perspective of events. In making an assessment of his contribution to modern India' we should examine the various influences, both of ideas and persons, that moulded and shaped his thought and personality.

"Leadership operates under the complex interaction of social forces - political aspirations, social relationships, economic wants, nationalism and religious beliefs. This factor explains the behaviour of different leaders operating differently even in contemporary conditions:. The situational factor is very important in understanding the various actions of a leader. Seeming contradictions in his behaviour can often be resolved only by unravelling the difficult knot of circumstances that ultimately contains all the contending influences in a given situation.

In 1909, Indian nationalists were annoyed when the British officials were playing up the differences between Hindus and Muslism. In a letter to Jawaharlal Nehru, Motilal wrote on March 25,1909 that the leaders of both the communities had no love amongst themselves. He explained to his son that the masses of both communities existed as good friends and the tension should not filter to the lower classes. Then nation building would be a thing of the past. Which the Anglo-Indian friends have distinctly scored. The emergence of the Hindu Mahasabha as a counterblast to Muslim League would weaken the foundation of the Congress.

Jawaharlal Nehru, was not only a fervent soul but always active. He felt that Gandhiji had electrified atmosphere by giving a new turn to the Congress and involving the people in the freedom struggle. His basic trait was aversion to communal politics. The moderate school usually consisted of communal politicians. He had seen that the leaders of Muslim League and Hindu Mahasabha were competitive in winning favours from the British government. When Poorna Swaraj. complete independence was the demand of the Congress leaders, the communal leaders were inquisitive of the respective positions their communities would possess in independent India. Nehru entered politics when Congress was an instrument of Indian nationalism under the influences of Tila, Mrs.Beasant and Gandhi.

The Constitutional Act 1919 which divided India into numerous divide compartments in the legislature was according to Nehru a dangerous proposition. He said "I am afraid I cannot get excited over this communal issue important as it is temporarily. It is after all a side issue and it ran have no real importance in the larger scheme of things. I have no fear and my vision of a future India contains no communalism". This beginning of nationalism should be viewed against this cultural background of intellectual ferment, with the westernised elite turning towards liberalism and the conservatives to Hinduism and Islam respectively. The liberal advocates of social and political reform were uncompromising due to their disapproval of traditional culture, which they thought that it was a retrogressive force, submerging the masses in superstition.

For a brief period after the 1916 Lucknow Pact, the relationship between India's Hindus and Muslims was amicable. Upto 1920, as long as Mohammed Ali Jinnah was a member of Congress tensions were less. After 1923, tensions flared up between the various communal groups and in Jawaharlal Nehru's view, the major goals of Congress were in grave danger of being jeopardized. Especially in North India there was deterioration of Hindu-Muslim relations.

The bitterness among the communal leaders at the top, led to the rigid political communal demands. The Muslim political reactionaries helped by the British Government became prominent. The Hindu political reactionaries also succeeded in raising the communal temper of the country. Congress was in a quandary and most of the Congressmen were communists under their national cloak. Due to this Sikhs as a particular communal group loudly voiced their particular demands. According to Gandhi communal problem could only be solved by goodwill and the generosity of the majority group and consented to Muslims demands. British government's policy in India was divide and rule. The Congress blamed the Government and communalist groups tor spreading communal ism and the latter blamed the Congress.

This problem could not have been solved by market place tactics. The third party is dominant and hands out its gifts to the prize boys of its choice. Our leaders thought within the narrow steel frame of the political freedom only without, considering any social change or economic freedom for the masses. It meant the removal of the financial links which was binding India to London, this inter-connection would have easily changed the social structure. The Indian leaders' outlook was reformist rather than revolutionary. The then atmosphere was not conducive for solving the communal problem by reformist - methods.

The situation demanded revolutionary outlook, planning and revolutionary solutions. Lack of clear ideals and objectives led to the spread of communalism. There was hardly any connection between the day to day sufferings and the fight for swaraj. Instincts of the people were exploited by the communalist in the name of religion. The leaders of the communal groups demanded a handful of jobs to upper middle classes and a special demand for additional seats in the legislatures symbolic of political power merely for patronage.

They were motivated by religious passions. Political reactionaries in the guise of communal leaders obstructed political advance. This was the unsavory situation "Muslim communal leaders said the most amazing things and seemed to care not at all for Indian nationalism or Indian freedom; Hindu communal leaders, though always speaking apparently in the name of nationalism, had little to do with it in practice, and incapable of any real action, sought to humble themselves before the Government, and did that too in vain. Both agreed in condemning socialistic and such like "subversive" movement:;, there was a touching unanimity in regard to any proposal affecting vested interests".

In mid-twenties a unity conference was held after which the Hindus and Muslims became tolerant and respectful of one another's religious practices and beliefs. Communal tensions further escalated when voting was based or separate electorates. It was painful tor Nehru when the troubles were in his home town Allahabad. In a letter to Dr.Syed Mahmud dated May 24, 1926, Nehru wrote, "I do not attach very much importance to political squabbles, but the communal frenzy is awful to contemplate. We seem to have been caught in a whirlpool of mutual hatred and we go round and round and down and down this abyss.

For months or even a year or more we have thought that the situation was so bad that it could not become worse. But it does (grow) worse and heaven knows where it will end. 'No country or people who are slaves to dogma....can progress, and unhappily our country and people have become extraordinarily dogmatic and little minded...

Religion as practised in India has turn out to be the old man of the sea for us and it has not only broken our backs but stultified and almost killed all originality of thought and mind. I have no patience left with the legitimate and illegitimate offspring of religion". He personally thought that it was impossible to cooperate with communalists provided the political objective was same. There is no meeting ground between progress and reaction, between those who struggle for freedom and those content with servitude. The political reaction covered with communalism takes advantage of the fear of each others community. Honest communalism was fear and false communalism was political reactions. The British government was supporting the reactionary leaders (Muslims) and ignoring the nationalists. Thus they were rearing communal feeling and simultaneously weakening the national struggle. History shows that this has always been done by rulers. *By* helping the Britishers, the Muslims were an addition to their proposed special powers and to show to the world how necessary their continued presence in India was.

INDIA'S FIRST PRIME MINISTER

Nehru and his colleagues had been released as the British Cabinet Mission arrived to propose plans for transfer of power. The Congress held a presidential election in the knowledge that its chosen leader would become India's head of government.

Once elected, Nehru headed an interim government, which was impaired by outbreaks of communal violence and political disorder, and the opposition of the Muslim League led by Muhammad Ali Jinnah, who were demanding a separate Muslim state of Pakistan. After failed bids to form coalitions, Nehru reluctantly supported the partition of India as per a plan released by the British on June 3, 1947. He would take office as the Prime Minister of India on August 15, and delivered his inaugural address titled "A Tryst With Destiny:"

"Long years ago we made a tryst with destiny, and now the time comes when we shall redeem our pledge, not wholly or in full measure, but very substantially. At the stroke of the midnight hour, when the world sleeps, India will awake to life and freedom. A moment comes, which comes but rarely in history, when we step out from the old to the new, when an age ends, and when the soul of a nation, long suppressed, finds utterance. It is fitting that at this solemn moment we take the pledge of dedication to the service of India and her people and to the still larger cause of humanity."

However, this period was marked with intense communal violence. This violence swept across the Punjab region, Delhi, Bengal and other parts of India. Nehru conducted joint tours with Pakistani leaders to encourage peace and calm angry and disillusioned refugees. Nehru would work with Maulana Azad and other Muslim leaders to safeguard and encourage Muslims to remain in India.

The violence of the time deeply affected Nehru, who called for a ceasefire and UN intervention to stop the Indo-Pakistani War of 1947. Fearing communal reprisals, Nehru also hesitated in supporting the annexation of Hyderabad State, and clashed with Patel on the Kashmir dispute and relations with Pakistan. Nehru asserted his own control over Kashmir policy while Patel objected to Nehru sidelining his Home Ministry's officials. Nehru felt offended by Patel's decision-making regarding the states' integration without consulting either him or the Cabinet. Patel asked Gandhi to relieve him of his obligation to serve. He knew that he lacked Nehru's youth and popularity, and believed that an open political battle would hurt India. After much personal deliberation and contrary to Patel's prediction, Gandhi on January 30, 1948 told Patel not to leave the Government, and to stay by Nehru's side in joint leadership. A free India, according to Gandhi, desperately needed both Patel and Nehru's joint leadership.

Nehru climbs atop the gate at Birla House to announce the death of Gandhi to the crowd outside. This photograph by Henri Cartier-Bresson is one of the most famous images of the 1940s.

Gandhi was assassinated on January 30, 1948. At Gandhi's wake, Nehru and Patel embraced each other and addressed the nation together. Despite working together, the two leaders would clash on various issues. Nehru declined Patel's counsel on sending assistance to Tibet in 1950 with the disputed entrance of the People's Republic of China and ejecting the Portuguese from Goa by military force. When Nehru pressured Dr. Rajendra Prasad to decline a nomination to become the first President of India in 1950 in favour of Rajagopalachari, he thus angered the party, which felt Nehru was attempting to impose his will. Nehru sought Patel's help in winning the party over, but Patel declined, and Prasad was duly elected. When Nehru opposed the 1950 Congress presidential candidacy of Purushottam Das Tandon, a conservative Hindu leader, he endorsed Jivatram Kripalani and threatened to resign if Tandon was elected. Patel rejected Nehru's views and endorsed Tandon in Gujarat, in a disputed election where Kripalani received not one vote despite hailing from that state himself.

In the years following independence, Nehru frequently turned to his daughter Indira to look after him and manage his personal affairs. Following Patel's death in 1950, Nehru became the most popular and powerful Indian politician. Under his leadership, the Congress won an overwhelming majority in the elections of 1952, in which his son-in-law Feroze Gandhi was also elected. Indira moved into Nehru's official residence to attend to him, inadvertently estranging her husband, who would become a critic of Nehru's government. Nevertheless, Indira would virtually become Nehru's chief of staff and constant companion in his travels across India and the world.

ACHIEVEMENTS AS PRIME PINISTER

In the 35 years from 1929, when Gandhi chose Nehru as president of the Congress session at Lahore, until his death as prime minister in 1964, Nehru remained—despite the Chinese debacle of 1962—the idol of his people. Nehru imported and imparted modern values and ways of thinking, which he adapted to Indian conditions. Apart from his stress on secularism and on the basic unity of India, despite its racial and religious diversities, Nehru was deeply concerned with carrying India forward into the modern age of scientific discovery and technological development. In addition, he aroused in his people an awareness of the necessity of social concern with the poor and the outcast and of respect for democratic values. One of the achievements of which he was particularly proud was the reform of the ancient Hindu civil code that finally enabled Hindu widows to enjoy equality with men in matters of inheritance and property.

Internationally, Nehru's star was in the ascendant until October 1956, when India's attitude on the Hungarian revolt against the Soviets brought his policy of nonalignment under sharp scrutiny. In the United Nations, India was the only non-aligned country to vote with the erstwhile Soviet Union on the invasion of Hungary, and thereafter it was difficult for Nehru to command credibility in his calls for non-alignment.

In the early years after independence, anticolonialism had been the cornerstone of his foreign policy, but, by the time of the Belgrade conference of non-aligned countries in 1961, Nehru had substituted non-alignment for anticolonialism as his pressing concern. In 1962, however, the Chinese threatened to overrun the Brahmaputra River valley as a result of a long-standing border dispute. Nehru called for Western aid, exposing the weakness of his non-alignment policy, and China withdrew.

Kashmir—claimed by both India and Pakistan—remained a perennial problem throughout Nehru's term as prime minister. His tentative efforts to settle the dispute by adjustments along the cease-fire lines having failed, Pakistan, in 1948, made an unsuccessful attempt to seize Kashmir by force. In solving the problem of the Portuguese colony of Goa—the last remaining colony in India—Nehru was more fortunate. Although its military occupation by Indian troops in December 1961 raised a furore in many Western countries, in the hindsight of history, Nehru's action is justifiable. With the withdrawal of the British and the French, the Portuguese colonial presence in India had become an anachronism.

Both the British and the French had withdrawn peacefully. If the Portuguese were not prepared to follow suit, Nehru had to find ways to dislodge them. After first trying persuasion, in August 1955 he had permitted a group of unarmed Indians to march into Portuguese territory in a non-violent demonstration. Even though the Portuguese opened fire on the demonstrators, killing nearly 30, Nehru stayed his hand for six years, appealing meanwhile to Portugal's Western friends to persuade its government to cede the colony. When India finally struck, Nehru could claim that neither he nor the government of India had ever been committed to non-violence as a policy.

Nehru's health showed signs of deteriorating not long after the clash with China. He suffered a slight stroke in 1963, followed by a more debilitating attack in January 1964. He died a few months later from a third and fatal stroke.

Assessment

While assertive in his Indianness, because of his modern political and economic outlook, he attracted the younger intelligentsia of India to Gandhi's movement of non-violent resistance against the British and later to rally them around him after independence. Nehru's Western upbringing and his visits to Europe before independence had acclimatized him to Western ways of thinking. Nehru has been held responsible for Wavell's recall, and his relationship with Mountbatten may have been responsible for smoothing things over during the transfer of power. In free India, Nehru as first prime minister laid the foundations of a democratic and secular India. If Gandhi was India's liberator, Nehru was its modernizer. Throughout his 17 years in office, he held up democratic socialism as the guiding star. With the help of the overwhelming majority that the Congress party maintained in Parliament during his term of office, he advanced towards that goal. The four pillars of his domestic policies were democracy, socialism, unity, and secularism. He succeeded to a large extent in maintaining the edifice supported by these four pillars during his lifetime.

Even during his lifetime, individual and collective perceptions of his leadership ranged from him being adored as a revolutionary and vibrant personification of the forward-looking spirit of India to being described as a pampered young man who accidentally acquired national leadership owing to the influence of his father and the favouritism of Mahatma Gandhi. Doubtless, Nehru was a leader of the freedom movement, as the founding father of institutional democracy in India and as the architect of India's policy in all its manifestations, and the longest serving prime minister of India (from 1946 to 1964). As an international statesman and as a popular leader, he was second only to Gandhi in this century.

Nehru came to such prominence in the freedom struggle primarily for two reasons. First, the Congressmen made him their leader because of their conviction that he was committed to the cause of freedom and to the service of the people of India. Second, Nehru worked his way up through municipal elections in Allahabad and through mass movements in Pratapgarh of Uttar Pradesh. After that there was no looking back from him.

Though Nehru accepted Gandhi as his mentor, they differed on many points. Gandhi's non-violence stemmed from his religious convictions, while Nehru believed in a liberal conception of ethics. Nehru believed in representative institutions, especially the dominance of the poorer classes in the elected institutions. In other words, he believed in the democratic empowerment of the poorer and lower castes. So if Gandhi was the father of India, Nehru was the principle architect of India's democracy and planning.

Nehru's only child, Indira Gandhi, served as India's prime minister from 1966 to 1977 and from 1980 to 1984. Her son, Rajiv Gandhi, was prime minister from 1984 to 1989. Nehru wrote extensively, especially during his interminable jail detentions—*Glimpses of World History* (1934-35) in the form of letters to his daughter Indira; his *Autobiography* (1936), largely a story of the nationalist struggle for independence; *Discovery of India* (1946), a foray into India's historical and cultural past; and *Selected Works* that contain several useful materials pertaining to India's freedom struggle.

NEHRU CRITIC OF HINDU MAHASABHA

Nehru was a critic of Hindu Mahasabha and so was the Hindu Mahasbha of Nehru. Hindu Mahasabha was against the Nehru Liaqat pact of April 8, 1950. In a speech in Nasik on September 1950, Nehru expressed his belief that secularism would provide great relief to the minority groups in India. He was devoted to scientific methodology stressing on rationalism. This evolved his nationalist political ideology laying emphasis on secularist democracy, a counterpoise to medievalism, obscurantism and religious dogmatism. Being a student of Indian thought, he added that secularism did not signify "merely material well being" Hence he wrote: "It must essentially have spiritual values and certain standards of behaviour, and, when we consider these, we enter immediately into the realm of what has been called religion".

Unfortunately the flexibility and compromises which Nehru exhibited in dealing with majority opinion as Congress leader regarding economic matters was lacking when he dealt with Muslim League. Though his rationale was different, his attitude towards Muslim League was in conformity with those of the dominant Congress leadership who considered the congress party as the sole representative of the Indian people and discarded aligned groups. Grasping the nature of the communal problem in India, he wrote a letter to his daughter Indira Gandhi in May 1933. In the letter he admitted that different groups, joined the non-co-operation movement led by Gandhi in 1920-22 with different motives. He came to the conclusion that there were three kinds of Nationalism in India: Hindu nationalism, Muslim nationalism and Indian nationalism, and he considered the last one as true nationalism. It was difficult for him to draw a sharp line between Hindu nationalism and Indian nationalism. "The two overlapped, as India is the only home of the Hindus and they formed a majority there. It was thus easier for the Hindus to appear as full blooded nationalists than for the Muslims, although each stood for his own particular brand of nationalism". He did not blame the Britishers for creating the Hindu-Muslim problem in India, but they made efforts to keep that problem alive and discouraged rapprochement among the communities. In his autobiography in 1935, he identified both Hindu and Muslim communalism with political and social reaction. He conceded that the struggle of the Congress Muslims, organised as the 'Nationalist Muslim Party', in order to combat the communal Muslim leaders had collapsed which was pitiful story.

The gone effects of the collapse were reflect in the results of provincial legislatures election which were held in 1937. The Congress Party could win seats in North-West Frontier Province where there was Muslim majority in the provinces. Congress emerged as the dominant party in almost all legislatures where Hindus had majority of seats. Throughout India, the total number of Muslim seats in provincial Assemblies were 482. The Congress contested 58 seats and won 26 Muslim League secured 108 and most of the Muslim seats had gone to provincial parties. Though it was not an impressive tally for the League, the Congress also did not exhibit a foothold among the Muslims, except in the North West Frontier Province. The need to win the confidence of the Muslim masses was inevitable for the Congress The talk of coalition between the Congress and the Muslim League failed to materialise. One of the major causes of this failure as per Nehru's assessment was that the Congress was negotiating with the communalist. Muslim parties could not reach the Muslim masses who were in the need of welfare. According to him, the calks of understanding between Muslims and Hindus represented a medieval mentality which had no place in the modern world.

In 1937 Nehru careful the Congress-League Coalition Ministry in Uttar Pradesh a myth. It was alleged by Maulana Abul Kalam Azad, that the talks of a Congress-League Coalition Ministry failed because of Nehru's insistence on the appointment of only one Minister from the Muslim League, while the latter wanted two of its representatives to be taken in. Nehru showed very little interest in the formation of the U.P. Ministry.

Although not the sole decision-maker, the fact is that he played a significant role in his home province in decision-making relating to the formation of a coalition ministry. He wrote to Govind Ballabh Pant, the then leader of the Congress Party in U.P, when he was interested in a coalition ministry : "I am personally convinced that any kind of pact, a coalition between us and the Muslim League, will be highly injurious.

It will mean that we almost lose our right to ask the Muslims to join directly. It will mean many other things also which are equally undesirable". After serious negotiations Nehru reluctantly absorbed two of the Muslim

Leauge's leaders into the Ministry but on conditions which he himself described as "stringent", and intended to secure "the winding up of the Muslim League group in the U.P. and its absorption in the Congress".

The talks failed when the conditions were unacceptable to the League leaders. It was generally accepted that this led the Muslim League leadership towards partition. Nehru considered the failure of the Congress-League Coalition in 1937 as "natural and logical" in the then existing circumstances, and he later on admitted that "the consequences of it on the communal question were unfortunate and it led to a feeling of grievance and isolation among many Muslims". This led to the first time in history, within a short span of two years, to emerge as a really powerful political organisation. The leaders of the Muslim League were determined to maintain their separate political and cultural identity of Muslims and secure a share in power commensurate with their historical and political importance.

Mountbatten plan was the basis for India's partition. Nehru had contributed a lot for this plan and it was legitimately known as Mountbatten - Nehru plan. Being pitted against powerful historical and social forces, Nehru failed to prevent India's partition in 1947. Jawaharlal Nehru as a national leader and Prime Minister shaped and articulated the concept of secularism. Thus India's struggle for independence proceeded with values of equal human worth, brotherhood, state does not identify itself with any one religion but is friendly and protects all religions.

The national identity transcends but never negates religious identity. This implies the separation of the rights and duties of a citizen in his public life from adherence, in his private life, to the beliefs and practices of his religion. To Nehru secular state means freedom of religion, conscience, including freedom for those who may have no religion. A caste-ridden society is not exactly secular but that which guarantees social and political equality is an ideal secular society. In India's intellectual heritage, Nehru's large concept of secularism as an equitable and humane social order where persons professing different faiths live in harmony in consonance with, marks a step forward.

Nehru's starting point was not religion but science and rational thought. In his view poverty and ignorance perpetuates injustice and oppression. Through education, economic and social change the disadvantage masses could be. rescued from vulnerability to the exploitation of religious sentiment by vested interests. He stressed the importance of the higher values of life. He defined secular democracy as promoting equal opportunities for a fuller life - a concept that strengthens inter-faith harmony. To him modernity and social change were a spiral movement retaining the roots in the past while aspiring to the future. The creative tension between the inertia of tradition and the thrust of modernisation would be resolved in a higher synthesis, secular and socialist democracy providing the framework for the transformation of an old society.

Jawaharlal Nehru was more than a Prime Minister since he had established a location in the national hierarchy of leadership prior to independence, when the Congress was under the coalition leadership of Gandhi and Nehru. Among his competitors in the Congress hierarchy before independence, none had the support of the masses as Nehru had. After independence he was a natural' choice to lead the country. He assured the masses since the pre-independent era that the mass poverty could be abolished after independence.

In his opinion, India would have a number of opportunities after independence. Nehru possessed a national base and legitimacy, due to mass-leader identification.

Because of this asset he became the Prime Minister. The masses were with Nehru since the politics of ballot confirmed it repeatedly. Other leaders of the Congress realized that Nehru was an unchallenged leader of the party as well as the government because he drew great support from the masses. For their political survival, other party and factional leaders accepted Nehru as an umpire in intra-party and inter-state conflicts. Nehru was accepted as an undisputed leader of the masses due to his role in the national movement and he was shrewd in being autonomous from party factions or regional barriers.

Position of Nehru in Indian political system Nehru's position was pre-eminent in the Indian political system, because of a decisive and crucial role in normal and emergency situations.

Nehru collected individuals he personally wanted in the Council of Ministers. Nehru thought that the talents of stalwarts in the party, like Patel and Azad and also non-party men like C.D.Deshmukh should be utilised in national building. He was dominant in selection of candidates at central and state level. He allotted crucial portfolios to his colleagues who possessed similar ideological persuasions as he. As head of the government, he gathered information about important happenings in the country through a network of intelligence service. Summing up, Nehru is an efficient Prime Minister of the country due to his supraconstitutional.

When religious wars were being fight in Europe, India was tolerant due to its eclectic culture. When we assess Nehru's personality we find that Nehru had imbibed the composite Indian culture. He had struggled to link past to the present and future. He was a staunch believer in democracy which resulted from his western education. The remedy he suggested to erase communalism was secularism. Scientific principle based on reason should dominate over superstition.

Being a Kashmiri Brahmin, under the patronage of Mughals, Nehru family occupied an eminent place due to their literary expertise and law profession. His western education had moulded him into a rational man who believed in the progress of the country through science and technology. He was proud of Indian culture, especially Buddhism due to its widespread influence in the East. He was aware of the drawbacks of religion, at the same time he knew its impact on the minds of people, hence advocated tolerance of all Religions which is the base of Indian secularism.

Nehru being the architect of modern India, his life and work reflect his secular spirit. Being an active member of the Congress he opposed the then prevailing communal parties. He was against separate electorates. He was of the opinion that the communal problem should be solved by mutual consensus. He wanted the communal leaders to be reformist rather than revolutionary. The communal leaders under the patronage of Britishers became political reactionaries. Nehru's main intention was providing a standard of living for the masses who were in abject poverty. Since the pre-independent era he had sown the seeds of secularism. With the partition of the country secularism became the inevitable basis of the polity to provide security to the masses Nehru as a Prime Minister worked for the separation of religion and politics, at some moments successful and at some moments failure in practical terms. He worked hard for the establishment of Indian nationalism. Due to his secular approach he succeeded in solving intra party and inter-state conflicts.

NEHRU'S WORKS IN POLITICS

Nehru came from a family of Kashmiri Brahmins, who had migrated to the plains early in the eighteenth century. He was the son of Motilal Nehru, a renowned lawyer and one of Mahatma Gandhi's prominent lieutenants. Jawaharlal was the eldest of four children, two of whom were daughters. His sister, Vijaya Lakshmi Pandit, later became the first woman president of the UN General Assembly. Until the age of 16, Nehru was educated at home by a series of English governesses and tutors. Only one of these, a part-Irish, part-Belgian theosophist, Ferdinand T. Brooks, appears to have made any impression on him. Gradually, he developed a taste for writers such as Walter Scott, Charles Dickens, Thackery, H.G. Wells, and Mark Twain, as well as for John Stuart Mill, Gladstone, John Morley, Bertrand Russell, and Bernard Shaw. Jawaharlal also had an Indian tutor who taught him Hindi and Sanskrit. In 1905 he went to Harrow, a leading English school, where he stayed for two years. Nehru's academic career was in no way outstanding.

From Harrow he went to Trinity College, Cambridge, where he spent three years earning an honours degree in natural science. On leaving

Cambridge, Nehru joined the Inner Temple in 1910 to read law, where in his own words he passed his examinations "with neither glory nor ignominy". It was here that he also confessed: "In my likes and dislikes, I was perhaps more an Englishman than an Indian." In London he was drawn to the Fabian socialists, also known as the Bloomsbury group. He returned home in 1912 after seven years of education in England. Four years after his return to India, in March 1916, Nehru married Kamala Kaul, who came from a Kashmiri family settled in Delhi. Their only child, Indira Priyadarshini, was born in 1917; she would later (under her married name of Indira Gandhi) also serve as prime minister of India.

POLITICAL APPRENTICESHIP

On his return to India, Nehru at first tried to settle down as a lawyer. But, unlike his father, he had only a desultory interest in his profession and did not relish either the practice of law or the company of lawyers. At this time he might be described, like many of his generation, as an instinctive nationalist who yearned for his country's freedom, but, like most of his contemporaries, he had not formulated any precise ideas on how it could be achieved.

Nehru's autobiography discloses his lively interest in politics. His letters to his father over the same period reveal their common interest in India's freedom. But not until father and son met Gandhi and were persuaded to follow in his political footsteps did either of them develop any definite ideas on how freedom was to be attained. The quality in Gandhi that impressed the two Nehrus was his insistence on action. A wrong, the Mahatma argued, should not only be condemned, it should be resisted. Earlier, Nehru and his father had been contemptuous of the run of contemporary Indian politicians, whose nationalism, with a few notable exceptions, consisted of interminable speeches and long-winded resolutions. Jawaharlal was also attracted by Gandhi's insistence on fighting Great Britain without fear or hate. Nehru met Gandhi for the first time in 1916 at the annual meeting of the Indian National Congress in Lucknow. Gandhi was 20 years his senior. Neither seems to have made any initially strong impression on the other. Nehru did not assume a leadership role in Indian politics, however, until his election as Congress president in 1929, when he presided over the historic Lahore session that proclaimed complete independence as India's political goal. Until then the objective had been dominion status. Nehru had joined the Allahabad High Court Bar in 1916, practising till 1920. But the legal profession did not hold him for long, and he found a meaningful vocation in politics. The year 1917 had seen the Russian Revolution, and it was also the year of agitation for

Home Rule, under the leadership of Annie Besant (1847-1933). Expelled from Bombay and then from the Central Provinces, she was finally interned. Jawaharlal signed up as one of the joint secretaries of the Home Rule League in the United Provinces with Motilal Nehru as president. "Home Rule has come and we have to take it if we stand up like men and falter not", so wrote Jawaharlal in a letter to *The Leader.* Nehru's close association with the Congress party dates from 1919 in the immediate aftermath of World War I. This period saw a wave of nationalist activity and governmental repression.

According to his testimony and that of his contemporaries, three events during 1919 and 1920 had a profound influence on Nehru's political career. The first was the Jallianwala Bagh massacre (April 1919), when General Reginald E.H. Dyer, a British officer, ordered his troops to fire on an unarmed crowd of Indians gathered for an anti-British political meeting. By the time the ammunition ran out, nearly 400 civilians were dead and 1,200 wounded. The massacre shook Nehru's faith in the beneficence of British rule. The second experience was Nehru's first-hand encounter with India's poverty in the countryside in the 1920s, and lastly, Gandhi's emergence during 1919-20, and his call for civil disobedience struck Nehru deeply. In fact, the Non-cooperation Movement (1920-22) of the Congress under Gandhi's leadership seemed to him to answer some of the major challenges of the time. Jawaharlal accepted the non-violent method as the only practical strategy that was then available.

Beginning his political career in the United Provinces (now Uttar Pradesh), during the Non-cooperation Movement, Jawaharlal came in contact with the impoverished peasants whose indomitable spirit defied the crushing economic burden, which an oppressive imperial regime imposed upon them. Nehru left a graphic account of the India which his sojourn in the rural areas opened up before him: "I went (to the rural districts near Allahabad) with some colleagues and we spent three days in the villages far from the railways and even the *pucca* (paved) road. The visit was a revelation to me. We found the whole countryside afire with enthusiasm and full of strange excitement...(The) people would come streaming out or even running as fast as they could.

They were in miserable rags, men and women, but their faces were full of excitement and their eyes glistened and seemed to expect strange happenings which would, as if by a miracle, put an end to their long misery....(A) new picture of India seemed to arise before me." He was, as he records, "filled with shame and sorrow....at the degradation and overpowering poverty of India", and this experience was to shape his later political thinking. The Non-cooperation Movement helped him emerge as a popular leader: "I took to the crowd and the crowd took to me." The movement also widened his political and social perspective. When, late in 1921, the prominent leaders and workers of the Congress party were outlawed in some provinces, Nehru went to prison for the first time. Over the next 24 years he was to serve another eight periods of detention, the last and longest ending in June 1945, after an imprisonment of almost three years. In all, Nehru spent more than nine years in jail. Characteristically, he described his terms of incarceration as normal interludes in a life of abnormal political activity.

His political apprenticeship with the Congress lasted from 1919 to 1929. In 1923 he became general secretary of the party for two years and again, in 1927, for another two years. His interests and duties took him on journeys over wide areas of India, particularly in his native United Provinces, where his first exposure to the overwhelming poverty and degradation of the peasantry had a profound influence on his basic ideas for solving these vital problems. Though vaguely inclined towards socialism, Nehru's radicalism had set in no definite mould. The watershed in his political and economic thinking was his tour of Europe and the erstwhile Soviet Union.

Nehru's explorations into the socialist theory after his visit to Europe in 1926-27, and his experiences with Nazi Germany marked a turning point in his social and political outlook. In 1927 he, as a representative of the Indian National Congress, attended the International Congress against colonial oppression and imperialism in Brussels. There he met some of the leading leftists of the world including George Lansbury, Ellen Wilkinson, Fenner Brockway, and Harry Pollitt, besides a large number of nationalists from Asia, Africa, and Latin America.

This was followed by his visit to Moscow where he was greeted by the newspaper *Pravda* as a "leader of the left wing of the Congress". There he had a first-hand glimpse of the reconstruction of a major society on the basis of socialism. His experience made him realise the need for an economic revolution, which would redeem India from the backwardness of its agrarian structure and, in fact, from its dependence on agriculture itself. He was convinced that the solution to India's socio-economic problems lay in socialism "not in a vague humanitarian way, but in the scientific economic sense." He thus involved himself with the Trade Union Movement and emerged as a champion of independence and socialism.

Nehru's radicalism came to the fore in 1927 over the debate on the extent and character of *swaraj* or self-government that the Congress was struggling for. In 1927, the British government sent an all-British commission (the Simon Commission), under the terms of the Government of India Act of 1919, to report as to "whether and to what extent it was desirable to establish the principle of responsible government, or to extend, modify, or restrict the degree of responsible government existing therein". The Congress gave a call for the boycott of the Simon Commission in its Madras (now Chennai) session (December 1927), with Nehru and his associates contributing to the success of the boycott.

The Simon Commission thus raised the issue of the type of constitution or the kind of independence that India should obtain for itself. So far *swaraj*, for the Congress leaders, had meant dominion status for India (similar to the position of self-governing Australia, New Zealand, and South Africa) within the ambit of the British Empire. But to Jawaharlal and his associates the acceptance of the dominion status implied recognizing the inevitability of British presence in India, as well as the perpetuation of imperialistic exploitation. In the Madras session in December 1927, Jawaharlal moved a resolution demanding real independence instead of dominion status. It was, however, at the Congress session at Calcutta (now Kolkata) in December 1928 that he, joined by Subhash Chandra Bose, pressed claim for complete independence as the Congress objective. The actual success of this demand came in the following year when as the newly elected president of the Indian National Congress at the Lahore session, Nehru gave the call for a new goal: *purna swaraj* (complete independence). When the clock struck at midnight on the night of December 31, 1929, Jawaharlal Nehru rose and led a solemn procession on the banks of the Ravi River. It was here that he raised India's national flag.

JAWAHARLAL NEHRU AND WORLD ORDER

It is now more than two decades since Jawaharlal Nehru passed away. For more than forty years he had been a major figure in the Indian national movement. For the first two decades he had been a loyal lieutenant of Mahatma Gandhi, disciplining himself to conform to the priorities of the national struggle, as defined by Gandhi, in spite of his skepticism about some of the methods adopted by his leader and some of the aims which appeared to him to be not so important.

In doing so, Nehru had the priceless advantage of having formulated, on his own, a few broad ideological guidelines to help him along uncharted paths: the essential principles of socialist planning, the need not merely not to forget but to stress the supreme importance of social justice in one's anxious search for political democracy and human rights; and the necessary collection of essential information and data about our vast country with its enormous diversity, both horizontally in regional and linguistic terms and vertically, in widely separate levels of development—all these preoccupied his attention. He was always excited over ideological niceties; the dilemmas between development and democracy, between discipline and the need to be totally unfettered in one's thinking, fascinated him.

In 1942, twentytwo years before he passed away, he was able to face the difficulties of decision-making in reconciling the needs of our nationalism with the competing requirements of global anti-fascism, without frustration or escapism; his decision was, in retrospect, sane and helpful to the national cause. He was able to do this, not least because of his over-riding loyalty to the cause of national sovereignty and to the leadership of Mahatma Gandhi. It is useful to recall this earlier part of Nehru's career because it will go a long way to explain the principles which guided his conduct in formulating foreign policy after the achievement of Independence.

During the years of his power he was always concerned with the challenges to sovereignty in a new world order, which had remarkable statutory elegance and an unprecedented coherence in the inter-relationship of the big powers. In this world order, the least powerful countries, the new entrants to the game of world politics, were expected to conform and be passive. Passivity meant continuity with the imperialist period, acceptance of earlier links of influence disguised by political independence and the membership of the United Nations. There was also a certain acceptance of the value systems developed by the departing empires and, as their extension, the new crusading ideology of the Western nations, after the ideological schism and the sudden onset of the Cold War which almost synchronised with Indian Independence. The first factor, therefore, which controlled Nehru's formulation of foreign policy was the preoccupation about preserving and defending sovereignty against adversaries, both old and new, both open and disguised. The second element was the need to recognise and build upon the integral link between sovereignty in international terms and freedom and justice for the individual and groups in the national domain. This meant a commitment to human rights, which, because of Nehru's personal disillusionment with the practice of the Western democracies during the imperialist epoch and, more specifically during the period immediately before war, a much more sensitive definition of and a much more scrupulous and detailed legislative attempt to guarantee democratic values.

The enormous burden of inequality and injustice, inherited down the centuries, the complications of the caste problem, the terrible deprivation under which the Harijans and tribals had been permitted to survive during the British period and the habits of gross indifference to poverty and sufferings, encouraged by the new elitism of the post-Independence generation, have made the ambitious attempt flawed from the beginning. Looking back today, we see as many failures as successes in our track record on domestic justice in political, economic and social terms, but the attempt was there solemnly enshrined in the Constitution and carefully tended for several years by that first generation of leaders in the national struggle, suddenly faced with the demands of responsibility and the difficult choice between many options in both domestic administration and management of external relations.

All this was further complicated by the unexpected major event of the country's partition. This impelled the Government of India after 1947 to have a conscious and assertive policy of secularism in direct and linear continuity with the programme of secular democracy, which the Indian National Congress leadership had stood for, against the attacks from the communalism of both the major communities. In this emphasis on secular values, Nehru had the immense advantage of total support of the Leftist parties, who differed from him on many other important matters. The developments in Kashmir and the tragic conflict which resulted made Secularism during the Nehru period not merely a decent ideology in democratic terms but excellent politics in international relations.

The acceptance and active pursuit of secular values in a Hindu majority country with a large and vocal Muslim minority, made the religious problem of minor relevance in our relations with those Muslim countries who also achieved independence about the same time as India and also with the older Islamic nations like Iran, Turkey and Egypt. This was an exceptionally important development in that Pakistan's desire and ability to exploit religious sympathies in other Islamic countries were neutralised by their acknowledgment of the essentially secular approach of the government in New Delhi.

The foreign policy of a country like India, with a rather special geographical situation at the cross-roads of communications both by land and sea, and an even more specific recent historical experience as a colony of a distant power, is bound to be primarily influenced by regional considerations. The division of India on a religious basis and the communal holocaust and exchange of populations which followed, were the major influences in the imposition of a certain defensive aspect to some aspects of India's foreign policy in these earlier years.

Then came the Kashmir problem, which was a direct result of the partition of the country, but not legally connected with it; it was an essentially strategic and political development in which there were several adversary influences, which we had to learn to cope with during the coming years. The Kashmir problem also made us realise the need to be careful about relations with both Britain and the United States; their sympathies were not necessarily with us in this or other future conflicts with Pakistan. What were domestic problems in pre-Independent India had become international issues after Independence, which attracted extra-regional pulls. The Kashmir experience also enabled us to be more familiar with the decision-making, pressure groups and lobbying within the UN, both in the Security Council and in the General Assembly. IT was a period of apprenticeship in which we had to learn the rules of the big power game in a world which had several small powers. The great powers were never particularly interested in reforming the world system, since they had devised it and were its principal beneficiaries. The great changes which came about during the next fifteen years in de-colonisation took place not within the limits of the world system, but outside it, initially tolerated and ultimately accepted by it in the form of granting membership to all the newly independent countries. There was, in the very last years of Nehru's life, even an activist phase in the UN policy on colonialism which promoted the self-government of the remaining colonies in Africa. This was something to which India had contributed effectively. This was also the policy associated with the names of Nehru and Krishna Menon during a creative phase in the history of the global struggle against imperialism.

While this was so, the UN as such was fractured by the divisions in the Security Council and this gave India an opportunity to break out of regional inhibitions and play a reasonably effective though modest role in some extra-regional disputes like Korea and Indo-China. In these disputes, India took the initiative of active negotiation, even without full credentials, between the major powers—a testimonial to the success of her efforts was the willing acceptance by all parties of India in a mediatory role in Korea. In Indo-China, India's involvement was more formal and continuous over a long period in an institutional form, as the Chairman of the International Supervisory Commission.

The Indo-China problem had been solved outside the UN system: a major participant, China, was a non-member. The Korean problem had, for more of its critical period, also a disputable link only with the UN because of the withdrawal of the Soviet Union from the Security Council. In later years, however, India played an activist role as a responsible member of the UN, carrying out some of the decisions of UN in keeping peace and guaranteeing order in conflictual and post-conflictual situations. This was the situation in the Middle East, the Congo and also Cyprus. The second extra-regional and global aspect of India's foreign policy during the Nehru years was the country's active association with the Commonwealth. India's decision to become a Republic and stay on in the Commonwealth was a major event in the evolution of that institution. This made it possible for the Commonwealth of nations to play an essentially minor, but useful, role on some matters during the next 20 years. It at least served in exposing the unwillingness of the Republic of South Africa to conform to civilised norms.

The third and in retrospect the most enduring feature of Nehru's foreign policy in those early years was the discovery of an Afro-Asian personality at

Bandung and its extension to an inter-continental nonaligned philosophy by the early sixties. There were other countries who played a notable role in the Afro-Asian conscience and in the ideology of nonalignment. Indonesia, Egypt, Yugoslavia and later Cuba—all had something unique and individual to give to the nonaligned policy. It was, however, Nehru, who articulated the essential need for any newly independent country to be detached from the major powers and, even more important, from the groups of major powers, to preserve the essence of sovereignty, which is "independence in foreign policy"; in his felicitous phrase, "all else is local self-government".

The period from the Asian Relations Conference in New Delhi in 1947 to the Afro-Asian gathering in Bandung in 1955 and then on to the first Non-Aligned Summit in 1961 represents to some extent the scope and reach of Jawaharlal Nehru's vision of the world system. In his picture of the newly organised world order, the small and medium states had a substantive role to play, both as sovereign nations and as representatives of new urges for remedying ancient injustices. Nonalignment in Nehru's conception was the solidarity of the weak, the articulation of the various economic and political grievances of the less powerful; it was a refusal to accept the over-riding authority of the major powers in the Security Council and the two global powers, the Soviet Union and the US in all matters, both when they disagreed and demanded loyalty and adherence and when they agreed on an odd issue and expected immediate compliance from the General Assembly.

Nehru's refusal to accept the policies of the major powers was directly connected with the greatest global problem of all in the modern world—the nuclear arms race. In this period he saw it more specifically as an environmental disaster and also as an attempt by the big powers to perpetuate their dominance. At the heart of Nehru's concept of nonalignment was his opposition to the nuclear weapons as an instrument of dominance by the global powers. In his mind and in India's policy as formulated by him, de-colonisation and nuclear disarmament were equally important, competing for precedence according to the specific demands of a particular occasion.

In 1961, at Belgrade, there was, however, a clear divergence of views between Nehru and some of his colleagues on the relative priority to be given to the problem of crusading for nuclear disarmament and de-colonisation. Nehru felt that, with the granting of independence to the French colonies, the major European empires had disintegrated. The rest were bound, inevitably, to be liberated soon. Some of his African colleagues and President Sukarno did not share his optimism. The years since then have confirmed to some extent both views. De-colonisation did score some major successes after a fairly fallow period when in the seventies, the Portuguese empire suddenly broke into pieces. It is important here to remind ourselves that a major factor in the Portuguese debacle was the support to the armed national liberation struggle in the colonies by the Third World countries. This new and assertive policy had, in fact, been indirectly heralded by India's military action in Goa only three months after Belgrade. Even while giving secondary importance to de-colonisation, Nehru had thus given a wholly new dimension to the anti-colonial struggle, which continues today to be essentially relevant in its new forms in Namibia and in South Africa, as it had been in Mozambique, Angola and Zimbabwe.

The anti-nuclear movement led to the partial test ban, which had, as its essential target, the preservation of the global environment. The two decades since then have thoroughly falsified Nehru's hopes. The fifth nuclear weapon power came on the world scene a few months after Nehru's death when China exploded its first bomb. The nuclear non-proliferation treaty in 1968 which Nehru's successors refused to endorse has, during the last eighteen years, only served to increase the danger from a nuclear disaster to the human race. Not even the earlier modest ambitions of Nehru and his contemporaries to bring to an end atmospheric tests has been realised—France and China refusing to cooperate, and the three nuclear weapon signatories of PTB and NPT accepting their refusal to sign agreements with considerable tolerance and understanding. Today India finds herself in a position of carrying forward this major aspect of Nehru's policy in other forms; we insist on opposing the non-proliferation treaty and its discriminatory provisions; we also insist on continuing to oppose atmospheric tests in the first instance and all tests later. Our own single peaceful nuclear explosion was an underground one with no threat of radiation to anyone either in our country or in the neighbouring states. We believe that only a comprehensive test ban treaty together with the outlawing of nuclear weapons and the graduated reduction of the stockpiles would lead to acceptable conditions in which the world community can survive and flourish.

Apart from these global strategic issues and specific disputes and conflicts in which India was involved, there was the equally important pervasive problem of economic development for the newly independent countries. Nehru's total world vision encompassed the evolution of a socially just society within India; for this purpose he devised in a certain pragmatic manner 'a mixed economy' in which the public sector was given a dominant role while the private sector was encouraged to be active within certain limits. This was the original vision. In actual practice, as we all know, things have not exactly turned out to be as he hoped for. We do have a substantial though much criticised public sector, but there is a much more active, even turbulent private sector more powerful and influential than had been scheduled either in the pre-Independence programming of the Congress Planning Committee under Nehru's chairmanship or in the successive Five-Year Plans produced by the government after independence.

As far as external relations were concerned, however, this decision to evolve a mixed economy at home led to inevitable policy consequences. The political and strategic decision to refrain from too much nearness to the major powers was complemented by an equally clear willingness to cooperate responsively with all nations in economic matters. From the very beginning, India has believed in international economic cooperation in the giving and receiving of credits and in the exchange of technical skills. The post-war economic system, the post-war monetary institutions etc. were found by our country to be extremely useful props to our own development efforts; more than that, we developed, in the first decade after independence, a certain expertise as an aid-giver and an aid-recipient in strictly limited circumstances and with comparatively small funds in the Colombo Plan. IT was against this background that the Soviet Union's willingness to help us in building a public sector steel mill became important. There were non-socialist developed nations like Britain and Germany who also assisted us in building new steel plants in the public sector. But the most important developed market economy, the United States, was hostile to the very idea. Over the years, the experience of Bhilai led to further collaborative arrangements between India's public sector and the Soviet Union and the other East European socialist countries. In domestic economic arrangements, these became organically linked with the external policy of detachment and also the selective cooperation, according to our terms, with foreign countries.

With the dwindling down of the Sterling Balances, India's exclusive dependence on Britain as supplier of defence material became obsolescent. Here again, the nonaligned policy became relevant. India began to make significant military purchases from all available suppliers who respected India's bonafides. The Soviet Union became a major supplier of defence equipment. It was never an exclusive supplier; on many occasions the option to buy from Moscow was taken after protracted negotiations with earlier suppliers had failed.

The policy of nonalignment, both in its negative and positive aspects and also in its strategic and economic aspects, had been accepted by a large majority within the country by the time the tragic conflict with China took place in 1962. This was, by any measure, a major disaster both in India's internal economic planning and its external obligations. There was a great deal of misunderstanding, misperception of India's policies and, also, intersection with other compulsions which made China commit this act of physical aggression against a friendly neighbouring country with such a long record of active cooperation and support on many political issues at a time when the People's Republic had been isolated and lonely in the world family.

The immediate damage was almost immeasurable; we are still to recover from some of the consequences of the distortions in our national planning brought about the diversion to defence expenditure of much-needed resources. The actual territorial dispute continues unresolved even though, over the years, both sides have learnt to live with it and slowly developed normal relations in other fields. The great achievement, in retrospect, during that traumatic experience was Jawaharlal Nehru's singleminded determination to preserve the nonaligned stance at all costs. This made it possible for a certain essential continuity to be preserved both in domestic and external policies during the next decade when the country faced new dangers both from without and within.

There have been, during the last three decades, several threats, some minor and some of major significance to the country's unity and integrity. The fact that they have been contained is primarily due to our federal democratic Constitution, which was devised by Nehru and his colleagues immediately after independence. Some inadequacies have been later located in that structure; all possible eventualities cannot be provided for in any human statute. Given that limitation, however, it is surprising how strong and durable the country's federal structure has proved. The purely domestic problems of Centre-State relations in a large country like India which can be compared to only a few other states in the world—the Soviet Union, China, Indonesia, Nigeria and Brazil—are inevitably complicated by neighbourhood dilemmas. India's relations with Nepal, Pakistan, Bangladesh, Sri Lanka and in earlier years, even with Burma, have all had a certain domestic connection. This is not very unusual or surprising in the modern post-imperial system. Retreating empires have left behind divided language groups and cultures, which demand unusual generosity towards each other, and statesmanship from political leaders in newly independent countries.

On the whole, India has been able to contain these problems except in the case of Pakistan where the Kashmir issue still remains unresolved. The two major conflicts in the first decade after Nehru's death did, in fact, lead to a certain greater stability in the relationship. Achievements like the Tashkent and Simla Agreements were possible only because of the long tradition of willingness to compromise and negotiate, as had been shown by Nehru during the many disputes with Pakistan in his time. The Nehru-Liaqat Ali Agreement of 1950 and the solution of the Indus river waters dispute under the World Bank auspices as well as the fairly straightforward manner in which the division of the economic assets of undivided India was carried out testify to an essentially sane, civilised and sometimes even magnanimous approach. In this, Nehru, of course, was inspired as well as assisted by Gandhi's precept and example.

There are other neighbourhood dilemmas in the Indian situation which we have learnt to live with. Political institutions in the neighbouring countries have been generally at variance with our own, with the single exception of Sri Lanka. Even in that case, the insistence on a unitary state and the consequent alienation of the Tamil minority does not approximate to India's constitutional situation or actual conduct as a federal nation.

This absence of ideological sympathy with almost all our neighbours has made the task of foreign policy difficult. It is, however, not impossible, because the very nature of the UN system makes it possible for ideologically different neighbour states to co-exist without too much difficulty. We must, however, recognise the fact that total non-interference even in the realm of ideas is a counsel of perfection; defensive elite groups and old-fashioned minority ruling classes easily develop a persecution mania about a large neighbour, particularly in our unique situation when these states have no common boundaries between each other but only with India. These problems were recognised in Nehru's time and solutions were found in some cases, options exercised in some others and when unavoidable, decisions postponed.

Today, more than twenty years after Nehru's death, some of these problems have become much worse. The process of nation-building in our country, we have discovered, has not advanced as much as we had thought. There are serious centrifrugal influences in any nation-state, however small, in this era and age, when the information explosion has activised hitherto quiescent areas in the world and layers in all population. This is common to most states, but a large state like ours has to contend with much more serious threats to the national integrity, threats which could be strengthened and encouraged by adversary forces outside our border. External relations thus become again linked in dramatic, near dangerous situations with the domestic situation. These problems will always be there, problems not merely of regional dissatisfaction or linguistic alienation; we have also learnt to recognise, over the decades, the continuing existence of deep-rooted resentments within our society not only between the rich and the poor, but, between the rich and the not so rich, between the very poor and the poor. Developmental achievements have been considerable, but have fallen far short of our expectations. We have tried to be a model member of the world monetary system trying to conform to the prescriptions given by multilateral aid institutions sometimes against our better judgment.

During the coming years the greatest single challenge to our national security will be in the economic sphere. If we are not able to become self-reliant without cost to social justice, if we are not able to record successes in distribution as well as production, we may find ourselves under the influence of global powers and multinational institutions. We may also find ourselves continuously under threat from neighbours who are seldom acting on their own. Jawaharlal Nehru's prescriptions for complete sovereignty in an inter-dependent world continues to be relevant in a generation which faces much more complicated problems than even he, with his historical vision, envisaged. New problems need new solutions; new institutions have to be constructed to be compatible with a changed environment. Basic principles are unchanged. It is these principles which he went on repeating throughout his adult political life to his countrymen both for the primary purpose of communication and for re-defining and revising them in his own mind which constitute his richest legacy.

LAST YEARS

Mr. Nehru had led the Congress to a major victory in the 1957 elections, but his government was facing rising problems and criticism. Disillusioned by intra-party corruption and bickering, Nehru contemplated resigning but continued to serve. The election of his daughter Indira as Congress President in 1959 aroused criticism for alleged nepotism, although Nehru disapproved of her election, partly because he considered it smacked of "dynastism"; he said, indeed it was "wholly undemocratic and an undesirable thing", and refused her a position in his cabinet. Indira herself was at loggerheads with her father over policy; most notably, she used his oft-stated personal deference to the Congress Working Committee to push through the dismissal of the Communist Party of India government in the state of Kerala, over his own objections. Nehru began to be frequently embarrassed by her ruthlessness and disregard for parliamentary tradition, and was "hurt" by what he saw as an assertiveness with no purpose other than to stake out an identity independent of her father.

Although the Pancha Sila (Five Principles of Peaceful Coexistence) was the basis of the 1954 Sino-Indian treaty over Tibet, in later years, Nehru's foreign policy suffered through increasing Chinese antagonism over border disputes and Nehru's decision to grant asylum to the Dalai Lama. After years of failed negotiations, Nehru authorized the Indian Army to annex Goa from Portugal in 1961. While increasing his popularity, Nehru received criticism for opting for military action. In the 1962 elections, Nehru led the Congress to victory yet with a diminished majority. Opposition parties ranging from the right-wing Bharatiya Jana Sangh and Swatantra Party, socialists and the Communist Party of India performed well.

In a matter of months, the border disputes with China turned into open conflict. Nehru assumed that as former victims of imperialism (India being a colony itself) they shared a sense of solidarity, as expressed in the phrase "Hindi-Chini bhai bhai" (Indians and Chinese are brothers). He was dedicated to the ideals of brotherhood and solidarity among developing nations. Nehru, naively, did not believe that one fellow Socialist country would attack another; and in any event, he felt secure behind the impregnable wall of ice that is the Himalayas. Both proved to be severe miscalculations of China's intentions and military capabilities. Following reports of his intention to confront Chinese occupation of the disputed areas-summarised in a memorable statement that he had asked the Army to "throw them (Chinese) out"-China launched a pre-emptive attack. In a matter of months, a Chinese invasion of northeastern India exposed the weaknesses of India's military as Chinese forces came as far as Assam. Widely criticised for his government's insufficient attention to defence, Nehru was forced to sack the defence minister Krishna Menon and accept U.S. military aid. Nehru's health began declining steadily, and he was forced to spend months recuperating in Kashmir through 1963. Upon his return from Kashmir in May 1964, Nehru suffered a stroke and later a heart attack. He died in the early hours of May 27, 1964. Nehru was cremated in accordance with Hindu rites at the Shantivana on the banks of the Yamuna River, witnessed by hundreds of thousands of mourners who had flocked into the streets of Delhi and the cremation grounds.

2

Nehru and Struggle for Indian Independence

After the Lahore session of 1929, Nehru emerged as the leader of the country's intellectuals and youth. Hoping that Nehru would draw India's youth, at that time gravitating towards extreme leftist causes, into the mainstream of the Congress movement, Gandhi had elevated him to the presidency of the Congress party over the heads of some of his seniors. The Mahatma also correctly calculated that, with added responsibility, Nehru himself would be inclined to keep to the middle way.

It was also in these years Nehru and Subhas Chandra Bose were communicating with the people in general and to the youth (through the Youth League, the Hindustani Seva Dal, the Naujawan Bharat Sabha and the Volunteers' Movement), the students (through the students' organizations and conferences), and the workers (mainly through the All India Trade Union Congress whose presidentship was taken over by Jawaharlal in 1929 and Subhas in 1931) in particular.

In 1931, Jawaharlal and his wife Kamala were arrested in connection with the salt *satyagraha*. Jawaharlal clearly defined the kind of independence the Congress must stand for. In his draft of the Fundamental Rights that was adopted in the Karachi session of the Congress (March 1931), he stated: "In order to end the exploitation of the masses, political freedom must include real economic freedom of the starving millions." The Congress, he hoped, could be converted into a real anti-imperialist "joint popular front", and he suggested as a first step "corporate membership" of trade unions and *kisan sabhas*. This indeed was an important step in the march towards Congress socialism and Nehru's emergence as a champion of civil liberties.

After his father's death in 1931, Jawaharlal moved into the inner councils of the Congress party and became closer to the Mahatma. Although Gandhi did not officially designate him his political heir until 1942, the country as early as the mid-1930s saw in Nehru the natural successor to Gandhi. The Gandhi-Irwin Pact of March 1931, signed between Gandhi and the British viceroy, Lord Irwin (later Lord Halifax), signalized a truce between the two. It climaxed one of Gandhi's more effective civil-disobedience movements, launched the year before, in the course of which Nehru had been arrested.

As an ardent anti-imperialist, Nehru was unhappy at the enactment of the Gandhi-Irwin compromise (March 1931), as well at the prospect of the Round Table Conference (September-December 1931) in London to resolve the Indian political question. He also saw no point in the formal withdrawal of the Civil Disobedience Movement (May 1933). In the closing stage of the Civil Disobedience Movement, Nehru had renewed his interest in the agitation of the Uttar Pradesh peasantry His commitment to the youth, the students, and the underprivileged inspired him towards a radical political temper. This eventually facilitated the formation of the Congress Socialist Party (May 1934) within the framework of the Congress organization. Though Nehru did not formally join the party, he drew its support on vital issues. He continued to give importance to the principles of Democratic Socialism in India, as well as a vision of an independent, liberated, and secular India.

After he was elected the Congress president in the Lucknow and the Faizpur sessions in 1936, Nehru offered his socialist ideas with greater clarity. He made significant advances on the agrarian question (by contributing to the formulation of a liberal Faizpur Congress Agrarian Programme), on the issue of constitution, and on the question of civil liberties (by ordering the Congress provincial ministries to release all political prisoners), on responsible government (especially by championing the cause of the *Praja Mandal* (peoples group) movement in the Indian states against the tyranny of their rulers) and on the world-wide campaign against Fascism (by taking the side of "forces of progress" in the Spanish Civil War, by protesting against the Italian attack on Ethiopia, and by organizing relief for China when it was attacked by Japan).

Hopes that the Gandhi-Irwin pact would be the prelude to a more relaxed period of Indo-British relations were not borne out; Lord Willingdon (who replaced Irwin as viceroy in 1931) jailed Gandhi in January 1932, shortly after his return from the Second Round Table Conference in London. He was charged with attempting to mount another civil-disobedience movement; Nehru was also arrested and sentenced to two years' imprisonment.

The Round Table Conferences in London, held to advance India's progress to self-government, eventually resulted in the Government of India Act of 1935, giving the Indian provinces a system of popular autonomous government. Ultimately, it provided for a federal system composed of the autonomous provinces and princely states. Although federation never came into being, provincial autonomy was implemented. During the mid-1930s Nehru was much concerned with developments in Europe, which seemed to be drifting towards another world war.

He was in Europe early in 1936, visiting his ailing wife, shortly before she died in a sanitarium in Switzerland. Even at this time he emphasized that in the event of war India's place was alongside the democracies, though he insisted that India could only fight in support of Great Britain and France as a free country. In the 1936-37 election campaign for the provincial legislatures under the Government of India Act of 1935, Nehru was the principal vote-getter for the Congress and came to occupy a powerful position in the ranks of the Congress party. When the elections following the introduction of provincial autonomy brought the Congress party to power in a majority of the provinces, Nehru was faced with a dilemma. The Muslim League under Mohammed Ali Jinnah (who was to become the creator of Pakistan) had fared badly at the polls. Congress, therefore, unwisely rejected Jinnah's plea for the formation of coalition Congress-Muslim League governments in some of the provinces, a decision on which Nehru had significant influence. The subsequent clash between the Congress and the League hardened into a conflict between Hindus and Muslims that was ultimately to lead to the partition of India and the creation of Pakistan.

JAWAHARLAL NEHRU AND THE INDIAN NATIONAL CONGRESS

Jawaharlal Nehru and the Indian National Congress maintained a close relationship that lasted for more than four long and eventful decades of Indian history. Nehru's relationship with the Indian National Congress officially started in 1919, two years after the birth of his daughter, Indira Priyadarshini, and seven years after his return from England. However, his close association with the Indian political scenario started much before his official initiation. Motilal Nehru, Jawaharlal's father, was a veteran Congressman of the moderate school and closely associated with the cause of India's freedom. Soon after his return from England in 1912, Jawaharlal found himself at the very midst of the Indian political scenario.

However, Jawaharlal was not very sure of the ideological position that would be effective for a rapid attainment of Indian Independence. On one side, there was his attachment to the extremist mode of protest, and then there was his loyalty towards his father. His initial dissociation from the ground realities of India also worked as a hindrance for him taking any definitive position.

He was overall disturbed at the state of the inane Indian response to the British rule, with Anglophile Indian elite at the helm. The emergence of Gandhi worked as a great impetus to the Indian freedom struggle, and provided Nehru with the much needed direction that he was in search of. Gandhi's success at Champaran and Ahmedabad introduced the power of Satyagraha to the Indian masses. Civic resistance seemed to be a new political weapon that was powerful enough to put even the greatest imperialist power on the back-foot on issues of rightful governance and public rights.

Jawaharlal Nehru as INC President: Jawaharlal Nehru's rise within the Indian National Congress (INC) was meteoric in the years following the Non-Cooperation movement. He, along with Subhas Chandra Bose, became two dynamic young leaders of the Congress to whom the Indians were glad to look up to for guidance. The Calcutta Congress of 1928 saw the Congress divided on the Nehru report prepared by Motilal Nehru on India's being awarded dominion status by the British government.

Jawaharlal himself took exception to the steps laid down by the Nehru report. Mahatma Gandhi worked towards a compromise, and also single handedly worked for Jawaharlal's election as the Congress President in the historic Lahore Congress in 1929. Despite the universally accepted organizational prowess of Vallabbhai Patel, Jawaharlal Nehru was elected as the Congress president at a young age of forty, prior to the extremely significant Lahore Congress of 1929. Nehru was prompt to use the platform in order to declare his dream of Purna Swaraj or Complete Independence.

Apprentice Congressman: Jawaharlal Nehru as a Congress apprentice started his political career soon after he returned from England. Although he worked in the legal firm of his father, yet it was India's predicament that concerned him more than his legal career. He was highly impressed by the Gandhian philosophy and way of life, and soon found in Gandhi the direction that he long yearned for. The entire Nehru family adopted Gandhian ways, however, but it was Nehru more than others who heartily accepted the Gandhian way of life, much to his father's dismay.

Nehru traveled the country extensively to preach Gandhi's ways and participate in the nationalist movements. The way he was received by the masses filled him with new confidence in his abilities and popular appeal. Gandhi himself was not slow to realize the great popular support that Nehru could harness with his background, charm and liberal education. These sojourns also provided Nehru with an opportunity to see the widespread exploitation that plagued every sphere of Indian civil life. The perils of the Indian populace that he witnessed first hand in these formative years shaped his policies during his tenure as a prime minister later on. Jawaharlal Nehru participated whole-heartedly in the Non-Cooperation movement. However, he did not join his father to part ways with Gandhi when Motilal Nehru formed the Swaraj Party with CR Das after the movement was called off by Gandhi following the Chauri Chaura incident. Jawaharlal Nehru was caught between divided loyalties between his father and Gandhi. However, his strong faith in Gandhian methodologies made him close ranks with Gandhi in this crucial period of his life. This tension between father and son would be a regular feature in Jawaharlal's life, and it was only after the death of his father that Nehru despite his grief, felt fully free to pursue his own political course. The ascendancy of Nehru in the fullest sense happened only after the death of Motilal Nehru.

Nehru's Prison Days: The monumental Lahore Congress introduced the Civil Disobedience Movement. Nehru plunged himself into the movement and courted arrest. It was not the first time Nehru went to prison, and it would not be the last time either. Over the period of the next decade, Nehru would spend most of the time of his life in prison as a political prisoner. However, he was determined to make his solitude count.

During the days of imprisonment, Nehru wrote extensively on a number of topics, particularly history and other social issues. He read a lot and often lectured fellow prisoners. However, with Motilal, Gandhi and Nehru imprisoned, the Indian freedom movement suddenly found itself without a clear direction. A number of factions both within Congress and outside were trying to undermine Satyagraha and offer alternate ways to India's freedom.

The Indian Independence and the INC: The new government was willing to provide self dominion to India. With Nehru as the Congress president, negotiations were being worked out between the British government and the Congress Party, which was by then elected to be the single most popular party in India. However, the British were willing to play the waiting game and see the outcome of the elections. Moreover, a common ground between the Indian National Congress and the Muslim League was yet to be reached. Nehru tried his best to work out a solution through talks with Jinnah. The talks, expectedly failed. There was an absolute deadlock between the parties, and Partition seemed to be the only way for India to finally attain freedom.

Nehru and the INC in the Years before Indian Freedom: Nehru spent most of the 1930s in prison, far from the Indian freedom struggle and the Indian National Congress. However, he kept a close watch on the course the movement was taking. On his return from prison to mainstream politics, Nehru had to employ all his reconciliatory skills to bring the warring factions within his party to a common platform. Although his Socialist ideals differed significantly from Gandhi's spiritual bent of civil resistance and the cultural aspects that came along with it. His differences with Gandhian modes came into the open in the Lucknow Conference of 1936.

Throughout the early forties, Nehru visited other Nationalist states as the Congress representative. He returned from China just before the World War II. The World War II brought in new problems for the Indian National Congress. Bose and his followers were willing to cooperate with the Axis forces in order to create pressure on the British officials, a move that Nehru summarily disapproved of. In the mean time, the Second Round Table Conference failed, and the Quit India movement was launched. Nehru was imprisoned once more. He was released in 1945 after the end of the War. Soon he started to work relentlessly towards forming the INA and preparing India for the hour of Independence. The end of the war brought the new Labor government in Britain, and the long held dream of Indian independence did not seem very far from then on.

The Indian Independence finally came in the year 1947; although the conditions of the much awaited freedom were far from what was expected. For Nehru as the President of the Indian national Congress, it was a bitter-sweet moment of truth. As the President of Congress, Nehru was the automatic choice as the first Prime Minister of Independent India. On 15th August, 1947 Nehru gave his famous 'Tryst with Destiny' speech from the Red Fort. However, it was hardly the end of his troubles. Mahatma Gandhi was murdered soon after and Patel died in 1950. Nehru was vested with the duty of steadying the rocking boat of the tottering economy of a newly emergent nation. This started the second phase of Nehru's work within the folds of the Indian National Congress, the post Independence phase.

Post-Independence Phase of INC and Nehru: Indian National Congress was committed to the primary idea of freeing India from British rule. Nehru thought otherwise, and he realized that the widespread popularity of the Congress could be used as a platform to address and solve much of the nation's problems. However, a sudden loss in a sense of direction was imminent in Congress. The Congress party itself had its due share of problems too. The Leftist forces provided a constant threat to the Party, as was the right wing within the Party who opposed Nehru's socialist ideals. At such a time, it was much because of Nehru's personal charisma that the integrity of the Congress could be successfully maintained.

Nehru's imposing internationalism somehow helped to soothe the problems back home. In fact, problems as mounting as the division of the provinces on linguistic lines and the Kashmir debate were also taken care of by Nehru's formidable success in foreign policies. It was with his stature, that Nehru managed to forge together the various warring forces within the

Congress. However, Nehru himself was well aware of the decadence that has infested the party ranks and is known to have warned his party members after the Congress victory of 1957.

Nehru's commitment to the Congress party was life-long, and he is still considered to be one of the greatest Congressmen. However, the greatness of Nehru remains in the fact, that he successfully transcended his Congress identity to become a major international political figure.

IMPRISONMENT DURING WORLD WAR II

When, at the outbreak of World War II in September 1939, the viceroy, Lord Linlithgow, committed India to war without consulting the autonomous provincial ministries, the Congress party's High Command withdrew its provincial ministries as a protest. Congress's action left the political field virtually open to Jinnah and the Muslim League. Nehru's views on the war differed from those of Gandhi. Initially, the Mahatma believed that whatever support was given to the British should be given unconditionally and that it should be of a non-violent character. Nehru held that non-violence had no place in defense against aggression and that India should support Great Britain in a war against Nazism, but only as a free nation. If it could not help, it should not hinder.

In October 1940, Gandhi, abandoning his original stand, decided to launch a limited civil-disobedience campaign in which leading advocates of Indian independence were selected to participate one by one. Nehru was arrested and sentenced to four years' imprisonment. After spending a little more than a year in jail, he was released, along with other Congress prisoners, three days before the bombing of Pearl Harbor in Hawaii. When the Japanese carried their attack through Burma to the borders of India in the spring of 1942, the British government, faced by this new military threat, decided to make some overtures to India.

Prime Minister Winston Churchill dispatched Sir Stafford Cripps, a member of the war Cabinet who was politically close to Nehru and also knew Jinnah, with proposals for a settlement of the constitutional problem. Cripps's mission failed, however, for Gandhi would accept nothing less than independence. Nehru played a significant role in negotiations with Sir Stafford Cripps as well as in the developments leading to the Quit India Movement (1942). Equally memorable is his role during the trial of the three officers of the Indian National Army in the Red Fort in November 1945, when he, along with Bhulabhai Desai and T.B. Sapru fought on behalf of the INA officers. He was also a chief negotiator during the Simla Conference (June 1945), Cabinet Mission (May 16, 1946), and June 3rd Plan (1947). The initiative in the Congress party now passed to Gandhi, who called on the British to leave India; Nehru, though reluctant to embarrass the war effort, had no alternative but to join Gandhi. Following the Quit India resolution passed by the Congress party in Bombay on August 8, 1942, the entire Congress working committee, including Gandhi and Nehru, was arrested and imprisoned. Nehru emerged from this — his ninth and last detention—only on June 15, 1945.

Though there were perceptible differences between Nehru and Gandhi, they were inseparable. Gandhi's verdict on him also points to Nehru's contribution to India's struggle for freedom: "Jawaharlal is as pure as crystal, he is truthful beyond suspicion. He is knight *sanspeur, sans reproche*. The nation is safe in his hands." The Mahatma regarded him as his political heir. Nehru adopted Gandhi's idea of non-violent struggle for liberating India from British rule, and believed that only the right means could produce right ends.

Within two years India was to be partitioned and free. A final attempt by the viceroy, Lord Wavell, to bring the Congress party and the Muslim League together failed. The Labour government that had meanwhile displaced Churchill's wartime administration dispatched, as one of its first acts, a Cabinet mission to India and later also replaced Lord Wavell with Lord Mountbatten. The question was no longer whether India was to be independent but whether it was to consist of one or more independent states. While Gandhi refused to accept partition, Nehru reluctantly but realistically acquiesced. On August 15, 1947, India and Pakistan emerged as two separate, independent countries. Nehru became independent India's first prime minister.

THE PRE-INDEPENDENCE ERA

Founded in 1885 with the objective of obtaining a greater share in government for educated Indians, the Indian National Congress was initially not opposed to British rule. The Congress met once a year during December. Indeed, it was a Scotsman, Allan Octavian Hume, who brought about its first meeting in Bombay, with the approval of Lord Dufferin, the then-Viceroy.

Womesh Chandra Bonerjee was the first President of the INC. The first meeting was scheduled to be held in Pune, but due to a plague outbreak there, the meeting was later shifted to Bombay. The first Session of INC was held from 28-31 December 1885, and was attended by 72 delegates.

A few years down the line, the demands of INC became more radical in the face of constant opposition from the government, and the party became very active in the independence movement. By 1907 the party was split into two halves: the *Garam Dal* of Bal Gangadhar Tilak, or Extremists (literally "hot faction"), and the *Naram Dal* of Gopal Krishna Gokhale, or Moderates (literally "soft faction"), distinguished by their attitude towards the British. Under the influence of Bal Gangadhar Tilak, the Congress became the first integrated mass organization in the country, bringing together millions of people against the British.

In its time as the nation's leader in the freedom struggle, it produced the nation's greatest leaders. Before the Gandhi Era came leaders like Bal Gangadhar Tilak, Bipin Chandra Pal, Lala Lajpat Rai, Gopal Krishna Gokhale, Mohammed Ali Jinnah (later leader of the Muslim League and instrumental in the creation of Pakistan), all starting with the first legendary icon of Indians: Dadabhai Naoroji, the president of the sister Indian National Association and later the first Indian Member of Parliament in the British House of Commons. With the rise of Mahatma Gandhi's popularity and his Satyagraha art of revolution came Sardar Vallabhbhai Patel, Pandit Jawaharlal Nehru (the nation's first Prime Minister), Dr. Rajendra Prasad (the nation's first President), Khan Mohammad Abbas Khan, Khan Abdul Ghaffar Khan, Chakravarti Rajgopalachari, Jivatram Kripalani and Maulana Abul Kalam Azad.

With the already existing nationalistic feeling combinded with Gandhi's popularity the Congress became a forceful mass organization in the country, bringing together millions of people by specifically working against caste differences, untouchability, poverty, and religious and ethnic boundaries. Although predominantly Hindu, it had members from virtually every religion, ethnic group, economic class and linguistic group. At the time of the Quit India movement, the Congress was undoubtedly the strongest political and revolutionary organization in India. The Indian National Congress could claim to be the true representative of the Indian people.

The 1929 Lahore session under the presidency of Jawaharlal Nehru holds special significance as in this session "Poorna Swaraj" (complete independence) was declared as the goal of INC. The 26th January 1930 was declared as "Poorna Swaraj Diwas," Independence Day although the British remained in India a number of years longer.

It was to commemorate this date particularly that The Indian Constitution was formally adopted on 26 January 1950 (even though it was passed on 26 November 1949). After the First World War the party became associated with Mahatma Gandhi, who remained its unofficial, spiritual leader and mass icon even as younger men and women became party president. The party was in many ways an umbrella organization, sheltering within itself radical socialists, traditionalists and even Hindu and Muslim conservatives.

The Post-independence Era

The party remained in power for thirty *continuous* years between independence in 1947 and its first taste of electoral defeat (at the national level) in 1977.

History of the Republic of India

The History of the Republic of India began on August 15, 1947 when India became an independent Dominion within the British Commonwealth. Concurrently the Muslim-majority northwest and east of British India was separated into the Dominion of Pakistan. Lord Louis Mountbatten, and later Chakravarti Rajagopalachari served in the office of the Governor General of India. Jawaharlal Nehru became the first Prime Minister of India and Sardar Vallabhbhai Patel became the Deputy Prime Minister of India and its Minister of Home Affairs.

1947–1950

Independent India's first years were marked with turbulent events — a massive exchange of population with Pakistan, the Indo-Pakistani War of 1947 and the integration of over 500 princely states to form a united nation.

AFTERMATH OF PARTITION

An estimated 3.5 million Hindus and Sikhs living in West Punjab, NWFP, Baluchistan, East Bengal and Sind migrated to India in fear of domination and suppression in Muslim Pakistan. Communal violence killed an estimated 1 million Hindus, Muslims and Sikhs, and gravely destabilized both Dominions along their Punjab and Bengal boundaries, and the cities of Calcutta, Delhi and Lahore. The violence was stopped by early September owing to the cooperative efforts of both Indian and Pakistani leaders, and especially due the efforts of Mohandas Gandhi, the leader of the Indian freedom struggle, who undertook a *fast-unto-death* in Calcutta and later in Delhi to calm people and emphasize peace despite the threat to his life. Both Governments constructed large relief camps for incoming and leaving refugees, and the Indian Army was mobilized to provide humanitarian assistance on a massive scale.

The assassination of Mahatma Gandhi on January 30, 1948 was a major setback to the young nation. Gandhi was murdered by Nathuram Vinayak Godse, allegedly affiliated with the Hindu nationalist movement, who held him responsible for partition and charged that Gandhi was appeasing Muslims. More than one million people flooded the streets of Delhi to follow the procession to cremation grounds and pay their last respects.

In 1949, India recorded close to 1 million Hindu refugees flooded into West Bengal and other states from East Pakistan, owing to communal violence, intimidation and repression from Muslim authorities. The plight of the refugees outraged Hindus and Indian nationalists, and the refugee population drained the resources of Indian states, who were unable to absorb them. While not ruling out war, Prime Minister Nehru and Sardar Patel invited Liaquat Ali Khan for talks in Delhi.

Although many Indians termed this appeasement, Nehru signed a pact with Liaquat Ali Khan that pledged both nations to the protection of minorities and creation of minority commissions.

Although opposed to the principle, Patel decided to back this Pact for the sake of peace, and played a critical role in garnering support from West Bengal and across India, and enforcing the provisions of the Pact. Khan and Nehru also signed a trade agreement, and committed to resolving bilateral disputes through peaceful means. Steadily, hundreds of thousands of Hindus returned to East Pakistan, but the thaw in relations did not last long, primarily owing to the Kashmir dispute.

Union's Integration

British India consisted of 17 provinces and a few hundred princely states. The provinces were given to India or Pakistan, in some cases in particular — Punjab and Bengal — after being partitioned. The princes of the princely states, however, won the right to either remain independent or join either nation. Thus India's leaders faced the prospect of inheriting a nation fragmented between medieval-era kingdoms and provinces organized by colonial powers. Under the leadership of Sardar Vallabhbhai Patel, the new Government of India employed political negotiations backed with the option (and, on several occasions, the use) of military action to ensure the primacy of the Central government and of the Constitution then being drafted.

There were three States that proved more difficult to integrate than others:

1. Junagadh – a December 1947 plebiscite resulted in a 99% vote to merge with India, annulling the controversial accession to Pakistan, which was made despite the people of the state being overwhelmingly Hindu.
2. Hyderabad – Patel ordered the Indian army to depose the government of the Nizam after the failure of negotiations, which was done between September 13 – September 17, 1948. It was incorporated as a state of India the next year.
3. The area of Kashmir in the far north of the subcontinent quickly became a source of controversy that erupted into the First Indo-Pakistani War which lasted from 1947 to 1949. Eventually a United Nations-overseen ceasefire was agreed that left India in control of two thirds of the contested region.

The Constituent Assembly adopted the Constitution of India, drafted by a committee headed by B. R. Ambedkar, on November 26, 1949. India became a federal, democratic republic after its Constitution came into effect on January 26, 1950. Rajendra Prasad became the first President of India.

1950s and 1960s

India held its first national elections under the Constitution in 1952, where a turnout of over 60% was recorded. The Congress Party won an overwhelming majority, and Jawaharlal Nehru began a second term as Prime Minister. President Prasad was also elected to a second term by the electoral college of the first Parliament of India.

NEHRU ADMINISTRATION (1952–1964)

Prime Minister Nehru led the Congress to major election victories in 1957 and 1962. The Parliament passed extensive reforms that increased the legal rights of women in Hindu society, and further legislated against caste discrimination and untouchability. Nehru advocated a strong initiative to enroll India's children to complete primary education, and thousands of schools, colleges and institutions of advanced learning, such as the Indian Institutes of Technology were founded across the nation. Nehru advocated a socialist model for the economy of India—no taxation for Indian farmers, minimum wage and benefits for blue-collar workers, and the nationalization of heavy industries such as steel, aviation, shipping, electricity and mining. An extensive public works and industrialization campaign resulted in the construction of major dams, irrigation canals, roads, thermal and hydroelectric power stations.

States Reorganization

Potti Sreeramulu's *fast-unto-death,* and consequent death for the demand of an Andhra State in 1953 sparked a major re-shaping of the Indian Union. Nehru appointed the *States Reorganization Commission,* upon whose recommendations, the States Reorganization Act was passed in 1956. Old states were dissolved and new states created on the lines of shared linguistic and ethnic demographics. The separation of Kerala and the Telugu-speaking regions of Madras State enabled the creation of an exclusively Tamil-speaking state of Tamil Nadu. On May 1, 1960, the states of Maharashtra and Gujarat were created out of the Bombay state. The creation of Punjabi Suba on November 1, 1966, an exclusively Punjabi speaking state of Punjab (India), occurred after a long struggle.

Foreign Policy and Military Conflicts

Nehru's foreign policy was the inspiration of the Non-Aligned Movement, of which India was a co-founder. Nehru maintained friendly relations with both the United States and the Soviet Union, and encouraged the People's Republic of China to join the global community of nations. In 1956, when the Suez Canal Company was seized by the Egyptian government, an international conference voted 18-4 to take action against Egypt. India was one of the 4 backers of Egypt, along with Indonesia, Sri Lanka, and the USSR.

India had controversially opposed the partition of Palestine and the 1956 invasion of the Sinai by Israel, Britain and France, but did not oppose the Chinese occupation of Tibet and the suppression of a pro-democracy movement in Hungary by the Soviet Union.

Although Nehru disavowed nuclear ambitions for India, Canada and France aided India in the development of nuclear power stations for electricity. India also negotiated an agreement in 1960 with Pakistan on the just use of the waters of seven rivers shared by the countries. Nehru had visited Pakistan in 1953, but owing to political turmoil in Pakistan, no headway was made on the Kashmir dispute.

1. India has fought a total of four wars/military conflicts with its rival nation Pakistan, two in this period.In the Indo-Pakistani War of 1947 fought over Kashmir, Pakistan occupied one third of Kashmir (which India claims as its territory), and India occupied three fifths (which Pakistan claims as its territory). In the Indo-Pakistani War of 1965 India attacked Pakistan on all fronts after attempts by Pakistani troops to infiltrate into Indian controlled Kashmir. #In 1961, after continual petitions for a peaceful handover, India invaded and annexed the Portuguese colony of Goa on the west coast of India.
2. In 1962 China and India engaged in the brief Sino-Indian War over the border in the Himalayas. The war was a complete rout for the Indians and led to a refocusing on arms build-up and an improvement in relations with the United States. While China withdrew from occupied lands in the northeast, it continues to occupy Aksai Chin in Kashmir. China disputes India's sovereignty over Arunachal Pradesh and until recently, Sikkim.

POST-NEHRU INDIA

Jawaharlal Nehru died on May 27, 1964. Lal Bahadur Shastri succeeded him as Prime Minister. In 1965 in the Second Kashmir War India and Pakistan again went to war, but without any definitive outcome or alteration of the Kashmir boundary. The Tashkent Agreement was signed under the mediation of the Soviet government, but Shastri died on the night after the signing ceremony. A leadership election resulted in the elevation of Indira Gandhi, Nehru's daughter who had been serving as Minister for Information and

Broadcasting, as the third Prime Minister. She defeated right-wing leader Morarji Desai.

The Congress Party won a reduced majority in the 1967 elections owing to widespread disenchantment over rising prices of commodities, unemployment, economic stagnation and a food crisis. Indira Gandhi had started on a rocky note after agreeing to a devaluation of the Indian rupee, which created much hardship for Indian businesses and consumers, and the import of wheat from the U.S. fell through due to political disputes.

Morarji Desai entered Indira's government as Deputy Prime Minister and Finance Minister, and with senior Congress politicians attempted to constrain Indira's authority. But following the counsel of her political advisor P. N. Haksar, Indira resuscitated her popular appeal by a major shift towards socialist policies. She successfully ended the privy purse guarantee for former Indian royalty, and waged a major offensive against party hierarchy over the nationalization of India's banks. Although resisted by Desai and India's business community, the policy was popular with the masses. When Congress politicians attempted to oust Indira by suspending her Congress membership, Indira was empowered with a large exodus of MPs to her own Congress (R). The bastion of the freedom struggle, the Indian National Congress had split in 1969. Indira continued to govern with a slim majority.

Nehru and States Reorganisation Act

The States Reorganization Act of 1956 was a major reform of the boundaries and governance of India's states and territories. The act reorganized the boundaries of India's states along linguistic lines, and amended the Indian Constitution to replace the three types of states, known as Parts A, B, and C states, with a single type of state. Although additional changes to India's state boundaries have been made since 1956, the States Reorganisation Act of 1956 remains the single most extensive change in state boundaries since the independence of India in 1947.

Political Integration after Independence and the Constitution of 1950

British India, which included most of present-day India as well as Pakistan and Bangladesh, was divided into two types of territories: provinces, which were governed directly by British officials, responsible to the Governor-General of India; and princely states, under the rule of local hereditary rulers who recognised British sovereignty in return for local autonomy, as established by treaty.

As a result of the reforms of the early 20th century, most of the provinces had elected legislatures and governors, although some of the smaller provinces were governed by a chief commissioner appointed by the Governor-General. The 20th century reforms of British India also established the principle of federalism, also known in British India as "dyarchy", which was carried forward into the governance of independent India.

On August 15, 1947, British India was granted independence as the separate dominions of India and Pakistan. The British dissolved their treaty relations with the over 600 princely states, who were encouraged to accede to either India or Pakistan. Most of the states acceded to India, and a few to Pakistan. Bhutan and Hyderabad opted for independence, although the armed intervention of India brought Hyderabad into the Indian Union.

During the 1947-1950 period, the territories of the princely states were politically integrated into the Indian Union. Most were merged into the existing provinces; others were organised into new provinces, like Rajputana, Himachal Pradesh, Madhya Bharat, and Vindhya Pradesh made up of multiple princely states; a few, including Mysore, Hyderabad, Bhopal, and Bilaspur, became separate provinces.

The Government of India Act 1935 remained the constitutional law of India pending adoption of a new Constitution. The Constitution of India, which went into effect on January 26, 1950, made India a sovereign, democratic republic, and a union of states (replacing provinces) and territories. The states would have extensive autonomy and complete democracy in the Union, while the Union territories would be administered by the Government of India. The constitution of 1950 distinguished between three types of states.

Part A states, which were the former governors' provinces of British India, were ruled by an elected governor and state legislature. The nine Part A states were Assam, West Bengal, Bihar, Bombay, Madhya Pradesh (formerly Central Provinces and Berar), Madras, Orissa, Punjab, and Uttar Pradesh (formerly United Provinces). The eight Part B states were former princely states or groups of princely states, governed by a rajpramukh, who was often a former prince, along with an elected legislature.

The rajpramukh was appointed by the President of India. The Part B states were Hyderabad, Saurashtra, Mysore, Travancore-Cochin, Madhya Bharat, Vindhya Pradesh, Patiala and East Punjab States Union (PEPSU), and Rajasthan. The ten Part C states included both the former chief commissioners' provinces and princely states, and were governed by a chief commissioner.

The chief commissioner was appointed by the President of India. The Part C states included Delhi, Kutch, Himachal Pradesh, Bilaspur, Coorg, Bhopal, Manipur, Ajmer-Merwara, and Tripura. Jammu and Kashmir had special status until 1957. The Andaman and Nicobar Islands was established as a union territory, ruled by a lieutenant governor appointed by the central government.

The Movement for Linguistic States

Political movements for the creation of new, linguistic-based states developed around India in the years after independence. The movement to create a Telugu-speaking state out of the northern portion of Madras State gathered strength in the years after independence, and in 1953, the 16 northern, Telugu-speaking districts of Madras State became the new State of Andhra. Other small changes were made to state boundaries during the 1950-1956 period. The small state of Bilaspur was merged with Himachal Pradesh on July 1, 1954, and Chandernagore, a former enclave of French India, was incorporated into West Bengal in 1955.

The States Reorganisation Commission

In December 1953, Prime Minister Jawaharlal Nehru appointed the States Reorganisation Commission to prepare for the creation of states on linguistic lines. This was headed by Justice Fazal Ali and the commission itself was also known as the *Fazal Ali Commission*. The efforts of this commission was overseen by Govind Ballabh Pant, who served as Home Minister from December 1954. The commission created a report in 1955 recommending the reorganisation of India's states.

The States Reorganisation Act

The States Reorganisation Act of 1956, which went into effect on November 1, eliminated the distinction between part A, B, and C states. It also reorganised the state boundaries and created or dissolved states and union territories.

India and the Non-Aligned Movement

India played an important role in the multilateral movements of colonies and newly independent countries that developed into the Non-Aligned Movement.

3

Nehru as a Social Reformer

Jawaharlal Nehru was the first Prime Minister of independent India. He was a key figure in the Indian independence movement. Nehru also initiated the process of social reform in the independent Indian Republic. The importance of Jawaharlal Nehru as a social reformer in Indian history cannot be denied. India gained independence on 15 August, 1947. The India that existed in the 1940's was a cauldron of social unrest.

The age-old problem of caste had reared its ugly head and was threatening to tear the social fabric apart. Religious tensions were also a reigning problem in India during those days. The partition of pre-independent India had divided the Indian sub-continent into two countries, India and Pakistan. Pakistan became an Islamic Republic as envisaged by its creator Mohamed Ali Jinnah. India became a secular republic by choice.

Jawaharlal Nehru inherited from the British a country that was bereft of social and economic stability. He inherited a mish-mash of people speaking as many as 16 different languages with different cultural moorings.

The genius of Jawaharlal Nehru as a social reformer shone through in this post-independence period. He took decisive steps to eradicate the evils of the all pervasive caste system. Nehru undertook corrective measures by changing existing Indian legal laws. Legal procedures were enacted to make caste discrimination illegal and punishable by law. The enacted laws were strictly enforced. Jawaharlal Nehru was one of the few Indian statesmen at that time who understood the need of proper intellectual development of the Indian populace. He had exposure to European educational ideals during his stay at England, where he received education. Nehru also knew that British stress on proper education to run their colonial empire. He understood the importance of proper and healthy intellectual development to run the nascent Indian state. Jawaharlal Nehru wished to combine the best of both worlds, the winning combination of western scientific prowess and Indian civilization wisdom.

Nehru realized that the only way the Indian Republic can reestablish its presence in the world stage is through the intellectual power of its citizens. Jawaharlal stressed on the teaching of science and its practical application fields. He took cognizance of the need of learning vocational science. The teaching of vocational science attracted him. Special focus was put on the development of technology. The famed Indian Institutes of Technology or IIT's were conceived and established during his Prime Minister-ship. The Indian Institutes of Technology are now regarded as one of the premier scientific institutes of higher technological learning throughout the world. IIT graduates are much in demand among the corporate sector. The establishment of such learning centers also indirectly contributed to the emergence of the Indian Republic as a pharmaceutical major in the late 1980's. The cheapest medicines in the world are produced and sold in India. The capabilities of the Indian software industry have also amazed the world.

Jawaharlal Nehru was born in an era when the principal mode of communication was the postal service. Telephones were affordable only by the minuscule economically empowered Indian populace. There were few government hospitals. The rural Indian population lived in pitiable conditions amidst abject poverty. Nehru was acutely aware of the rural situation of India. He had contested and won democratic elections in Pratapgarh district of Uttar Pradesh. Jawaharlal Nehru knew the many problems faced by the rural populace.

The rural environment was feudal at that time. Literacy was low and social tensions were simmering below the societal surface. Nehru initiated the construction and functioning of a number of schools. The schools provided primary and secondary education to the rural population. The schools are spread throughout India. Primary education was provided free of cost.

The government schools also provided free meals to its students. This scheme was the trump card of Jawaharlal Nehru. The great statesmen understood the importance of food to attract students to schools.

The purchasing power of the rural Indian population at that time was very low. A majority of the rural population subsisted on one meal a day. All members of the family were required to work to keep the home-fires burning. The children were also roped in to earn for the family. Jawaharlal Nehru knew the importance of food in the educational scheme. The food acts as a magnet for the impoverished hungry child. The family of the prospective student was also happy with the subsequent tangible cost savings.

The food given in the primary education programs included milk in addition to pulses for a healthy meal. The specter of malnutrition in the 1950's and 1960's India were fought in this way. Jawaharlal Nehru also established vocational schools for adults. Adult education centers were created both in rural and urban areas. Higher technical schools were also established.

The Indian Republic has a substantial population. Almost half of the population is women. Jawaharlal Nehru enacted laws to guarantee practical universal suffrage to the women population of the country. The laws aimed to secure the social freedoms of Indian women. Female legal rights were also increased under Nehru's able Prime Ministership.

Jawaharlal Nehru was a highly educated man. His western education catalyzed his aspirations for equality of the Indian populace. Nehru actively promoted and brought about the system of reservations in the Indian job sector. A certain percentage of government jobs were reserved for persons born into scheduled castes and scheduled tribes. This was done to ensure the participation of the less privileged Indian population to the mainstream.

Jawaharlal Nehru had many social successes to his credit. He was responsible for promoting the rights of religious minorities. His swift judgment along with his mentor Mahatma Gandhi at the time of independence ensured that the Indian Republic became a secular state. He understood the basic social nature of the Indian population. The Indian population is largely secular, plural and civil and has a number of practicing religions. Nehru fostered the need for tolerance of all religions and respect for people unlike own.

The success of Jawaharlal Nehru's reforms is apparent throughout the modern Indian Republic. The booming economy of contemporary India underscores this fact.

CIVIL DISOBEDIENCE

The mystic strain in Bose character survived and remained with him until his death in an air crash in Formosa on the eve of the Japanese surrender in World War II. Politics imbued with philosophy and religio-mystic thought lead to strange idealisations. They were to lead Subhas into an association with Fascism and Nazism for the liberation of his country.

Bose was not greatly influenced by Gandhi, with whose methods and philosophy he often vigorously disagreed. His only political guru was Deshbandhu Das, whose death in 1925 left him bereft of a secure anchorage. Bose had no patience with Gandhi's nonviolence, and was irritated by the intricate permutations and combinations of the Mahatma's political processes. There he differed from Nefara, who by rationalising Gandhi's inconsistencies sought to reduce his teachings to an intellectual pattern of thinking. Temperamentally and intellectually Bose and Gandhi were poles apart. Eventually this was to influence Bose's place in the Congress hierarchy. Nehra, while still critical of many phases in the Mahatma's political thought, found in him a lodestar that never ceased to attract. He found too that he was beginning to share with Gandhi an immense and unusual popularity with the masses. He could not but realise that he had become a national hero. Songs were written about him and legends grew around him. He was showered, as is the Indian way, with titles. He was hailed as Bharat Bhushan (Jewel of India) and Tyagamurti (Embodiment of Sacrifice).

If this adulation sometimes went to Nehru's head, as he confesses it did, he had his wife and sisters to provide the necessary corrective. The new conferred on Jawaharlal were a for and fun.

At the he was adjured by one of them, "O of pass me the better," or sometimes even little Indira "O of Sacrifice, what is the time?" the affectionate amusement But was not amused. To her the adulation showered on her son by the a perfectly natural reaction. the Motilal 7 at his son's suggestion and Gandhi, decided to give over his house Anand to the renaming it Swaraj. The family the to a new house, christened after the old, which a and the offices of the All-India Candid not live to complete the legal formal of later done by Jawaharlal, who in accord his created a trust of the property to the independence pledge-taking cere OB demonstrated the depth and strength of pop only awaited the signal to launch on civil disobedience. As Nefara was to write in a letters to his daughter three 1930 "with the air dark with the shadow of coining a 315! Gandhi suddenly announced his so-called Eleven his willingness to put off civil disobedience if Brit by his Points,, would grant the substance of independence. He eleven things: (1) total prohibition of alcohol; (2) tie restoration of the exchange rate of the rupee to is good; (3) of land revenue by 50 per cent; (4) abolition of the salt tax; (5) reduction of military expenditure by at least 50 per cent; (6) of the salaries of civil servants by half; (7) a protective cloth; (8) enactment of a coastal reservation bill in of Indian shipping; (9) release of all political prisoners not for murder or attempted murder; (10) abolition or control of the Criminal Investigation Department, whose principal target. He her Happiness "became, by its new name, Hie Abode of Independence, was the Congress; and (11) of forearms for self-defence, to popular control.

"Let the Viceroy" declared Gandhi "satisfy us with regard to very simple but vital of India. He will that hear no talk of civil disobedience. It was a startlingly miscellaneous list of demands designed obviously to appeal to various sections of the people the masses, classes businessmen and intellectuals. But to Nehru this curious melange of social and political reforms seemed to bear no relation whatever to the basic demand for independence.

Once again he was peeved and puzzled. What, for instance, had the abolition of the salt tax to do with civil disobedience? Gandhi was soon to let the country and the Congress know. There is no article like salt, outside water, by taring which the State can touch the starving millions, the sick, the maimed and the utterly helpless" Gandhi proclaimed. The tax constitutes therefore the most inhuman poll tax the ingenuity of man can devise."

Like the hated gabette which formed a rallying cry for the French peasantry before the onset of the French Revolution,, salt suddenly became the symbol of revolt in India. By calling on the people deliberately to break the salt law and "manufacture" at on the open beaches, Gandhi gave a dramatically rebellious significance to a simple act.

On March 2nd the Mahatma wrote a letter to the Viceroy, Lord Irwin, addressing him as "Dear Friend," in the course of which he said: Even the salt he [the peasant] must use in order to live is so taxed as to make the burden fall heaviest on him, if only because of the heartless impartiality of its incidence. The tax shows itself more burdensome to the poor man for salt is the one thing he must eat more than the rich, individually and collectively.

After enumerating the various burdens heaped on the Indian people, Gandhi went on to write: if you cannot see your way to deal with these evils and my letter makes no appeal to your heart, on the eleventh day of this month I shall proceed with such co-workers of the ashram as I can take, to disregard the provisions of the salt laws. I regard this tax to be the most iniquitous of all from the poor man's standpoint As the independence movement is essentially for the la the a will "be made with this evil. The is that we to the creel monopoly for so long. It is, ready, in a disciplined manner, to take up the me, in the act of disobeying the Salt Act, to lay them to the of a law that should never have disagreed the maas to the Viceroy through an English mesa by the name of Reginald Reynolds was formal, and merely regretted that the Mabe "contemplating a course of action which is clearly to violation of the law, and danger to the public peace."

On 30th, at 6:30 in the morning, Gandhi, accompanied by set out on his famous march from his ashram at for the small sea-side village of Dandi, 241 miles away. He was He strode briskly, staff In hand, speaking at towns to crowds which swelled progressively, and as he a ire of patriotic fervour Eared through the land.

At about halfway between Sabarmati and Dandi, Motilal cm their way back to Allahabad from a meeting of the Congress Committee at Ahmedabad, met the Mahatma a few hole is with him there, and then walked a little dis him. Fattier and son finally bade him farewell. 'That," "was my last glimpse of him then as I saw him, in marching along at the head of his followers with firm a peaceful but undaunted look It was a moving sight" It was a which stirred Nehru deeply and brought welling to the ardour and impatience of his impetuous spirit. He to plunge into the struggle which had still to begin. At this he turned to the country's youth, who, like him, were at the leash, and in a message to them even as the Mahatma onward he apostrophized: "The pilgrim marches onward. The of battle lies before you, the flag of India beckons you, and herself awaits your coming. Do you hesitate now, you who but yesterday so loudly on her side? Will you be mere lookers-on in this straggle and see your best and bravest face the might be a empire which has crashed your country and her children?

Who If India dies? Who dies if India lives?" On March list the All-India Congress Committee meeting at Ahmedabad prepared for the now inevitable struggle. It was arranged that as each President was arrested, his should succeed him, appointing in tarn a new Working Committee to replace those members who were also arrested. This applied not only to the Central Congress organisation bet to provincial and local committees.

Earlier Gandhi had indicated that while a sporadic act of violence would not lead him to call off the movement as he had done in the last civil-disobedience campaign eight years earlier, he would not tolerate violence as in any way part of lie movement. In his march towards Dandi he preached the message of nonviolence incessantly, and as was his wont spoke frankly on the decencies of himself and the Indian people: "We are not angels. We are very weak, tempted. There are many lapses to our debit". On April 7th Gandhi with his followers reached Dandi, and on the following day, after his morning prayers, the Mahatma walked to the beach and, picking up a lump of crude salt, symbolically broke the law. In the event of his arrest he nominated a veteran Muslim Congressman, the white-bearded Abbas Tyabji, to succeed him in the leadership, and on Tyabji's arrest he announced that Mis. Sarojini Naidu should succeed.

Gandhi's action was the signal for a country-wide breaking of the salt law. "It seemed," wrote Nehru, "as though a spring had been suddenly released."

The British authorities, inclined at first to dismiss the Mahatma's march as a futile political pantomime, now took alarm. They resorted to firing and to lathi charges on demonstrators. Once again Gandhi adjured his people to remain steadfastly nonviolent in the face of repression. "If we are to stand the final heat of the battle" he urged, "we must learn to stand our ground in the face of cavalry or baton charges and allow ourselves to be trampled under the horses, hoofs or be braised in the charges."

On April 14th Nehra was arrested while entraining from Allahabad for Raipur in the then Central Provinces. 5 He had earlier, after addressing a huge meeting and leading a vast procession, ceremoniously "manufactured" some contraband salt. He was charged with breach of the salt law, tried summarily behind prison walk and sentenced to six this his term of imprisonment. Jawaharlal was in fail years, being detained this time in his province. He was to remain there, with an of until January 26, 1931. The with repression increasing on the one and mounting on the other. Nehra had to him as the Congress President during his in jail, bat the declined, and Jawaharlal then nomihis as his Although ailing and stricken by the first of the which ten months later was to end in his over the of responsibility with his accused the movement with determination and discipline was in the early hours of May 5th while sleeping in his hut at Dandi "At the dead of night like thieves they to away," wrote Mira Ben, his English disciple. "For to lay hands on him they feared the multitude him for a prophet in arrest civil disobedience had acquired a new and on crowds and lathi charges grew to be or occurrences. From breach of the salt laws the movement into other directions. Foreign cloth shops were booths boycotted.

A of the movement was the remarkable awakening of Indian left their sheltered homes in thousands and took their by menfolk in the fight for freedom. Many hundreds of arrested and imprisoned. From this period derives the of and emancipation which henceforth was increasingly to feminine progress in India surprisingly, the women of the Nehra household were foreign the fray. For many hours daily Jawaharlal's mother, sisters and under the hot summer sun picketing foreign cloth shops, others of their sex the rudeness and indignities to which sometimes subjected by the police. Motilals patriarchal outnot easily accoromodate itself to the idea of his wife, ami daughter-in-law participating in such activities. But he did not interfere, and secretly took pride in the courage and energy which they displayed, later, he Jawaharlal in jail, he spoke with affectionate of doings.

Most surprising of all was the and ardour by the ailing Kamala, whose determination while it Jawaharlal also moved him deeply. In the months of 1930, as civil disobedience loomed large on the horizon, he had for the first time Kamala's eager desire to prove a worthy political comrade. Now, from behind prison walk, he followed with amazement his wife's efforts to galvanise the movement in Allahabad city and district, and her energy, well and organising capacity left him with a feeling of proud if baffled astonishment. Kamala, although ill and weak, was trying to justify herself in her husband's eye.

"She made up for inexperience by her fire and energy" Nehra wrote much later, "and within a few months she became the pride of Allahabad." From then onwards he saw Kamala in a new light, and this sense of political affinity grew a deeper personal communion between them. Prison and his own political preoccupations had so far prevented Jawaharlal from seeing that what Kamala wanted above all was not to be a mere shadow of her husband but his companion and helpmate. But now at long last he saw and understood.

Daily the movement gathered in strength. As prohibitive laws grew in number, the civil resisters discovered new foci for defiance. There were large-scale raids on salt pans and depots, resulting in the arrest of many top-ranking leaders of Congress; but despite their imprisonment the movement continued with unabated fervour. In the course of this peaceful and determined straggle in which vast masses participated in villages, towns and cities, nearly 100,000 persons wait to prison.

The most spectacular demonstration of nonviolence was seen in the hitherto turbulent Northwest Frontier Province, which is peopled largely by the Pathans and other martial tribesmen. Here Khan Abdul Ghaffat Khan, a brother of Nehru's old friend Dr. Khan Sahib, had organised the movement whose followers were known as Khudai Khidmatgars (Servants of God) and who were pledged to nonviolent service. Because of the rough rust-coloured blouses they wore they were popularly called Red Shirts though they had no Communist affiliations whatever.

Khan Abdul Ghaffar Khan's father had been the chief of a clan of on a in Peshawar district on the border of as it Pakistan. Ghaffar Khan was a of habits, and had been associated with tic the days of the Rowlatt Act, though his were not in active cooperation the Gandhi as Ghaffar Khan came to be known, was by the nonviolent teachings of the Mahatma, and to his followers. In an area such as the Northwhere the rule of an eye for an eye and a for a this was a highly ambitious undertaking. But the in his message of nonviolence, which the minds of the hitherto aggressive tribesmen, out in their thousands to demonstrate peacefully the Raj. Armoured cars were moved against them, and in the British authorities resorted to indiscriminate But the were not easily cowed; and although there a few of violent retaliation, the Khudai Khidmatgars and faced uneinchingly the bullets and bay of flick. So impressive was the forbearance and patience of Hindu-Muslim tribesmen that on one occasion in two of British-led Hindu troops, the 18th Royal Rifles, to fire on them when ordered to do so, and back to their barracks under arrest. The Frontier was imprisoned along with many hundreds of his followers.

Nehru followed eagerly the trend of events outside. He has with a sense of elation and pride. The bearing of Indian particularly of his wife, mother and sisters, exhilarated him, and he was moved also by the strangely peaceful behaviour of the Pathans under the leadership of Khan Abdul Ghaffar Khan or later he knew his father would join him in prison. On June was arrested in Allahabad shortly after he had been on a visit to Bombay, one of the chief citadels of civil resistance in the He was sentenced to six months' imprisonment, and joined his son in his barrack in Naini Central Prison.

Jawaharlal was confined, for the first time by finished was a small circular enclosure roughly one hundred feet in and by a feet high. In the centre of this enclosure a squat drab containing cells, occupied too of as a lavatory.

The enclosure bow an It was in the jail as Kuttaghar the Doghouse. Nehra found the circular wall of his prison-house more oppressive than the rectangular to which he so far in jail. The summer months were uncomfortably and at night he slept in the open, in the narrow corridor the inner building and the enclosing wall, his bed being heavily chained to the ground, probably to prevent its use as a ladder of escape! At night the jail, like a jungle, was full of strange sounds the clatter of the sentries, footsteps, the clanking of keys, the weird shouts and cries of the watchmen on guard, and the hundred and one small noises that break lie vast stillness of a prison asleep.

Lying on his bed ? Nehru liked to watch the open sky and the clouds as they moved across the star-studded canopy of the heavens. Sometimes he would try to work out the approximate from the position of a familiar constellation. A constant stellar companion was the pole star, which peeped cheerfully at him every night from just over the rim of the prison wall.

Nehra rose very early in the morning, about 3:30 or 4:00 A.M. As usual, he planned his day carefully, devoting nearly three hours to spinning on his own charkha, and another two or three hours to weaving. He read a great deal, exercised himself within the narrow ambits of his enclosure, washed his clothes, and generally tidied up the place.

Daily newspapers were not permitted, but a Hindi weekly journal carried accounts of the civil-disobedience movement, and Nehra often found this dramatic reading. Although the principal Congress leaden were in jail, the movement continued steadfastly. There were daily lathi charges, firing at demonstrators was not uncommon, and martial law was declared at a few places, including Sholapur in western India, where the penalty for carrying the national flag was ten years' imprisonment.

Many hundreds were arrested and imprisoned daily throughout the country. But their place was taken by many hundreds of others.

Women, workers and students were prominent in the movement of men-women and children who in at street to street singing patriotic a of calve in 1930. Throughout the day clad in saris shops purveying foreign goods, and by the autumn of 1930 imports of had to between a third and a fourth of the In Bombay sixteen British-owned mills and in the larger cities came out frequently in helping to paralyse production. By July 6th the was commenting caustically on the "defeatism" "demoralization" of the Europeans in India, while the Statement conceded that "everybody admits the of the and all classes of traders are seriously "be the situation. Yet, the temper of the people if aroused was often Hikmet Bayiry former Turkish ambassador to Afghanistan, while touring India in 1930 when Gandhi and in he was entertained to tea by an Indian super of a jail in northern India. There were other Indian guests, having tea in the garden, loud cries of Gandhi's ears. On inquiry he found that it was the of flick prisoners in that jail to greet the setting sun with are there here?" he asked to Nine thousand, they told him.

And many wore there here in 1921? a thousand. "And many do you think there will be ten years hence?" he The laughed and pointed good-humouredly at the stipermlendent fee will be in" Nehru discovered that the tingle and excitement of outside were infecting some of the convict inmates. "Swaraj is coming" they exclaimed. "Will Swaraj take us out of this" patriotic songs in the morning. For a month Jawaharlal alone in his barrack and was joined by another Narmada Prasad Singh – arrival was a relief. Two and a half later, on the last day of June 7 1930,, he was pleasantly when his father strode into the enclosure accompanied by Dr. Syed Mahmud, now Minister for External Affairs in Nehru's cabinet Motilal had been arrested early that morning while he was still in bed. "And now we are together again," he remarked. Seeing his son – he was in great good humour. Motilal had barely seven months to live but neither father nor son realised it.

TRYST WITH DESTINY

Jawaharlal Nehru's Tryst with Destiny Speech

Tryst with Destiny was a speech made by Jawaharlal Nehru, the first Prime Minister of the Republic of India. The speech was made to the Indian Constituent Assembly, on the eve of India's independence, towards midnight on August 14, 1947. It focuses on the aspects that transcend India's history.

It is considered in modern India to be a landmark oration that captures the essence of the triumphant culmination of the hundred-year Indian freedom struggle against the British Empire in India.

Text

Long years ago we made a tryst with destiny, and now the time comes when we shall redeem our pledge, not wholly or in full measure, but very substantially. At the stroke of the midnight hour, when the world sleeps, India will awake to life and freedom. A moment comes, which comes but rarely in history, when we step out from the old to the new, when an age ends, and when the soul of a nation, long suppressed, finds utterance. It is fitting that at this solemn moment we take the pledge of dedication to the service of India and her people and to the still larger cause of humanity.

At the dawn of history India started on her unending quest, and trackless centuries are filled with her striving and the grandeur of her success and her failures. Through good and ill fortune alike she has never lost sight of that quest or forgotten the ideals which gave her strength. We end today a period of ill fortune and India discovers herself again. The achievement we celebrate today is but a step, an opening of opportunity, to the greater triumphs and achievements that await us. Are we brave enough and wise enough to grasp this opportunity and accept the challenge of the future?

That future is not one of ease or resting but of incessant striving so that we may fulfil the pledges we have so often taken and the one we shall take today. The service of India means the service of the millions who suffer. It means the ending of poverty and ignorance and disease and inequality of opportunity. The ambition of the greatest man of our generation has been to wipe every tear from every eye. That may be beyond us, but as long as there are tears and suffering, so long our work will not be over.

And so we have to labour and to work, and work hard, to give reality to our dreams. Those dreams are for India, but they are also for the world, for all the nations and peoples are too closely knit together today for any one of them to imagine that it can live apart Peace has been said to be indivisible; so is freedom, so is prosperity now, and so also is disaster in this One World that can no longer be split into isolated fragments.

We have to build the noble mansion of free India where all her children may dwell. The appointed day has come-the day appointed by destiny-and India stands forth again, after long slumber and struggle, awake, vital, free and independent. The past clings on to us still in some measure and we have to do much before we redeem the pledges we have so often taken. Yet the turning-point is past, and history begins anew for us, the history which we shall live and act and others will write about. It is a fateful moment for us in India, A new star rises, the star of freedom in the East, a new hope comes into being, a vision long cherished materializes. May the star never set and that hope never be betrayed! We rejoice in that freedom,

The future beckons to us. Whither do we go and what shall be our endeavour? To bring freedom and opportunity to the common man, to the peasants and workers of India; to fight and end poverty and ignorance and disease; to build up a prosperous, democratic and progressive nation, and to create social, economic and political institutions which will ensure justice and fullness of life to every man and woman. We have hard work ahead. There is no resting for any one of us till we redeem our pledge in full, till we make all the people of India what destiny intended them to be. We are citizens of a great country on the verge of bold advance, and we have to live up to that high standard. All of us, to whatever religion we may belong, are equally the children of India with equal rights, privileges and obligations. We cannot encourage communalism or narrow-mindedness, for no nation can be great whose people are narrow in thought or in action.

To the nations and peoples of the world we send greetings and pledge ourselves to cooperate with them in furthering peace, freedom and democracy. And to India, our much-loved motherland, the ancient, the eternal and the ever-new, we pay our reverent homage and we bind ourselves afresh to her service.

Jai Hind.

WRITINGS OF JAWAHARLAL NEHRU

Jawaharlal Nehru's imprint on the history of postcolonial India has been extraordinary. The contingencies that put Nehru at the helm of India's fledgling polity after the departure of the British in 1947 ensured that the decisions he took on behalf of the Indian nation-state had far-reaching ramifications. Nehru's view of the historical possibilities available to India at the dawn of its independence were shaped by his understanding of the West's historical trajectory, in which he saw universal significance. At the heart of this view lay his belief that independent India's national state should direct economic development; but also construct a constitutional, secular government, build economic opportunities for its predominantly agrarian population, and maintain sovereignty in the international arena through a policy of "non-alignment" in the Cold War. That this vision was constantly forced to make adjustments and compromises in the face of political instability is now a moot point. What emerges from a perusal of Nehru's voluminous writings is a sense of how, as a political leader, he was forced to be imaginative and creative with his worldview.

The two-volume collection entitled *The Essential Writings of Jawaharlal Nehru* ed. Sarvepalli Gopal and Uma Iyengar is a significant contribution to our understanding of the intellectual history of twentieth century India. Gopal, one of the co-editors of the book, died in 2002, and will always be remembered for his rich interpretations of the life and writings of Jawaharlal Nehru (and his biographies of the English Viceroys Ripon and Irwin, as well as Gopal's father, the distinguished philosopher-statesman Sarvepalli Radhakrishnan).

Apart from writing the three volumes of *Jawaharlal Nehru: A Biography*, he was general editor of *The Selected Works of Jawaharlal Nehru*; thirty one volumes in the first series and thirty in the second series. The latest, volume

31, came out in December 2002 after his death. He also edited *Jawaharlal Nehru: An Anthology,* which was published in 1980. His collaborator in *The Essential Writings,* Uma Iyengar, has dedicated this feast of an anthology in two volumes to Gopal's memory. The work was completed in his lifetime. Sadly, he did not live to see its publication.

Volume 2 of the anthology contains nearly five-hundred extracts from Nehru's writings, correspondence, and interviews, covering themes ranging from his views on Indian culture and polity to his thoughts on nature, science, and religion. The selections reflect his thinking on a range of topics, and perhaps most valuably, allow the reader to construct a composite picture of Nehru. Except for a few texts in the first section on "Polity and Governance" which are of more than individual significance, official statements of policy and documents that merely transmit his point of view have been largely set aside. Instead, the editors have compiled Nehru's more reflective pieces. The depth of Gopal's lifelong commitment to the study of Nehru's life and works is revealed in these selections. Ramachandra Guha, in a recent piece on Gopal's contributions and legacy has described this commitment in evocative detail ("Remembering").

Although it is impossible to describe the contents of this rich collection in a review of this kind, some aspects are worth mentioning. The early writings included in this anthology are dominated by Nehru's experiments with articulating the ideological contours of nationalism (as in the essay "A National State"). These give way to essays describing his preoccupation with issues of nation-building, the idea of India as a nation-state, the legacy of Mahatma Gandhi, and the pressures of nation-building. Nehru's commitment to socialist development and the imperatives of modernization are apparent from the excerpts in the section on "Polity and Governance" which is particularly rich.

His description of what comprises the "essence of a democractic state" reveals his debt to Gandhi. Like Gandhi, with whom he was very close, Nehru contradicted himself frequently, which is hardly surprising since he often had to make adjustments to suit the vagaries of an unstable political environment. His fascination with India's past, evident from works like *The Discovery of India,* and his letters to his daughter Indira Gandhi from prison, bear testimony to his own preoccupation with shaping the contours of India's future, and indeed what he perceived as his own legacy.

He strongly advocated the development of science and technology, which he believed would propel India into the age of modernity. He also envisioned India's active role in international affairs. One of the most fascinating sections deals with Nehru's views on the place of science and technology in the development state. His advocacy of nuclear technology played a critical part in shaping India's nuclear program (a member of which is the President of India today), although it is clear from his speech "Pernicious Influence of Technology" that he was aware of the dangers of valorizing science and technology. Nehru's desire to promote the role of technology led to the foundation of many engineering and medical colleges, at the pinnacle of which are the Indian Institutes of Technology, many graduates of which are members of India's transnational intelligentsia preoccupied with the expansion of information technology.

Later sections on the book reveal Nehru's views on peace and disarmament, the need to move beyond facile dichotomies like the "orient and the occident," and the urgency of creating an international community free from the ideological divide at the heart of the Cold War. The sections on international affairs (entitled "India and Beyond," "India, Pakistan and Kashmir," and "War, Peace and Disarmament") present announced view of Nehru's justifications for non-alignment.

Discussions of the Kashmir issue are particularly poignant, revealing Nehru's deep concerns about the region's descent into political instability. In many of his pronouncements about the dangers of political extremism, he reveals himself to have been remarkably prescient. In addition to expounding on political matters, Nehru also wrote extensively on his love for nature, which is evocatively captured in his musings on wildlife and the environment.

In the history of the Indian state, the period between 1947 and Nehru's death in 1964 witnessed the stabilization of the state following the turmoil of the Partition, and its emergence as an agent of development. Under Nehru's prime minister-ship, the Indian government attempted to penetrate many areas of social life while experimenting with democratic institutions and practices. These agendas, shaped by Nehru's socialist, democratic vision so poignantly outlined in his Discovery of India were implemented through processes of negotiation and adjustment.

The second volume in this two part series demonstrates, with depth and rigor, the diverse ways in which historical contingency played a critical role in shaping Nehru's ideas, and the subtle ways in which in engaged with a diverse range of issues confronting his times. Comprehensive in scope, the volumes reveal Jawaharlal Nehru's complexity as a thinker and politician. Even though there have been many anthologies of Nehru's work, it is fair to say that taken together, the two volumes that make up *The Essential Works of Jawaharlal Nehru* are an invaluable resource for those interested in the history of the challenges confronting not just contemporary India, but many postcolonial societies.

NEHRU'S POLICIES

Prime Minister Jawaharlal Nehru's administration created the policies that formed the backbone of India's social and economic development, national defence and position in world affairs for decades. Although Nehru's policies were mostly imitation of other countries', instead of realisation of India's uniqueness.

Jawaharlal Nehru-Foreign Policy

Nehru's foreign policy was supportive of anti-colonialism, and the freedom movements in Tanzania, Algeria, Indochina and the abolition of apartheid in South Africa. Nehru was also one of the founding statesmen of the Non Aligned Movement, of Asian and African nations seeking to stay away from the pressures of the alliances created by the USA and USSR. Nehru also condemned the invasion of Suez in 1956 by Israel, Britain and France.

However, Nehru's neutrality was strongly criticised when he failed to condemn the USSR's invasion of Hungary in 1956-58.

On November 27, 1946, Nehru appealed to the United States and the Soviet Union to end nuclear testing and to start nuclear disarmament, stating that such an action would "save humanity from the ultimate disaster."

Nehru's personal charisma extended to the world stage where, because of his leadership, India was often seen to be "punching above its weight." As Prime Minister, he pursued a foreign policy of non-alignment and became a founder and leader of the Non-Aligned Movement.

He pursued India's claim to Kashmir in the face of Pakistani opposition, resulting in the First Kashmir War (1947-49). Not wishing to confront China, Nehru did not protest the Chinese conquest of Tibet, despite the fact that it meant the disappearance of a buffer state that had separated China and India, although the Dalai Lama was permitted to set up a government-in-exile at Dharamsala.

Military defeat at the hands of the People's Republic of China in the Sino-Indian War in October 1962 brought strong criticism of military unpreparedness and Nehru's policy of excessive trust in China, which had, to its credit, truthfully indicated its intention to occupy Tibet, including parts of it claimed by India.

Jawaharlal Nehru-Home Front

Nehru was leading a combination of old and young Indians all energised by patriotism and the opportunity to finally put their dreams and vision for India into practice. The Nehru years were generally peaceful, with the generation of freedom-fighters controlling the Union and state governments and political parties. Nehru also engineered major social and political reforms in India.

Laws were passed abolishing caste discrimination, dowry weddings and suttee, and extending legal rights and social freedoms to Indian women, all against tough opposition from orthodox Hindus. Discrimination based on casteism was outlawed. Nehru championed a nationwide campaign to enrol every Indian child in a primary school and encourage higher education. The famous Indian Institutes of Technology were established during Nehru's reign.

In 1957, the States Reorganisation Commission led by P.C. Mahanalobis promulgated a plan to create new Indian states whose territorial boundaries would be defined by the majority language of the resident population.

While generally supported, this plan caused sectarian violence in Mumbai, Andhra Pradesh and Tamil Nadu, where states argued about the territorial demarcation, and violence erupted between different ethnic communities. Once he saw that both party and country wanted it, Nehru yielded to the formation of linguistic states-a policy he was personally opposed to. The debate of making Hindi the national language also heated up as a result, claiming a number of lives amidst times of disorder.

Nehru also encouraged peaceful generation of nuclear energy, financing work at the Bhabha Atomic Research Centre in Mumbai. He solicited economic and technical support from the USA, Canada, the UK, France and the USSR, all who helped establish major industrial factories, steel plants and India's first nuclear reactors. Major dams and irrigation canals, roads and highways, electric power stations and a host of other public works were constructed.

THE ORIGINS OF NEHRU'S SOCIALIST THINKING UP TO 1947

Although Nehru did not produce any major works during these years his autobiography provides insight to his economic thinking. This era is important because it contains several very significant events in his life as well as some of the earliest expressions of his emerging socialist thinking. These events provided stimulus and influence for the growth of his socialist thinking. In India Nehru's formal education began with home tutors. In his autobiography Nehru notes that one British tutor in particular was very influential, Ferdinand T. Brooks. Nehru claimed that, in addition to introducing him to theosophy, Brooks nurtured his interest in science and his "taste for reading," especially English books. Nehru then went to Harrow and on to Cambridge where, although he took the Natural Sciences Tripos, he gained a wide exposure to economic and social matters. It is evident that Nehru's interest in socialist thinking developed at Cambridge. Nehru specifically noted in his autobiography that he discussed George Bernard Shaw's prefaces at Cambridge.

In an interview in 1956, he maintained "that it was really at Cambridge that, broadly speaking certain socialistic ideas - partly Fabian socialism, partly some slightly more aggressive socialistic ideas - developed." Whilst studying for the Bar, Nehru claimed that he "simply drifted, doing some general reading, vaguely attracted to the Fabians and socialistic ideas." However, on the evidence of the autobiography and Nehru's works during this era his primary concern was with nationalism rather than socialism. Writing in his autobiography at the time when he first met Gandhi, at the Lucknow Congress in 1916, he states: "It was all nationalism and patriotism and I was a pure nationalist, my vague socialist ideas of college days having sunk into the background." Nevertheless, it is evident that Nehru was exposed to a very formal British style education which acquainted him with British literature, writers and thinkers and introduced him to current social and scientific growths.

The influence of George Bernard Shaw is also long-established in a letter Nehru wrote to his daughter Indira from prison in 1935. He encouraged Indira to: "Read more of him. Almost all his plays are worth it and his prefaces to these plays are equally important." Nehru's familiarity with Shaw's work and his admiration for the man are mentioned in another letter to Indira. Nehru wrote: "I have been reading Bernard Shaw's plays again. Twice I have read them previously and seen some of them on the stage. And now for the third time I am going through the lot." He continued: "What a wise man he is, full of the deepest understanding of life." Nor was it only with Shaw's plays and prefaces that Nehru was familiar. In a letter to his sister in 1944 he advised: "Someone has sent me Bernard Shaw's new book *Everybody's Political What's What.*"

Significantly Nehru explains: "I talk about this so that you might not send it. It is the kind of book you might feel inclined to send me." The abiding influence of Shaw is revealed in a letter that Nehru wrote to him in 1948. Nehru recalled Shaw's address he had heard as a Cambridge undergraduate and noted how he had "grown up in company with" Shaw's writings and books and as a result he had "been moulded by that reading." This connection with Shaw provided an early entry into Fabianism and British socialism more generally which would remain a substantial influence on Nehru's socialist thinking. The next significant event for Nehru was his trip to Europe, and especially Russia, in 1926-1927. Whilst in Europe Nehru visited England during the general strike and attended the Congress of the Oppressed Nationalities, as the representative of the Indian National Congress, in Brussels in February 1927. In Brussels Nehru met many European socialists as well as other Asian nationalists, including the Labour Party politician George

Lansbury (1859-1940) and Madame Sun Yat-sen (1892-1981), the wife of Sun Yat-sen. Later Nehru claimed that as a result of the Congress he "turned inevitably with good will towards Communism." However, Nehru claimed he was acquainted with only the "broad features" of communism and was attracted by the "tremendous changes taking place in Russia." As well as being somewhat superficial Nehru's interest in communism was tempered by his irritation with the "dictatorial ways" and "aggressive and rather vulgar methods" of communists. At the same time, Nehru's speeches at the Congress reflected his growing anti-imperialism, and he emphasised its exploitative nature. Nehru expressly condemned British imperialism in India, describing it as a era in which "free-booters prowled about and committed plunder and robberies in the land in an unbridled manner." Nehru's visit to Russia, after the Brussels' Congress, stimulated his developing interest in communism. His comments on the visit reveal his pragmatism which became most apparent towards the end of his life. In his account of the trip Nehru stated that in the new Russia: 'The real test of success can only be in the measure of happiness of the masses of the people." Nehru was also interested in what he witnessed in Russia because he felt India, which was also a large, under industrialised, agricultural country, could learn from the Russian experience. Nehru's most significant and extensive declaration of his socialist thinking at this time came in his Presidential Address to the Lahore session of the Indian National Congress in 1929. According to Nehru the world was in a state of transition, he described it as "one vast question mark," as the old order gave way to the new. Nehru proceeded to offer his solution:

I must frankly confess that I am a socialist and a republican and am no believer in kings and princes, or in the order which produces the modern kings of industry, who have greater power over the lives and fortunes of men than even kings of old, and whose methods are as predatory as those of the old feudal aristocracy.

Next Nehru outlined some of the points of his programme which included, the ending of poverty, the introduction of minimum wages and reform of the land-laws. As such the programme sought to remedy many of the problems caused or exacerbated by British imperialism. Nehru explicitly rejected Gandhi's theory of trusteeship and noted: "Englishmen consider themselves the trustees for India, and yet to what a condition they have reduced our country."

For Nehru the only type of "trusteeship that can be fair is the trusteeship of the nation and not of one individual or group." Finally, and significantly, Nehru held that the programme he outlined should be obtained by "legitimate and peaceful" methods. By this time Nehru had demonstrated the foundations of his socialist thinking, which included his concern with poverty, industrial growth and his critique of capitalism and imperialism. Of particular importance was Nehru's connection of capitalism and imperialism. It is likely that Nehru's bitter experience of British imperialism had turned him against capitalism as the predominant economic system in Britain.

The leftward drift of Nehru's socialist thinking is confirmed in his essay, "Whither India?" It is widely held to be an important contribution to Nehru's socialist thinking. In his autobiography Nehru observed that "Whither India?" had "attracted considerable attention" but this was not really warranted: 'There was nothing novel or original in these articles for any one in touch with recent growths and modern Western thinking."

Nehru begins by surveying the world situation, then the Asian situation and finally the Indian situation and identifies the problems and presents his solution. Nehru's analysis of the world situation offers a distinctly Marxist interpretation of history: "The tremendous importance of economic events in shaping history and forms of government is almost universally admitted now." In line with this Marxist interpretation Nehru summarised the expansion of capitalism in the west and particularly in Britain: "India's gold, in the early stages helped in the further industrialization of England." The exploitation of India "brought much wealth to England" some of which "trickled down to the working class" and "took the edge off working-class discontent." Nehru believed that the growth of capitalism, following its introduction by the British, was inevitable and he stated that "the processes of history and economics cannot be stopped for long." In this way imperialism had helped in the initial growth of capitalism and had alleviated the problems of its maturity. However, imperialism was only a temporary expedient and capitalism was now in crisis. Nehru claimed that the "ill distribution of the world's wealth" had created a paradox, of increased production and increased unemployment and poverty under capitalism, which "grows with it till it eats and destroys the very system which created it." Nehru observed that amongst the capitalist countries only in the United States was "some attempt being made today towards lessening to a slight extent inequalities in wealth by State action." Having provided this background of the world situation Nehru turned to Asia and India.

Nehru considered Asia "the main field of conflict between nationalism and imperialism." Consequently the nationalist struggle for political freedom was the primary urge in Asia. However, this struggle was "becoming a social struggle also for economic freedom." This process was causing a tension between the two forces which was exemplified by the situation in India which was part of the "great struggle going on all over the world for the emancipation of the oppressed." Nehru stated:

The whole basis and urge of the national movement came from a desire for economic betterment, to throw off the burdens that crushed the masses and to end the exploitation of the Indian people.

Therefore, the solution that Nehru offered was both economic and political: "Politically, it must mean independence and the severance of the British connection" and "economically and socially it must mean the ending of all special class privileges and vested interests." In summary, the change would have to be "fundamental" and "revolutionary" for it would be "a foolish waste of energy to think and act in terms of carrying on the existing regime and trying to reform it and improve it" Nehru concluded by answering the question in the title of the essay, "Whither India?," as follows: Surely to the great human goal of social and economic equality, to the ending of all exploitation of nation by nation and class by class to national freedom within the frame-work of an international co-operative socialist world federation. In sum, Nehru held that the Indian situation could not be considered apart from the wider world situation. In essence the crisis of the world situation necessitated an economic dimension to the nationalist struggle.

Nehru's action of the rise of socialism in the west in *Glimpses of World History* and his analysis of recent world events reveals much of his developing socialist thinking. *Glimpses of World History* is widely held to reveal Marxist influence, Dutt for example, observed Nehru's "acceptance of the Marxist view of the scientific explanation of the historical process." In his account of the growth of socialism in Europe he contrasts the growth of the more moderate, "conservative" and "evolutionary" British brand, including Owenism, Chartism and Fabianism, with the more "radical and revolutionary" continental variety. Returning to a theme developed in " Whither India?" Nehru also attributed the "moderation of English thinking" to English prosperity, which was in part due to "the exploitation of India and other colonial possessions."

For Nehru, the "British brand of socialism was represented by the Fabian Society with a very mild programme of distant change." However, Nehru believed that this evolutionary type of socialism was "weakening" and the difference between it and "other non-socialist groups" was "thinning away." Therefore, Marx's "clear-cut and cogently argued" theory of "scientific socialism" was now "considered the general socialist creed." Marxism's "basic idea" was that "production and distribution and other important activities should be largely socialized or controlled by the State." The Marxist interpretation of history, according to Nehru, was a "grand process of evolution by inevitable class struggles." Crucially, Nehru observed that even Lenin, "the greatest modern exponent of Marxism," warned against considering "Marxism as a dogma."

Nehru's acceptance of the Marxist interpretation of history is demonstrated by his explanation of what he called the "crisis of capitalism" during the 1930s depression in those terms. For Nehru, it was not due to a "temporary crisis," as suggested by various "capitalist experts," but a much "deeper" trouble: the "beginning of the final death agony" of capitalism, which was due to a fundamental "inequality in the distribution of wealth." It was not only capitalism that had failed; parliaments too, especially the English parliament, had failed, since they had perpetuated the vested interests of the "possessing classes" in upholding the capitalist system. In support of this interpretation Nehru quoted Laski, who held that the British government had "become an executive dictatorship tempered by fear of parliamentary revolt." The "essential contradiction between the capitalist system and democracy" meant there was no "real democracy" in England; for Nehru democracy included "economic and social equality" as well as the right to vote.

Nehru's autobiography also discussed the paradox he detected in Gandhi which touches on the nature of Nehru's socialist thinking. Writing of 1933-1934 Nehru observed that he and Gandhi "differed considerably" but he was "grateful" that Gandhi has come "as far as he could" towards his position. On this subject Nehru attacked those "parlour socialists" who "did little themselves" except "criticize others," particularly Gandhi, and who "make high socialist doctrine a refuge for inaction." Nehru remarked of Gandhi:

Occasionally he calls himself a socialist, but he uses the word in a sense peculiar to himself which has little or nothing to do with the economic framework of society which usually goes by the name of socialism. Following his lead a number of prominent Congressmen have taken to the use of that word, meaning thereby a kind of muddled humanitarianism.

According to Nehru, Gandhi's peculiar use of the term was despite the fact that he had "read many books on economics and socialism and even Marxism." The implication is that despite Nehru's own qualified acceptance of Marxism his socialism was not muddled humanitarianism. Additionally, Gandhi had "no desire to raise the standards of the masses beyond a certain very modest competence" whilst Nehru saw this as essential.

For Nehru, Gandhi's "idea of trusteeship" whereby the rich are "the trustees of the poor" resembled a "religious attitude" which was "bound up with the world of long ago." Nehru recognised, like Gandhi, that "the industrial age has brought many evils" but, and contrary to Gandhi's view, it had also "laid down a basis of material well-being which makes cultural and spiritual progress far easier for large numbers." According to Nehru, these benefits were not available in India because India had "not profited by industrialism" but had "been exploited by it" and therefore: 'The fault is not of industrialism but of foreign domination." Nehru then dismissed Gandhi's "self-Nehru expanded on this point in a letter to Krishna Kripalani in 1939.

He acknowledged that: "Violence and monopoly and concentration of wealth in few hands are produced by the present economic structure." However: "It is not large scale industry that brings any injustice and violence but the misuse of large scale industry by private capitalists and financiers." In accordance with this analysis Nehru stated: "It is possible, I think, to eliminate the evil and the violence of the big machine by changing the economic structure of capitalism. It is essentially private ownership and the sufficient village" as "an impossible objective" and called for the "establishment of a socialist order." However, Gandhi's "khadi movement," whilst it was not a serious "solution of any vital present-day problem," could serve as "a temporary measure" possibly "for some time to come."

In the concluding chapter Nehru returned to the classification of his socialist thinking. He stated:

As these pages will show, I am very far from being a communist My roots are still perhaps partly in the nineteenth century, and I have been too much influenced by the humanist liberal tradition to get out of it completely.... I dislike dogmatism, and the treatment of Karl Marx's writings or any other books as revealed scripture which cannot be challenged, and the regimentation and heresy hunts which seem to be a feature of modern communism.... But still I incline more and more towards a communist philosophy.

As always Nehru's admiration for and tendency towards socialism and communism is qualified and reserved. The autobiography represents a further attempt to place the Indian situation in the context of the wider world situation. It revealed that Nehru accepted the economic interpretation of history in general terms. In particular Marx's insight was, for Nehru, "due to the scientific method he adopted."

Early in 1936 Nehru received a letter from Lord Lothian criticising the growth of socialism in India. In his reply Nehru acknowledged that Marx's "interpretation of history is the only one which does explain history to some extent." Secondly, whilst "a great deal of private initiative may be left" under socialism "nationalization of the means of production seems to be inevitable." Finally, Nehru considered that in "theory" it might be possible to "establish Socialism by democratic acquisitive form of society that encourage a competitive violence."

However, in "practice" there "are likely to be very great difficulties, because the opponents of Socialism will reject the democratic method when they see their power threatened." This of course raises the question whether Nehru advocated the establishment of socialism by non-democratic or violent means. He tends further toward this more extreme position a little later, "constitutional methods" had "no meaning" if there is no democratic constitution.

It is instructive to contrast this analysis with Nehru's discussion in his autobiography of Tawney's concerns during the 1930s that it might not even be possible for a Labour government in Britain to gain "real power" in the face of institutional resistance from "the privileged classes." Nehru considered that if this is the case in Britain which has "democratic parliamentary institutions" and "a long tradition of civil liberty" the chances of success in India were remote. The fact that in reality the first post-war Labour government was able to implement much of their programme was probably not lost on Nehru. In 1950 he remarked that: "England is obviously pursuing a socialist policy and has been pursuing it with considerable courage during the last four or five years since the war ended." For Nehru, England was not only pursuing socialism; even its capitalism had altered. In a speech in 1956, Nehru observed that "capitalism even in England is different from what it was in the nineteenth century." Nehru's concern for individual freedom, which often conflicted with his socialism, could well be attributable to Tawney. For example, Nehru noted in 1939 that he was "far from being an orthodox Marxist" and claimed that he thinking it possible to combine Socialism with "a great deal of freedom for the individual."

Another important contribution to the growth of Nehru's socialist thinking was Presidential Address to the Lucknow session of the Indian National Congress in 1936. The address follows Nehru's usual style beginning with an outline of the problem which includes a survey of recent history and the world situation. Nehru saw the world situation as one of crisis and conflict in which "two rival economic and political systems faced each other." On one side "was the capitalist order which had inevitably developed into vast imperialisms" and which "in its difficulties" had taken to fascism. On the other side was "the new socialist order of the U. S. S. R." and the "rising nationalisms of the eastern and other dependent countries." Nehru declared that the Congress stood, "ranged against fascism and imperialism," and as long as imperialism remained: 'The exploitation of our masses will still continue and all the vital social problems that face us will remain unsolved." Nehru emphasised the importance of his concern with the poverty of the masses and his desire that it should be incorporated within the nationalist movement. He believed that: 'The Congress must be not only for the masses, as it claims to be, but of the masses; only then will it really be for the masses."

In presenting his solution Nehru stated: "I am convinced that there is intimate connection between world events, and our national problem is but a part of the world problem of capitalism-imperialism." Nehru expanded on his current thinking on economic and social matters and clarified much of the earlier vagueness and provided a clear statement of his socialist thinking: socialist or an individualist? Is there a necessary contradiction in the two terms? Are we all such integrated human beings that we can define ourselves precisely in a word or a phrase?" For Nehru the explanation was that he was "temperamentally and by training an individualist" but "intellectually a socialist." In fact Nehru was in favour of socialism not because it would "kill or suppress individuality" but because it would "release innumerable individuals from economic and cultural bondage." Nehru to Bose, April 3, 1939 in *A Bunch of Old Letters,* 350-352.

I am convinced that the only key to the solution of the world's problems and of India's problems lies in socialism, and when I use this word I do so not in a vague humanitarian way but in the scientific sense. Socialism is, however, something even more than an economic doctrine; it is a philosophy of life and as such it appeals to me. I see no way of ending the poverty, the vast unemployment, the degradation and the subjection of the Indian people except though socialism.

Nehru proceeded to detail some of the features of "this new civilization," a "glimpse" of which he had observed in the Soviet Union, including, "the ending of private property," and "rapid industrialization." However, he noted that although he regarded some growths in the Soviet Union as "a great and fascinating unfolding of a new order" other growths had "pained" him "greatly." Nehru concluded by expressing a "wish for the advancement of socialism" in Congress and India, whilst accepting that it did not "fit with the present ideology of the Congress" and therefore he would not "force the issue" and "create difficulties" which may hinder the "struggle for independence." Whilst Nehru favoured large-scale industrialization he did not exclude Gandhian village-based growth. Even at the height of Nehru's Marxist phase when he was most impressed by the Soviet experiment, and consequently turned more towards large and heavy industry, he still left room for village industries. For example, at Lucknow Nehru stated that he believed "khadi and village industries have a definite place in our present economy." Nehru also repeated his belief that that "even in imperialist

In 1931 at Karachi the Congress had passed a Resolution on Fundamental Rights and Economic Policy. This resolution, amongst other things, promised economic arrangements which would "conform to the principle of justice," state protection of industrial workers' wages and conditions, and reform of the land tenure system. Indian National Congress Resolution on Fundamental Rights and Economic Policy, passed at Karachi, as amended by All-India

Congress Committee - August 6-8, 1931 in *Nehru,* vol. 1, ed., Norman, 248-251. According to Nehru: "In the Karachi resolution... [the Congress] took a step, a very short step, in a socialist direction by advocating nationalisation of key industries and services, and various other measures to lessen the burden on the poor and increase it on the rich." However, this "very short step" was indeed only a step for Nehru and it "was not socialism at all," since "a capitalist state could easily accept almost everything contained in that resolution." More generally the ideology of the Congress was undoubtedly Gandhi's 'muddled humanitarianism.'

This British influence is important in its own right and also for the glimpse it gives of the nature of Nehru's socialist thinking during the 1930s.

There are a variety of reason why Nehru turned to Marxism to the extent reflected in his socialist thinking at this time. Firstly, he had visited Russia, and been impressed by achievements there, before many of the negative aspects emerged later in the 1930s. His own experience of Russia seemed to have been vindicated by the accounts of others who had visited Russia, most notably the Webbs. Secondly, his frustration with the lack of success of the nationalist movement caused him to explore more radical possibilities. This was reinforced by the policies of the British Labour Party, which had not moved as fast towards obtaining a solution to the Indian situation as Nehru would have liked, and thereby served to sustain British imperialism. Contemporaneously, growths elsewhere in the world, the rise of fascism and the crisis of capitalism, were in stark contrast to the successes that Nehru saw in Russia and socialism. Finally, Nehru's frustrations with Gandhi and in particular his economic policies, whilst never insurmountable, were at their height

The work of Harold Laski was another influence on Nehru's Marxism. It has already been demonstrated that Nehru knew Laski and was well versed with his work. In Laski's critical work, *Communism* (1927), he nevertheless accepted the materialist interpretation of history and the belief that the distribution of political power should be accompanied by the distribution of economic power. Laski's position altered somewhat during the 1930s. In *The State in Theory and Practice,* Laski adopted a more Marxian analysis which resembled Nehru's position at that time. According to Laski, capitalism had lasted as long as it had due to rising prosperity but when it was in crisis it 'could not afford a liberal policy." Therefore, the "owners of property" were reluctant to give up "their legal privileges" which resulted in fascism in some countries and "resistance to social reform in Britain." A similar view was expressed by Nehru in his letter to Lord Lothian in 1936: "[T]he opponents of Socialism will reject the democratic method when they see their power threatened." This is comparable with Laski who stated: "As always when the fundamental idea of poverty is threatened, its owners fell into a panic. Political democracy was seen to be the enemy." Laski proceeded to call for communal ownership of the means of production "to secure the total well-being of a society" as Nehru did at Lucknow and afterward.

An important feature of Nehru's Marxism was its qualified, and ultimately temporary, nature. This can be accounted for in several ways. Firstly, it was always tempered by Nehru's acceptance of peaceful, non-violent Gandhian methods. Nehru may have accepted the goals of Marxism but he only ever flirted with the violent methods associated with it. This was supported by Nehru's knowledge of the Soviet experiment which had been to him unacceptably violent Nehru was also especially attracted to Gandhi's approach after his visit to the rural Indian villages. This visit had impressed upon Nehru the necessity of making the nationalist movement, which had traditionally been a purely middle class movement, relevant to the masses. Therefore, Gandhi's identification with the masses had appealed to Nehru. Secondly, Nehru consistently expressed a strong belief in democracy and individual freedom, which was always incongruous with an unrestrained Marxism. This too had been backed by Nehru's knowledge of the Soviet experiment which, he believed, had suppressed individual freedom and had been overly regimented. Thirdly, Nehru believed that the solution must be suited to the unique conditions existing in India, which European socialism did not address, and consequently it should be of the Indian genius. This feeling also inclined Nehru towards Gandhi who was uniquely a product of India.

Nehru's concluding history, *The Discovery of India* contains much useful insight to his socialist thinking immediately prior to Indian independence. In the introduction, Nehru admits that he has "changed a good deal" and become more "contemplative" since he wrote his autobiography. Nehru begins by surveying recent events, including the growth of his own ideas. It was the "desire to experience life through action" and the "desire to discover the past in its relation to the present" that had dominated his thinking. Nehru recalled that Marx and Lenin had "produced a powerful effect" on his mind and the "practical achievements of the Soviet Union" had "advanced human society by a great leap." But Nehru declared that he was "too much of an individualist and believer in personal freedom to like overmuch regimentation." That said whilst he "accepted the fundamentals of the socialist theory" he had "little patience with leftist groups in India" that clung to a "fixed doctrine." For Nehru at this time: "A living philosophy must answer the problems of today." Having stated his guiding philosophy Nehru was able to embark on his discovery of Indian history. Interestingly, Nehru felt that he was able to do this "almost as an alien critic" since he had come to India "via the West."

Arriving at the present Nehru discussed his views concerning growth and planning. Nehru, in contrast to Gandhi's views, stated his ideaion of India's growth:

I am all for tractors and big machinery, I am convinced that the rapid industrialization of India is essential to relieve the pressure on land, to combat poverty and raise standards of living, for defence and a variety of other reasons.

Nehru also claimed that Gandhi's views toward "the use of machinery" had undergone a "gradual change." According to Nehru, Gandhi "came to accept the necessity of many kinds of heavy industries and large-scale key industries and public utilities." Nehru equated rapid industrialization with the socialist ideal and thus village industries would only be necessary during the transition. However, Nehru observed that the rapidly changing world situation, to which Nehru was always attuned, meant "an attempt to build up a country's economy largely on the basis of cottage and small industries" was "doomed to failure." He continued, linking his faith in science with his desire for industrialization: "If technology demands the big machine, as it does today in a large measure, then the big machine with all its implications and consequences must be accepted." In a crucial passage Nehru reveals an interesting aspect of his ideaion of socialism:

We are sometimes told that the present Government of India, with its ownership and control of railways, and a growing control of and interference in industry, finance, and indeed, life in general, is moving in a socialist direction. But this is something utterly different from democratic state control, apart from being essentially foreign control.... This is very far from socialism; indeed, it is absurd to talk of socialism in a country dominated by an alien power.... Even a complete nationalization (so-called) of industry unaccompanied by political democracy will lead only to a different kind of exploitation, for while industry will belong to the state, the state itself will not belong to the people.

Thus for Nehru imperialism had not only "arrested" the "normal growth" of India, which had consequently become "static," it had prevented the growth of more progressive forms of society. Significantly, Nehru quoted Tawney in support of this change or choice, which "is not between monopoly and competition, but between monopoly which is irresponsible and private, and a monopoly which is responsible and public." For Nehru this would entail "the public ownership of the basic and major industries," "the co-operative or collective control of the land," and "careful and continuous planning." Nehru's quotation of Tawney is taken from *The Acquisitive Society:* 'The choice before him [the consumer]... is not between competition and monopoly, but between a monopoly which is irresponsible and private and a monopoly which is responsible and public." This influence is interesting for Nehru was, if not always an atheist, passionately secular and the moral and spiritual dimension of Tawney's socialism would not necessarily have appealed to him. However, Nehru seems to have been influenced by Tawney's critique of capitalism.

INDIA 1947-1966

Consolidation; Foreign Policy: In 1947 the moment for India's independence had finally come. However, the colony of British India was split in two countries, the Republics of India (with a dominating Hindu majority) and Pakistan (with a dominating Muslim majority).

Both governments-in India a government of the Congress Party under Prime Minister Jawahrlal Nehru-were not willing to accept the continued independence of India's over 500 princely states; the princes or the people of these states had to make choices. While many accepted their fate and saw their statelets annexed into India or Pakistan, the Nizam of Hyderabad did not; in a brief 1948 war, his principality was conquered by Indian forces and annexed, placed under military administration and in 1956 split over three Indian states.

Another problem arose in the case of Jammu and Kashmir: the Maharaja opted for India, while an estimated 90% of the population was Muslim and desired integration into Pakistan (the K in Pakistan stands for Kashmir). In the end, Kashmir was partitioned into a part held by Pakistan and a (larger) part held by India. Both sides continue to claim all of Jammu and Kashmir.

The separation of British India and the princely states into India and Pakistan was violent; c. 8.6 million of Hindus and Sikhs fled from Pakistani territory, c. 7.9 million of Muslims from Indian territory. Mohandas K. Gandhi was assassinated by a radical Hindu Nathuram Godse. India and Pakistan fought a brief war in 1948.

In foreign policy, the Nehru administration criticised colonialism and pursued an independent course between the two blocks.

Nehru was a leading figure in the early Non-Aligned Movement. At the end of the Korean War, India assumed the presidency in the NNSC (Neutral Nations Supervisory Council) that was to supervise the armistice on the peninsula.

In 1954, India absorbed French India; in 1961, Indian forces occupied Portuguese India; both were annexed into India. In 1962, India and China fought the Sino-Indian War; the Chinese occupied a part of Kashmir and Himalayan border regions in Arunachal Pradesh; China still holds on to part of Kashmir.

India's own conquests, her wars with Pakistan and her dispute with China discredited India as a leading force in the Non-Aligned Movement; it rather came to be regarded as a regional power. After Nehru's death in 1964, a Second Indo-Pakistani War (1965) was fought. Administration: India adopted a Federal Constitution, with some of her member states having a population larger than that of former mother country, the UK. In 1950 India proclaimed the Republic. The country earned the title "largest democracy on earth", despite the fact that many different languages are spoken within its borders, the country is a religious caleidoscope and despite high analphabetism.

Upon independence, India inherited a territorial structure based on British conquests, annexations, administrative divisions and princely states, which did reflect historical feudatory structures rather than India's social, economic and cultural reality. From 1948 to 1960 India's political landscape was repeatedly altered, in order to abolish remnants of feudalism and to create viable states based on the common language of her inhabitants.

The new Republic of India adopted a policy of respecting cultural differences within the federation, but taking action against any secessionist movement, such as the suggested Dravidastan (southern India).

The establishment of Andhra Pradesh as the state of the Telugu-speaking people marks the beginning of reshaping India into a federation of nation states; in 1956 Kerala (Malayalam), Mysore (now Karnataka, Kannada), Rest-Madras (today Tamil Nadu, Tamil) followed, in 1960 Maharashtra (Marathi), Gujarat (Gujarati).

The feudal states were abolished in 1956. In 1966, Hindi-speaking Haryana was separated from the (East) Punjab. Hindi was to replace English as the national (*i.e.* federal) language by 1965; when this policy was to be implemented, it caused riots in non-Hindi speaking areas.

Domestic Policy: After the assassination of Mohandas K. Gandhi in 1948 and the death of Sardar Patel in 1950, the leading figure in Indian politics was Jawaharlal Nehru; he died in 1964 and was succeeded by Lal Bahadur Shastri, who died in 1966. The Indian National Congress, whose actions had brought about the British withdrawal from India, in 1947 began a transformation into a political party. It was to occupy a dominant position in Indian politics for the coming decades, both in the federation and on state level.

India was a functioning multiparty democracy, in which the Congress Party occupied the central position. Other parties held only a fraction of seats and often were not capable to cover the entire country, but could form a formidable alternative to Congress on state level. The Congress Party administration pursued a social policy of cautious modernisation, emphasising the emancipation of the untouchable (dalits). Positions in public administration were to be granted without consideration to India's traditional caste system; the army and universities also were to be open for people from all social groups. Nehru advocated secularism and a non-dogmatic form of socialism.

In 1961, village self-government was introduced in many states (BBoY 1962).

The Economy: In the early years of independence, India suffered food shortage. The state launched a programme constructing dams in order to provide water reservoirs for irrigation projects. In 1953, rationing and price controls were abolished in large parts of the country.

Rice production in the Republic of India amounted to 32 million metric tons in 1947; the figure rose to 45.6 million metric tons in 1966 (IHS)

B.R. Mitchell has established a table showing the total values of exports and imports in aggregate current values. Imports exceeded imports throughout the period from 1947 to 1966; in 1966, in aggregate current (2003) values, total exports amounted to 11.5 billion Rupees, imports to 20.1 billion Rupees (IHS).

India's political leaders in the years immediately after independence blamed the British administration for having prevented Indian development by failing to improve the education of the masses and by preventing the country to industrialize.

Many institutions of higher learning were established (where English maintained importance, at least as one of several languages of instruction); the state pursued a protectionist economic policy and, in Five Year Plans, attempted to promote industrialisation of the country. The first Five Year Plan was implemented 1951-1956. In 1958, India adopted the metric system (BBoY 1959).

Social History: In 1947, the population of the Republic of India was estimated at 345 million; in 1966 at 493 million. The policy of planned industrialisation went along with a policy intending to weaken caste structures and abolishing social discrimination against the dalits. The policy was of moderate success; while new economic structures were established, they struggled because of bureaucratic reglementation, partially also because large segments of India's population were unaccustomed to the requirements of an industrial society.

Resistance against the well-intended policies by the state was strongest in the countryside. However, increases in GNP failed to significantly raise the standard of living of the population, because of continued high population growth.

In 1955 a monogamy was introduced by law, as was divorce for Hindus. Untouchability was abolished, the Dalits now described as scheduled classes; the treatment of a person as an untouchable was made a criminal offence (BBoY 1956).

THE VARIETY AND UNITY OF INDIA

With such background as legacy, Nehru expressed his cherished dream to see a unified India despite multiple ethnic diversities with differing religious beliefs that were embraced by its multitude populace as expressed in his work, the 'Discovery of India'. This book is his last major work wherein he sets out to discover his own country. Coverage of the book ranges from the earliest days of Indian history to the dawn of independence. This survey provides clear interpretations of history and the complexity of contemporary problems as revealed through the mind and personality of one of the noble sons of India whose importance in the framing of policies is as ever more relevant in contemporary India than before. Instance of his vision is found in that:

"The Pathan and the Tamil are two extreme examples, the others lie somewhere in between. All of them have their distinctive features; all of them have still more the distinguishing mark of India. It is fascinating to find how the Bengalis, the Marathas, the Gujaratis, the Tamils, the Andhras, the Oriyas, the Assamese, the Canarese, the Malayalis, the Sindhis, the Punjabis, the Pathans, the Kashmiris, the Rajputs, and the great central block comprising the Hindustani-speaking people have retained their peculiar characteristics for hundreds of years, have still more or less the same virtues and failings of which old tradition or record tells us, and yet have been throughout these ages distinctively Indian, with the same national heritage and the same set of moral and mental qualities. There was something living and dynamic about this heritage which showed itself in ways of living and a philosophical attitude to life and its problems. Ancient India, like ancient China, was a world in itself, a culture and a civilization, which gave shape to all things. Foreign influences poured in and often influenced that culture and were absorbed. Disruptive tendencies gave rise immediately to an attempt to find a synthesis. Some kind of a dream of unity has occupied the mind of India since the dawn of civilization. That unity was not conceived as something imposed from outside, standardization of externals or even of beliefs. It was something deeper and, within its fold, the widest tolerance of belief and custom was practiced and every variety acknowledged and even encouraged.

"Differences, big or small can always be noticed even within a national group, however closely bound together it may be. The essential unity of that group becomes apparent when it is compared to another national group, though often the differences between two adjoining groups fade out or intermingle near the frontiers, and modern developments are tending to produce certain uniformity everywhere. In ancient and medieval times, the idea of the modern nation was non-existent, and feudal, religious, racial, or cultural bonds had more importance. Yet I think that at almost any time in recorded history an Indian would have felt more or less at home in any part of India, and would have felt as a stranger and alien in any other country. He would certainly have felt less of a stranger in countries which had partly adopted his culture or religion.

Those who professed a religion of non-Indian origin or, coming to India, settled down there, became distinctively Indian in the course of a few generations, such as Christians, Jews, Parsees, Moslems. Indian converts to some of these religions never ceased to be Indian on account of a change of their faith. They were looked upon in other countries as Indians and foreigners, even though there might have been a community of faith between them.

"Today, when the conception of nationalism has developed much more, Indians in foreign countries inevitably from a national group and hang together for various purposes, in spite of their internal differences. An Indian Christian is looked upon as an Indian wherever he may go. An Indian Moslem is considered an Indian in Turkey or Arabia or Iran, or any other country where Islam is the dominant religion." It speaks volumes of his concept of Indian 'Unity in diversity' which still binds the people of India together.

POPULAR CULTURE

The speech is referenced in the 1998 Hindi film *Earth* directed by Deepa Mehta. The film portrays the main characters listening to the speech on radio, against the backdrop of the Hindu-Muslim riots following the Partition of India. This provides an interesting juxtaposition between the realities of Partition and the optimism that followed Independence.

1947, First-hand between Karachi and Delhi

I shall skip past her delightful account of the Karachi ceremony—which took place on August 13 and 14 within eyeshot of a bronze statue of Mahatma Gandhi in a nearby circle—even though some of her irreverent comments are worth quoting even now ("Jinnah, whose smile muscles seem to be permanently out of order..."). Karachi was still a Hindu-majority city, and large sections of the population were understandably subdued at the partition of the country.Delhi's mood was altogether more joyous. The Talbots arrived at the Constituent Assembly just in time after a hair-raising journey from Pakistan on the afternoon of August 14. Mildred describes Nehru's famous "tryst with destiny" speech, recounts the now-forgotten exuberance of a delegate who marred the decorum of the occasion by shouting a cheer for the Mahatma, and then tells a story I have not come across elsewhere: "At the moment when the clock was chiming the [midnight] hour there was a rude interruption which startled everyone. A conch shell was blown long and loudly from the rear of the hall. Involuntarily every head turned.... It was revealing to witness the [...] relief [...] when they saw that it was one of the most highly respected members of the Assembly, a devout Hindu, simply invoking the gods to witness this ceremony.... I happened to spot Nehru just as he was turning away, trying to hide a smile by covering his mouth with his hand." Mildred describes the pressure of the throngs outside the Assembly clamouring for a glimpse of their idol, Nehru, whom the police obliged "to slip out by a back entrance". As an American, she was struck by the fact that when the crowds got out of hand it was the VIP who changed his plans. There are numerous fascinating vignettes in her letter of the next morning's Independence Day events: of Nehru's horror at seeing a horse fall (he only turned his attention back to the ceremony when he saw the horse rise again and move); of the U.S.

Ambassador's irritation that President Truman's cable of congratulations had been omitted when other leaders' greetings were read (it turned out that it had been misplaced); of Mountbatten's demeanour of "sincere pleasure", a sharp contrast with his stiffness in Karachi ("Here he was relaxed and at home among friendly companions... his good wishes were obviously heartfelt.") Mildred's harrowing account of the evening's ceremony, ruined by rain and by 5,00,000 people turning out for an event planned for 25,000, is too long to summarise here, but for one detail: amidst the chaos, Indira Gandhi "looking woebegone and bedraggled. Her sari was torn, her hair straggling, her fingernails ruined. And she was one of the dignitaries!"

The Flag Goes up

But the highlight of Mildred's account is of the morning of August 15, 1947, when the national flag was raised over the Council Hall: "the multitudes had gathered as far as the eye could see in the two-mile long parkway approach to the Secretariat, on tops of buildings, in windows, on cornices, in trees, perched everywhere like so many birds. The raising of that first flag was the single most thrilling experience of the entire celebration.... The first who spotted it pointed like eager childen; others... looked up and tried to push their way to a vantage point so they too could see this miracle. For a few minutes there was almost a subdued hush over the whole crowd; then a soft bass undertone slowly swelled until, perhaps when the flag reached the top,...

there was a breathtaking roar of cheering, shouting, and excited cries which others said penetrated to the hall inside and made their spines tingle. While I was being stirred by the sheer power and grandeur of the spectacle,... the Indians either stood mute, immersed in their own overwhelming thoughts, or were shouting almost uncontrollably. It was a grand emotional experience that left most of us with shaky voices or complete inability to speak."

These are the words not of an Indian nationalist but of a young American woman. Mildred Talbot wrote to her American friend two weeks after witnessing that first flag-raising: "The memory of the feelings that surged up within us as we watched their [i.e. the Indian masses'] excitement and awe still brings tears to my eyes." Fifty-seven years later, the memories of that first Independence Day have faded in all but a tiny percentage of our population. But the power of that magical moment when India became free, and the hopes raised of what we would make of that freedom, must never be forgotten. Today is the day to remember that moment, and to rededicate ourselves to its promise. It is a promise every Indian can do his or her own part to fulfil.

Gandhi & Nehru

They were opposite in nature, but they shared a passion for freedom and justice, and together created a giant of democracy.

The 20th century produced many remarkable leaders, but few nations were blessed with a pair quite like India's Mahatma Gandhi and his protégé Jawaharlal Nehru. Gandhi was idealistic, quirky, quixotic and determined, a cross between a saint and a ward politician; like the best crossbreeds, he managed to distill the qualities of both and yet transcend their contradictions. Nehru was a moody, idealistic intellectual who felt an almost mystical empathy for the toiling peasant masses; an aristocrat who had passionate socialist convictions; a product of Harrow and Cambridge who spent over 10 years in British jails; an agnostic radical who became an unlikely follower of the deeply spiritual Mahatma. Together they brought a nation to freedom and laid the underpinnings for the world's largest democracy.

Gandhi was the extraordinary leader of the world's first successful nonviolent movement for independence from colonial rule. To describe his method, he coined the expression *satyagraha*—literally, "holding on to truth" or, as he variously described it, truth force, love force or soul force. He disliked the English term passive resistance because *satyagraha* required activism, not passivity. If you believed in truth and cared enough to obtain it, Gandhi felt, you could not afford to be passive. You had to be prepared actively to suffer for truth. It was *satyagraha* that first bound Nehru to Gandhi, soon after the latter's return to India in 1915 from a long sojourn in South Africa, where his morally charged leadership of the Indian community against racial discrimination had earned him the sobriquet of Mahatma ("Great Soul," a term he detested).

Gandhi's unique method of resistance through civil disobedience, allied to a talent for organization, gave the Indian nationalist movement both a saint and a strategist. His singular insight was that self-government would never be achieved by the resolutions passed by a self-regarding and unelected élite pursuing the politics of the drawing room. To him, self-government had to involve the empowerment of India's suffering multitudes in whose name the upper classes were clamoring for Home Rule. This position did not go over well with India's political class, which consisted largely of maharajahs and lawyers—men of means who discoursed in English and demanded the rights of Englishmen. To put his principles into practice, Gandhi lived in near-absolute poverty in an ashram and traveled across the land in third-class railway compartments, campaigning against untouchability, poor sanitation and child marriage, while also preaching an eclectic set of virtues from sexual abstinence and frequent enemas to the weaving of hand-spun cotton cloth. That he was an eccentric was beyond doubt. That he had touched a chord amongst the masses was equally apparent. That he was a potent political force soon became clear. He captured the imagination of the nation by publicly breaking English law in the name of a higher law ("the voice of conscience") and challenging the British to jail him. Despite differences over both tactics (Nehru wanted independence immediately whereas Gandhi believed Indians had to be made ready for their own freedom) and philosophy (the agnostic Nehru had little patience for the Mahatma's spirituality), the two men proved a formidable combination. Gandhi guided Nehru to the political pinnacle; Nehru in turn proved an inspirational campaigner as President of the Indian National Congress, electrifying the nation with his speeches and tireless travel. Gandhi took the issue of freedom to the masses as one of simple right and wrong and gave them a technique to which the British had no response.

By abstaining from violence Gandhi wrested the moral advantage. By breaking the law nonviolently he demonstrated the injustice of the law. By accepting the punishments imposed on him he confronted his captors with their own brutalization. By voluntarily imposing suffering upon himself in his hunger strikes he demonstrated the lengths to which he was prepared to go in defense of what he considered right. Gandhi's moral rectitude and Nehru's political passion made the perpetuation of British rule an impossibility.

Of course there was much more to Gandhism—physical self-denial, self-reliance, a belief in the human capacity for selfless love, religious ecumenism, idealistic internationalism, and a passionate commitment to equality and social justice. The improvement of his fellow human beings was arguably more important to him than the political goal of ridding India of the British. But it is his central tenet of nonviolence in the pursuit of these ends that represents his most significant original contribution to the world. Martin Luther King in the U.S., Adolfo Pérez Esquivel in Argentina, Nelson Mandela in South Africa and Aung San Suu Kyi in Burma all sought inspiration from the Mahatma's teachings.

Upon Gandhi's assassination in 1948, a year after independence, Nehru, the country's first Prime Minister, became the keeper of the national flame, the most visible embodiment of India's struggle for freedom. Gandhi's death could have led Nehru to assume untrammeled power. Instead, he spent a lifetime trying to instill the habits of democracy in his people—a disdain for dictators, a respect for parliamentary procedures, an abiding faith in the constitutional system. He himself was such a convinced democrat that, at the crest of his rise, he authored an anonymous article warning Indians of the dangers of giving dictatorial temptations to Jawaharlal Nehru. "He must be checked," he wrote of himself. "We want no Caesars." During Nehru's 17 years as Prime Minister, democratic values became so entrenched that when his daughter Indira suspended India's freedoms with a State of Emergency for 21 months, she felt compelled to return to the Indian people for vindication, held an election, and comprehensively lost it.

While the world was disintegrating into fascism, violence and war in the 20th century, Gandhi taught the virtues of truth, nonviolence and peace. The principal pillars of Nehru's legacy—democratic institution-building, staunch pan-Indian secularism, socialist economics at home and a foreign policy of nonalignment—were all integral to a vision of Indianness that sustained the nation for decades. Today, both legacies are fundamentally contested, and many Indians have strayed from the ideals bequeathed to them by Gandhi and Nehru. Yet they, in their very different ways, each represented that rare kind of leader who is not diminished by the inadequacies of his followers. The American editor Norman Cousins once asked Nehru what he hoped his legacy to India would be. "Four hundred million people capable of governing themselves," Nehru replied. The numbers have grown, but the very fact that each day over a billion Indians govern themselves in a pluralist democracy is testimony to the deeds and words of these two men.

Nehru Declined offer of Permanent U.N. Seat'

Jawaharlal Nehru "declined a United States offer" to India to "take the permanent seat on the United Nations Security Council" around 1953 and suggested that it be given to China, according to the United Nations Under-Secretary General, Sashi Tharoor.

In his latest book, "Nehru — The Invention of India," Mr. Tharoor writes that Indian diplomats who have seen files swear that Nehru declined the offer about the same time as he turned down "with scorn" John Foster Dulles' support for an Indian Monroe Doctrine.

Nehru had suggested that the seat, till then held by Taiwan, be offered to Beijing instead. He wrote that "the seat was held with scant credibility by Taiwan."

Rafiq Zakaria, historian and scholar, and Murli Deora, MP, highlighted the disclosure at a function organised here to release the book. Manmohan Singh, Leader of Opposition in the Rajya Sabha, handed over the first copy to the Maharashtra Chief Minister, Sushilkumar Shinde.

Later, talking of the book, brought out by Penguin Viking, Mr.Tharoor spoke of Nehru's legacy which included four elements — democratic institution building, socialism, a non-aligned foreign policy and secularism, and said the legacy was far too important not to be re-looked at from the point of view of the 21st century.

In Nehru's time, India had no foreign policy and it was correct to say "Nehru had a foreign policy."

Often, other politicians and the foreign office mandarins came to know about the policy when they heard Nehru speak on the issue, Mr. Tharoor said.

He had been alive, Jawaharlal Nehru would have been 110 years and one month old at the turn of the century. It is 36 years since his moving away from the centrestage of Indian and world politics. With death and with the passage of time, great leaders undergo a process of demystification. Distances in terms of time and the elimination of the physical presence of these larger-than-life figures enable succeeding generations to a assess their lives more objectively, without being afflicted by their charisma and power, whatever the ingredients of that power might have been.

Nehru even during his life-time went through the spectrum of individual and collective reactions to his leadership, from being adored as a revolutionary and vibrant personification of the forward-looking spirit of India to being described as a pampered young man who accidentally acquired national leadership due to the influence of his father and the favouritism of Mahatma Gandhi. He has been admired as a leader of the freedom movements, as the founding father of institutional democracy in India and as the architect of India's policy in all its manifestations, being the longest serving prime minister of India (from 1946 to 1964).

It would be pertinent to evaluate Nehru as a leader and a statesman because of the decisive and over-arching role that he played in Indian history in the 20th century. Regardless of criticisms, he was one of the most influential leaders of our freedom struggle. He was a pioneering articulator of Asian resurgence and was an unusually idealistic advocate of conscience in international politics. India's parliamentary democracy, free judiciary and media, the apolitical civil servants and armed forces, the commitment to secularism, social justice and equality before law, all originated in the blue print for free India which he worked out.

Nehru had a profound belief in India's destiny as a moral and stabilizing force in inter-state relations. He had faith in the Indian people and an equally strong hope that their maturity and civilisational wisdom would ensure for India an important role in the world. His education in the West, and his exposure to the political movements of Europe in the first three decades of this century, combined with his eclectic sense of history, made him realise that science, technology and economic modernisation and development were essential pre-requisites to fulfill the vision of a free India that he had in mind and to which he devoted three-fourths of his life. These ingredients and influences, cannot be denied in generic terms but in is necessary to assess Nehru through the prism of India's realities today, and to judge him in the context of criticisms leveled against him as an individual and as a public figure. This exercise should necessarily be an assessment of him as a leader of the freedom struggle, as a founding ideologue of the Indian Republic, as the prime minister, as an international statesman and as a leader beloved of the people of India, second only to Gandhi in this century. I can do no better than to recall two remarks made by senior members of the Congress over his role as leader of the freedom struggle. Acharya Kripalani, speaking at a seminar of the Gandhi Vichar Parishad in Wardha in 1954, said Nehru became a prominent leader of the freedom struggle basically because of the colonial mindset of the Indians. "He is an Englishman in Indian clothing." So the respect for him. I was one of the audience to which this remark was made. Though we were very young, we did not accept this assessment. We attributed it to the breaking away of Jayaprakash Narayan and Kriplani from the Congress at the point of time.

The second view was expressed years later by former prime minister P.V. Narasimha Rao when I asked him how Nehru came to such prominence in the freedom struggle. He said Congressmen made him their leader because of their conviction that he was committed to the cause of freedom and to the service of the people of India. But he also reminded me that Nehru had worked his way up through municipal elections in Allahabad and through mass movements in Pratapgarh of Uttar Pradesh.

As the ideologue of the Indian Constitution and the Indian polity, Nehru's contributions cannot be denied. It is his implementation of the doctrine of secularism and his approach to harmonizing the diversities of India which seem flawed in retrospect. The basic reasoning of secularism which he put forward was valid—that a plural, multi-religious, civil society like that of India's could remain harmonious and united only if it is underpinned by religious tolerance and separation of religion from politics. The flaw, however, was that he did not underline the fact that the secular ethos of Indian society was rooted in two factors. That Hindus constituted the majority of the people of the country and that Hindu ethos at the profoundest intellectual and spiritual levels believed deeply in religious tolerance and respect for other religions.

If the majority of people in India were not Hindus, India would not have been a secular country. Instead of emphasising this, Nehru put the Hindu majority somewhat on the defensive, predicating Indian secularism on certification by the minorities, that the majority is secular. This resulted in a certain defensiveness and self-conscious denial of their religious and cultural identity by the Hindu community, which has perhaps made secularism a surface phenomenon in India's socio-political processes.

Similarly, Nehru's decision to reorganise the states on the basis of languages, while being good-intentioned, perhaps germinated the seeds of the present centrifugal territorial demands, affecting the unity of our country. While he was the builder of democratic institutions and conventions, one has to acknowledge that he did not groom a second generation of leadership in the party or the country, nor did he show any awareness of the need for anchoring the Congress in a trained cadre of party workers. He presumed that the commitment and organisational cohesion of the Congress during the freedom struggle would continue which was not to be because the party in a freedom movement is always different from a party in power in terms of ethos and motivations.

It is fashionable now to criticise Nehru's economic policies. He is castigated for making the public sector occupy the commanding heights of Indian economy. He is criticised for not linking up with western market economies.

It has to be remembered that the Indian private sector did not have the resources and motivation to invest in infrastructural sectors of the economy which required long-term investments and gestation periods. More importantly, between 1947 and 1955, all his efforts to get the major western powers involved in infrastructural development did not get a positive response. It was in consequence of this predicament that he entrusted the responsibility of mobilising resources and channelling them to fundamental sectors of the Indian economy to the government and the public sector. While the decisions that he took seem logical and relevant to those times, the question to be answered is whether he would have continued the same policies had he lived into the '80s. Whatever his faults, he was alert and sensitive to changing domestic and international situations. Who knows, he might have been an equally active participant in the process of economic liberalisation and modernisation?

As an international statesman and foreign minister, there is a questioning of his founding the Non-Aligned Movement and its relevance today. It is true that the movement has not been very effective in safeguarding the interests of its member countries, particularly India. Two facts have to be kept in mind while evaluating Nehru's adherence to the movement. First, he made a distinction between being "non-aligned" and being part of "the Non-Aligned Movement".

He believed in non-alignment as a guiding principle of India's foreign policy so that India is assured of having the freedom of choice in making decisions responsive to its national interests without being subject to external influences. He articulated apprehensions about being part of a movement which in itself could become a bloc of countries. It was Krishna Menon who ultimately persuaded him to make India join the movement, arguing that the parallel interests of the countries of the movement would increase their influence in international transactions.

He did not believe in the non-aligned movement as a dogma. He rightly believed in non-alignment (as distinct from neutrality) as a guiding principle of India's foreign and security policies. Nehru can certainly be faulted for his idealism and belief in the sanctity of international law and agreements, in the light of his decision to go to the United Nations on the Kashmir issue and his faith in morality and goodwill as effective principles in inter-state relations. It was only at the end of 1962 after the military debacle against China that he acknowledged this reality, but it was too late. He can be blamed with Vallabhbhai Patel for the impatience which led to Partition about which Maulana Azad has written. In retrospect, Partition was good. It is preferable to India facing more profound centrifugal alienations than it is facing now.

Nehru was the beloved leader of his people. But when one intermeshes his individual persona with his public persona, one cannot but come to the conclusion that he was for the people, was committed to India's destiny being governed by the people but to a great extent was not "of the people". He was essentially a remote, aristocratic, glamorous and private person. Gandhi, Patel and Ambedkar were perhaps more immersed in the mass identity of Indians. Regardless of the fault lines, Nehru remains the most important architect of free India. The words of Justice Oliver Wendell Holmes come to mind here. "A great man represents a great ganglion in the nerves of society, or to vary the figure, at a strategic point in the campaign of history and his greatness consists in seizing that opportunity and being there at that particular strategic point."

Interim Prime Minister

Nanda was the interim Prime Minister of India twice for thirteen days each: the first time after the death of Prime Minister Jawaharlal Nehru in 1964, and the second time after the death of Prime Minister Lal Bahadur Shastri in 1966. His both terms were uneventful, yet they were important because of potential danger to the country following Nehru's death soon after a war with China in 1962, and Shastri's death after a war with Pakistan in 1965.

4

Nehru and Nationalism

Nehru's nationalist thought in order to assess the nature and extent of the influence of British political thought and practice. The next section will examine the period up to 1933 and the following section the period from then until Indian independence in 1947. The last section will consider Nehru's nationalist thought following Indian independence. Finally, a conclusion will summarize the findings of the chapter.

THE ORIGINS OF NEHRU'S NATIONALIST THOUGHT, UP TO 1933

Discussing his education in England in his autobiography Nehru portrayed himself as having been a fervent nationalist who had sought Indian independence from his youth. There is some evidence that his early education may have kindled these sentiments. For example, Nanda described an examination paper that Nehru encountered at Harrow:

The English History paper for the Christmas term, 1906, included combustible material for a future rebel against the British Raj. One of the questions was: 'For what reasons did the American colonies revolt? Why was it impossible to subjugate them?'

Nanda recognised the irony that the English public schools, which he called the "nurseries of the governing classes," instilled a range of attributes which Nehru put to the opposite use to that which they were normally employed: "The qualities which went to the making of the 'guardians' of the Empire were equally serviceable in hardening the fibre of the future rebel against the British *Raj*." Nanda also claimed that Nehru experienced a degree of racial prejudice at Cambridge:

At a ceremonial function held at Cambridge to award honorary degrees to a number of distinguished persons, including the Aga Kahn and the Maharaja of Bikaner, young Nehru's sharp eyes noted that the Vice-Chancellor did not deign to get up from his chair when giving the degrees to the Indians, although he had stood up for everyone else.

The awareness of the racial aspects of British imperialism in India and its impact of Nehru's nationalist thought became an important theme in Nehru's later work.

Nehru discussed theosophy and in particular Annie Besant in his autobiography and this constitutes a further potential British influence from this period. Although Nehru seemed to de-emphasise the extent of the influence in his autobiography he did devote a chapter to theosophy. Reflecting on this subject years later Nehru admitted that he considered theosophy to be "totally ineffective" and that "the Theosophical Society seemed to be cut off from the world's problems." Despite this, Nehru conceded: "Mrs. Besant had a very powerful influence on me in my childhood. And later, many years later, when I had come back on the political plane, again she had a powerful influence on me."

It is interesting to note that Das's study of Nehru's political thought does not mention Besant in the context of Nehru's nationalist thought or his political thought in general. However, according to a recent study, some of Besant's ideas "recur time and again" in Nehru's thought and especially his later work.

Besant's more positive assessment of Indian culture and its spiritual nature is mirrored in Nehru's later work which emphasised India's long heritage prior to the arrival of the British. In addition to the spiritual aspects of the influence of theosophy and Besant's critique of the economic impact of British imperialism, which seem to have manifested themselves in Nehru's later work, it is likely that Besant's support of Indian independence also encouraged his early nationalist thought.

In his autobiography, Nehru explain that following his return to India from England, he was "a pure nationalist" and the "vague socialist ideas" he entertained whilst at Cambridge had "sunk into the background." He claimed: "Nationalistic ideas filled my mind. I mused of Indian freedom and Asiatic freedom from the thraldom of Europe. I dreamt of brave deeds, of how, sword in hand, I would fight for India and help in freeing her." These comments resemble the sentiment of Meredith's "For the 'Centenary of Garibaldi'" that appeared at the beginning of Trevelyan's *Garibaldi and the Thousand,* two verses of which Nehru quoted in *Glimpses of World History.*

Nehru also identified two further significant influences that contributed toward the development of his nationalist thought at this time and are of particular relevance to his British connection. Firstly, Nehru explained that he had received "one of G. M. Trevelyan's Garibaldi books" as a prize whilst at Harrow. He claimed that this work "fascinated" him and he subsequently "obtained the other two volumes of the series and studied the whole Garibaldi story in them carefully."

Nehru described the impact of this study: "Visions of similar deeds in India came before me, of a gallant fight for freedom, and in my mind India and Italy got strangely mixed together." Secondly, Nehru claimed that during the Boer war all his "sympathies were with the Boers" and that he had followed events in the press. Thus through his British connection Nehru learned of the struggles of the Boers and the Italians for national freedom. The example of Italian nationalism became a recurring subject in Nehru's nationalist thought and is discussed below whilst the Boers' struggle, although Nehru never returned to it, constitutes an important early source of influence.

It is thus reasonable to contend that Nehru was influenced by the kind of liberal nationalism that he discovered in Trevelyan's work. Das's study of Nehru's ideaion of nationalism located it within the "liberal humanitarian" variety, prevalent in the nineteenth century, as opposed to the "conservative and authoritarian" tradition commonly associated with fascism. In particular, Das described Nehru's nationalism in terms that have been attributed to Trevelyan and the kind of liberalism that he espoused in the Garibaldi trilogy. For Das, Nehru's nationalism included "an urge to fight against domination or despotic governments, faith in the individual liberty and rights of men, aspirations for greater liberty, equality and happiness for all" and favoured "national self-determination." Thus Das considered that Nehru "saw in his ideaion of nationalism not a narrow and fanatical urge but a healthy force." It is evident that Nehru developed this ideaion relatively early in his career and Trevelyan would seem to be an important source.

However, these early liberal influences were supplanted by socialist influences from the 1920s onwards. One potential British source of this growing socialist influence on Nehru, which is of particular relevance to the development of his nationalist thought, is the work of Harold Laski. Laski's *A Grammar of Politics* contains a discussion of nationalism which resembles that contained in Nehru's nationalist thought. In discussing the development of nationalism, Laski mentioned the example of Italy and Austria:

It became the chapter of the nineteenth century that States composed of various nationalities were monstrous hybrids for which no excuse could be offered; hence, for example, the passionate sympathy of Victorian England with the Italian crusade against Austria.

However, Laski recognised that the growth of nationalism had been accompanied by industrialism and conflict between states, which had tempered his acceptance of it as a wholly progressive force. For Laski, it was because industrialism had "created a world-market, and a world-market implies foreign competition" that "nationalism becomes transformed into imperialism." Therefore, according to Laski: "A nationalism that implies the sovereign right of self-determination is, therefore, a principle of which the consequences are far from different from those envisaged by men like Mazzini and Mill." It was for these reasons that Laski felt nationalism must be checked: "A nation is entitled to live. But because it cannot live to itself alone, the question of how it is to live is not a question it is entitled to determine alone." Ultimately, although Laski accepted "the rational desire for self-government" he considered the solution to these problems would be found in "world-government" and observed that any "order based upon compulsion can never permanently maintain itself and gave the examples of India, Ireland and Austria-Hungary.

There exists in Laski's position here the same tension between nationalism and the desire for independence and socialism that is evident in Nehru's nationalist thought. It is evident that Laski was one of the major socialist sources from which Nehru drew to develop his understanding of nationalism. The Development of Nehru's Nationalist Thought 1933-1946 Nehru's essay, "Wither India?," which reveals substantial socialist influence, further develops his attempt to reconcile nationalism and internationalism. Nehru sought to place the Indian freedom struggle in the context of the world situation and his wider political thought.

He began by explaining that Indian nationalism drew attention to "the inherent conflict between national interests" in the case of the British Government's claim that "they were the trustees" for India. However, Nehru admitted, "nationalism does not make us realize the equally inherent and fundamental conflict between economic interests within the nation." Nehru described the world situation in terms of a crisis of capitalism: 'The growth of industries and nationalist movements in all the countries of the East checked Western exploitation, and the profits of Western capitalism began to go down." Moving to Asia, Nehru claimed that it was "the main field of conflict between nationalism and imperialism." Then Nehru explained why "the strongest force in Asia" was nationalism rather than internationalism:

This is natural as a country under alien domination must inevitably think first in terms of nationalism. But the powerful economic forces working for change in the world today have influenced this nationalism to an ever-increasing extent, and everywhere it is appearing in Socialistic garb.

For Nehru, India was a part of this wider "Asiatic problem" and it too possessed "a struggle today between the old nationalist ideology and the new economic ideology." Having described the background, Nehru outlined his policy: "Politically, it must mean independence and the severance of the British connection, which means imperialist domination." However, Nehru also dismissed narrow nationalism: "National isolation is neither a desirable nor a possible ideal in a world which is daily becoming more of a unit."

Consequently, Nehru's nationalist thought sought to take account of this reality: "Our ideal and objective cannot go against this historical tendency, and we must be prepared to discard a narrow nationalism in favour of world co-operation and real internationalism." However, Nehru distinguished this internationalism from that implied by Dominion status:

British statesmen of the Liberal and Labour variety often point out to us the ills of a narrow nationalism and dwell on the virtues of what used to be known as the British Empire and is now euphemistically called the British Commonwealth of Nations. Under cover of fine and radical words and phrases they seek to hide the ugly and brutal face of imperialism and try to keep us in its embrace of death.

Finally, Nehru remarked: 'The British Empire and real internationalism are as the poles apart, and it is not through that empire that we can march to internationalism." In this essay Nehru - for all his unease at nationalism - attempted to justify his belief that Indian independence must take precedence over the kind of internationalism required by socialist influences. Thus despite the evidence of substantial socialist influence, Nehru maintained a strongly nationalist position.

Nehru's conversation of Italian nationalism in *Glimpses of World History* is particularly germane to the analysis of British influences on his nationalist thought. Firstly, Nehru admitted that he first learned of Italian nationalism through his reading of Trevelyan's study of Garibaldi. In the chapter devoted to the development of modem Italy, Nehru recommended to Indira that if she wanted to acquaint herself "with the joy and anguish of the struggle" she should read "three books by Trevelyan - *Garibaldi and the Fight for the Roman Republic, Garibaldi and the Thousand,* and *Garibaldi and the Making of Italy.* " Secondly, Nehru made clear that he was familiar with the positive British attitudes towards Italian nationalism and in particular he quoted George Meredith's poetry praising the Italian nationalist leaders. However, Nehru observed that the English attitude to Italian nationalism revealed an inconsistency when contrasted with the attitude towards other cases. Nehru remarked:

At the time of the Italian struggle the English people sympathized with Garibaldi and his red-shirts, and many an English poet wrote stirring poetry about the fight. It is strange how the sympathies of the English often »o out to struggling peoples provided their own interests are not involved.

It is likely that Nehru had in mind British attitudes toward Indian nationalism as a case where the British interest was threatened. It is evident that Italian nationalism constituted an important influence on Nehru's nationalist thought and as well as being an influence in its own right it can also be considered as part of British influences on Nehru. In his autobiography, Nehru expanded on the similarities between India and Italy to which he had alluded in *Glimpses of World History.* These similarities had two aspects, the first was that between India and Italy and Nehru remarked:

There is some similarity between Italy and India. Both are ancient countries with long traditions of culture behind them, though Italy is a newcomer compared to India, and India is a much vaster country. Both are split up politically, and yet the ideaion of Italia, like that of India, never died, and in all their diversity the unity was predominant.

It is significant that Nehru emphasised the cultural unity of Italy and India, rather than the racial, religious or geographic, and this ideaion of nationalism was central to his later nationalist thought. Similarly, the belief that the cultural unity of India had been dormant, rather than extinguished, and that the unity was amid diversity were themes that Nehru was to develop later in *The Discovery of India.* The second aspect of the similarity between the Italian and Indian situations was that between the 'conquering' nations of Austria and Britain. Nehru also draw a parallel between these two countries:

More interesting is the comparison of England with Austria, for has not England of the twentieth century been compared to Austria of the nineteenth, proud and haughty and imposing still, but with the roots that gave strength shrivelling up and decay eating its way into the mighty fabric.

The parallel that Nehru drew admitted that Britain, as in the Austrian case, had become corrupt and thus lost any legitimacy it may have possessed. In drawing the analogy Nehru was likely to have surmised that British rule was neither inevitable nor irreversible. Nehru's discussion of the rise of Mussolini and Italian fascism in *Glimpses of World History* is pertinent because it addresses Nehru's concern with the development of overly narrow nationalism. Nehru explained the development of fascism as due to specific factors in Italy in the 1920s and 1930s, which included economic problems, the large numbers of demobilized soldiers and the divisions in the Italian left. However, Nehru's condemnation of fascism provides a striking contrast with his previous praise of the development of Italian nationalism and he ignores any possible link between the two phenomena. According to Nehru, Mussolini was able to take advantage of "divisions and splits" amongst Italian socialists to increase his own power whilst he "spoke in favour of the rich one day, and in favour of the poor the next day" so as "to play one off against the other." Although Mussolini may have portrayed himself as a champion of the poor, according to Nehru, he was "essentially... the champion of the propertied classes." For Nehru, fascism was both devoid of "fixed principles" and "any apologetic attitude towards violence," in contrast to "Communism or Marxism" which possessed "an intricate economic theory and interpretation of history, which requires the hardest mental discipline." For Nehru, fascism's inherent violence spilled over to Italy's foreign policy, which became imperialistic and confrontational. The rise of fascism in Italy had also caused disappointment for Trevelyan but he explained it as a misunderstanding of the Italian people rather than in Nehru's Marxist terms.

Nehru's Presidential Address at Lucknow in April 1936 placed his nationalist thought into the context of his world view, which at that time saw "the world divided up into two vast groups today - the Imperialist and Fascist on one side, [and] the Socialist and nationalist on the other." Nehru claimed that: "Nationalism in the east... was essentially different from the new and terribly narrow nationalism of fascist countries; the former was the historical urge to freedom, the latter the last refuge of reaction." Thus Nehru rejected any solution short of complete independence for India:

According to Cannadine,. "the dramatic rise of Fascism suggested that in some fundamental sense Trevelyan had misread the Italian past and the Italian people." Later Trevelyan suggested that the Italians had lacked the same faith in constitutional government that he observed in the British.

Between Indian nationalism, Indian freedom and British imperialism there can be no common ground, and if we remain within the imperialist fold, whatever our name or status, whatever outward semblance, of political power we might have, we remain cribbed and confined and allied to and dominated by the capitalist world. The exploitation of our masses will still continue and the vital social problems that face us will remain unsolved.

Nehru believed that "a clear and definite fascist mentality" was evident amongst the British in India. According to Nehru, British rule in India had been mutually detrimental:

It is astonishing to find to what depths of vulgarity our rulers have descended in their ardent desire to hold on to what they have got and it is depressing, though perhaps inevitable that some of our own countrymen, more interested in British Imperialism than the British themselves, should excel at this deplorable game.

These problems were, according to Nehru, inherent in the nature of British rule: "I have watched this process of moral and intellectual decay and realized, even more than I did previously, how autocratic power corrupts and degrades and vulgarizes." Finally, Nehru castigated the communal leaders as "political reactionaries" and hence he regarded the communal issue was divisive, harmful to the cause of Indian nationalism and a diversion from more important economic issues. This address marked the peak of socialist influences on Nehru's nationalist thought.

Nehru's anxiety with international developments, and particularly the polarisation that he perceived during the late 1930s, is illustrated clearly in his comments on the Spanish civil war. In his Presidential Address at Faizpur in December 1936, Nehru described an "organic connection between world events" and in particular a struggle between nationalism and democracy and the combined forces of fascism and imperialism. In this context, Nehru regarded the Spanish civil war as the most obvious manifestation of this struggle of which India was also a part: "And the struggle today is fiercest and clearest in Spain, and on the outcome of that depends war or peace in the world in the near future."

Nehru observed that the League of Nations had been ineffective for "while fascist powers helped the rebels, the League Powers proclaimed a futile policy of non-intervention." Nehru's concern with events in Spain is also revealed in his correspondence with his daughter at the time. This correspondence reinforces the depth of Nehru's concern with the Spanish civil war and also the fact that Indira kept him informed of British attitudes towards conflict.

In a 1937 article requesting food aid for the Spanish people, Nehru explained that the "same basic forces are in conflict elsewhere as in India." In particular Nehru referred to the Spanish civil war in this context:

This conflict of world forces is most evident in Spain, where bloody and inhuman war has waged for over seven months, and where a brutal Fascism and militarism have sought to crush and annihilate Spanish democracy and reduce to dust and ashes the rights of the Spanish people.

Nehru described how the Republicans in Madrid had faced the combined "forces of reaction, the Fascist Powers, foreign legionaries, mercenaries, [and] the farce of nonintervention." Nehru's dismissal of the policy of non-intervention is significant because he associated it with the British Government: "In this struggle British imperialism, with its so-called policy of non-intervention, has hindered and obstructed the Spanish people in their fight for freedom."

Thus Nehru drew a parallel between the British policy of non-intervention toward Spain which favoured fascism, by accident or design, and imperialist policy toward India, which was anti-democratic, and essentially fascist. Finally, Nehru claimed that India could not be indifferent to the outcome of the Spanish civil war: "For Fascism and imperialism march hand in hand, they are blood brothers." This analysis of the Spanish civil war represents an attempt by Nehru to integrate his own nationalist thought within a wider struggle between democracy and nationalism on the one side and imperialism and fascism on the other. According to Brecher, Nehru's psychoanalysis of the developments of the 1930s, and particularly that given in *Glimpses of World History,* was similar to that made by John Strachey:

> Nehru's analysis of the rise of Fascism and Nazism, the cause of the Great Depression, the growing disunity among the Western Powers, and the approach of war bears a marked resemblance to Strachey's The *Coming Struggle for Power,* though not quite as outspoken in its Marxism.

Although Brecher does not cite any, the evidence for the potential influence of Strachey's work is compelling. The 'struggle' that Strachey described was between monopoly capitalism, which had developed into fascism and imperialism, and nationalism. Consequently, for Strachey, as for Nehru, the crisis of the 1930s could only be solved by the replacement of the capitalist system with a socialist alternative. Throughout *The Coming Struggle for Power,* Strachey's analysis touched on themes that can also be found in Nehru's nationalist thought. In particular there are some striking similarities between Strachey's work and each of the most important elements of Nehru's nationalist thought most relevant to his British connection.

In constructing his Marxist analysis, Strachey viewed the state, and specifically the British state, as a tool constituted for material ends in the pursuit of capitalism. In doing view, and specifically G. M. Trevelyan, whom he considered the foremost member of that school. Strachey also criticised H. G. Wells, describing him as "the chief living theorist of the capitalist class." Strachey singled out Wells's *The Outline of History* as the evidence for this assessment, and although he regarded it as a "considerable work" and one of the few of its kind, it did not adequately explain imperialism. Finally, Strachey remarked that although George Bernard Shaw was "endowed with [a] mind of keener edge than his contemporary" Wells, and had familiarised himself with Marx's *Capital,* it had led him in the "strange" direction of joining "the Fabian Society." It is difficult to gauge the extent to which Nehru may have been influenced by Strachey's criticism of Trevelyan and Wells. In the latter case *The Outline of History* was one of the very few sources of any kind available to Nehru whilst in jail and even Strachey admitted that the work filled a void, since there were few if any "outline[s] of world history" available.

However, Strachey's criticism of Shaw and the Fabians is more significant. It is likely that during the 1930s Nehru was more influenced by Strachey's Marxism than by Fabianism and some members of the Fabian Society. However, in later life, Nehru rejected many Marxist influences and arrived at a more moderate socialism that found a significant role for the state.

Strachey also discussed the relationship between Britain and the Dominions in the context of his analysis of the development of capitalism. For Strachey there was an "indissoluble connection between the whole inevitable drift to monopoly *within* states and the intensification of enmity *between* states."

In summary, Strachey considered that: 'The capitalist system is dying and cannot be revived." A consequence, and one of the symptoms of ailing capitalism, was the development of imperialism, which attempted to prolong the capitalist system by reserving "the vast natural resources, and the vast markets, of the British Empire for the exclusive exploitation of Empire entrepreneurs."

However, Strachey identified a problem with this policy that had two aspects. Firstly, he considered "that the interests of the British capitalists and the Dominion capitalists are flatly contradictory" and claimed: "It is proving almost impossible to secure agreement between the British and the Dominion entrepreneurs as to a division of the spoils." This analysis of conflicting interests is similar to that used by Nehru in *Glimpses of World History* and it follows that conflicts would be greater between Britain and India, which had even less in common than the self-governing, white Dominions. Secondly, Strachey believed that the conflicts between Britain and the self-governing Dominions could not be resolved by simply exploiting "the non-self-governing Empire" to a greater extent, simply because it was not possible because the populations there were already "half-starved." This would certainly have accorded with Nehru's analysis of Indian poverty and the British contribution towards it. Such an analysis led Strachey and Nehru to conclude that capitalism and the British Empire was facing an unavoidable crisis or ' struggle for power.'

Strachey's analysis of the decay of capitalism and its implications for the British empire led him to draw an analogy between it and the fate of a nineteenth century empire. Strachey likened Britain to Austria:

Now there is little doubt that in principle the power of the British Empire is in decline. Great Britain is the Austria of the twentieth century. The stage of the nineteenth century was, it is true, the narrower stage of Europe: the stage upon which the complex tragedy of the twentieth century is being enacted, is the whole world. But, with this qualification, the parallel is obvious. The Austrian Empire was, and the British Empire is, a conglomeration of extremely dissimilar parts: no ties of blood, religion, race, or tradition being common to these parts. Both have been the result of long processes of historical accretion, in which pieces and bits of territory have been slowly brought together. Both have been continually disturbed by nationalist movements, and at intervals by open revolts, in one or more of their parts.

This is significant given Nehru's use of a similar parallel in his autobiography and also the discussion of Austria by Trevelyan and Laski.

Additionally, Strachey's insistence that the British Empire was "indisputably a waning and not a waxing influence in world affairs" may have helped to instil in Nehru the belief that Indian independence was inevitable. This analogy also provides a connection between the influence of Trevelyan earlier in Nehru's life and the later influence of Strachey.

One of Nehru's most significant contributions to his nationalist thought was *The Discovery of India.* It reveals the gradual shift in emphasis in Nehru's nationalist thought from the overtly Marxist anti-imperialism of the early 1930s to the later position which stressed Indian cultural unity. Das identified *The Discovery of India* as the work that contained the essence of Nehru's thoughts on Indian nationalism. According to Gopal, it offered a "buoyant message" in "the dark years of Indian nationalism" and stressed "the necessity of revitalizing the Indian people." However, Gopal also believed that Nehru became "engrossed" in Indian culture to such an extent that it led to some "woolly writing" and a lack of "analysis, elegance and clear thinking." In sum, for Gopal, who recognised the irony in the work, Nehru had "in an astonishingly narrow nationalist tradition... put together a version of India's cultural history derived from secondary sources and studded with testimonials from European observers." For Brecher, it was a "rambling and discursive history" of India, which examined Nehru's own "cultural heritage" and reveals "the specifically Indian influences on his character.

In *The Discovery of India,* according to Gopal: "Jawaharlal is no longer primarily interested in social and economic change, in action and great men, or in Marxist analysis of class struggles." Although Nehru had shifted from Marxism his anti-British rhetoric was as clear and critical as ever. However, Gopal's comments on this aspect of *The Discovery of India* reveal something of the nature of his British connection: 'The chapters on the war years blend into a general, scathing account of British rule in India. The severe criticism it not so much unfair as uncharacteristic of Jawaharlal." It is perhaps more accurate to claim that Nehru's criticism is uncharacteristic of his later sentiment, after independence had been obtained.

Firstly, Nehru placed his nationalist consideration into the wider context of Indian nationalism during the last years of British rule. At that time, Nehru explained, Indian nationalism was "inevitable" because "national freedom must be the first and dominant urge." Nehru observed that although this sentiment may have been contrary to the spirit of internationalism, it was nevertheless a reality and the "nationalist ideal" was "not a thing of the past with no future significance." In this way Nehru defended Indian nationalism, and his own nationalist thought, from the charge, from the left, that it was not progressive. Then, as he had done elsewhere, Nehru dismissed those who advocated the internationalism implied by the British empire: Sometimes we are told that our nationalism is a sign of our backwardness and even our demand for independence indicates our narrowmindedness.

Those who tell us seem to imagine that true internationalism would triumph if we agreed to remain as junior partners in the British Empire or Commonwealth of Nations. They do not appear to realize that this particular type of so-called internationalism is only an extension of a narrow British nationalism, which could not have appealed to us even if the logical consequences of Anglo-Indian history had not utterly rooted out its possibility from our minds.

Nehru believed that independence was a priority for India: "Internationalism can indeed only develop in a free country, for all the thought and energy of a subject country are directed towards the achievements of its own freedom." Discussing the second world war, Nehru revealed a motivation for his nationalism in his criticism of British imperialism:

Repeatedly we pointed out the inconsistency of condemning fascism and nazism and maintaining imperialist domination. It was true that the former were indulging in horrid crimes whilst imperialism in India and elsewhere had stabilized itself. The difference was one of degree and of time, not of kind.

Here Nehru repeated some of the convictions of his earliest nationalist thought when he stated that India must attain independence prior to embarking on any reforms of society of the economy.

Secondly, as well as being divisive, Nehru considered that the combination of racialism and imperialism was harmful to both India and Britain:

Imperialism and the domination of one people over another is bad, and so is racialism. But imperialism plus racialism can only lead to horror and ultimately to the degradation of all concerned with them. The future historians of England will have to consider how far England's decline from her proud eminence was due to her imperialism and racialism, which corrupted her public life and made her forget the lessons of her own history and literature.

The decline of British civilization was a theme that Nehru discussed elsewhere in *The Discovery of India* and it is evident he regarded it positively:

Nevertheless Britain has had in the past, and has still, remarkable qualities -courage and the will to pull together, scientific and constructive ability and a capacity for adaptation. These qualities, and others she possesses, go a long way to make a nation great and enable it to overcome the dangers and perils that confront it.

Nehru identified falling population growth as another manifestation of the decline of the civilization: "In England a steady fall in the fertility rate has been noticeable since the eighties of the last century, and it is the lowest now in Europe except for France." For Nehru this phenomenon was indicative of a deeper malaise:

It would seem that the kind of modern civilization that developed first in the west and spread elsewhere, and especially the metropolitan life that has been its chief feature, produces an unstable society which gradually loses its vitality.

For Nehru, declining population was another aspect of the racial issue: "What is wrong with modern civilization which produces at the roots these signs of racial decadence?" Finally, Nehru also dismissed the possibility of Dominion status on racial grounds: "The idea behind dominion status, of a mother country closely connected with her daughter nations, all of them having a common cultural background, seemed totally inapplicable to India." In justifying this belief Nehru cited the treatment of Indians around the Empire and Commonwealth: "The racial discrimination and treatment of Indians in some of the British dominions and colonies were powerful factors in our determination to break from that group."

Given the possible influence of Laski and Strachey it is necessary to mention the Left Book Club (L. B. C.) which linked them with Nehru in the 1930s. Along with Harold Laski and the publisher Victor Gollancz, Strachey was a founder of the L. B. C. and, according to Michael Newman, he was its "dominant intellectual influence." The L. B. C. operated between 1936 and 1948 but was most influential in the period from its foundation until the outbreak of the second world war. It published many socialist works, including those by the Webbs, Laski and Strachey and, according to Hugh Thomas, *The Coming Struggle for Power* "was regarded as a prescribed text." Due largely to the predominance of Strachey's influence the L. B. C. positioned itself to the left of the mainstream Labour Party. In fact the L. B. C. was dominated by the Communist Party through Strachey and according to Samuels: "In most people's minds the Left Book Club and the Communist Party were virtually indistinguishable." Significantly, Strachey sought to establish a united front organisation against fascism through the L. B. C. and to this end "the Club became preoccupied with the struggle in Spain" and held rallies in aid of that cause. The analysis of the world situation fostered by the L. B. C. was agreeable to Nehru and Indian nationalism and he was aware of its activities and the principal promoters. For example, his daughter Indira discussed the L. B. C. in a letter to Nehru in 1936:

I am thinking of becoming a member of the Left Book Club. Have you heard of it? Its aim is to help in the terribly urgent struggle for World Peace & a better Newman, *John Strachey,* 54. It is worth noting that Gollancz was also Nehru's publisher. Samuels, "The Left Book Club," 66-81. Samuels noted that the L. B. C. obtained 57,000 members by April 1939 and estimated a readership of a quarter of a million. Its influence was greatly diminished after the Nazi- Soviet pact of August 1939.

In his reply Nehru advised Indira: "Certainly join the Left Book Club. I have myself been thinking of doing so."

The L. B. C.'s anti-imperialism and support for the Spanish republic is mirrored in much of Nehru's work of this period. Certainly there is evidence to suggest that the L.B.C. was an important influence on Nehru at this time. A number of these themes, especially those found in *The Discovery of India,* are also found in the work of the British socialist writer and acquaintance of Nehru, H. N. Brailsford (1873-1958).

In particular, Bradford's *Subject India,* which was published in 1943 as part of the L. B. C. series discussed the Indian situation from a perspective similar and sympathetic to that of Nehru. In common with much British historiography, Brailsford detected an element of cowardice and unmanliness in the Indian character: 'There is some truth in the usual English belief that part at least of the Indian population is unwarlike."

Brailsford scrutinised the idea of Indian unity and argued that although there were several races and languages and that the British had sought to "divide and rule," there was nevertheless a "common heritage of culture" and a "cultural unity."

Brailsford, like Nehru, also considered that the princely states were "backward and reactionary." Finally, Brailsford also emphasised the difference between India and the Dominions and appraised it in much the same way as Nehru. For Brailsford, "the Dominions are countries are peopled by our kinsmen" and the implication for relations between Britain and the Dominions was founded on this basis:

The political relationship, vaguely defined, with no organised institutional structure, befits the informal dealings of kinsmen. This tie, unlike anything else in history or the contemporary world, works best when the Dominion is solidly Anglo-Saxon, as New Zealand is, and very ill when it is alien in blood, as Eire is.

Obviously Brailsford appreciated, as Nehru did, the difficulty of incorporating India into the Commonwealth structure. It is worth noting that the racial aspect expressed here and by Nehru is rather more sophisticated than a simple English or Indian dichotomy. Nehru's nationalist thought recognised, as Brailsford does, differences between the British and or Anglo-Saxon races and the other 'white' races, like the Irish or Spanish. It is likely that if Brailsford did not provide a British source direcdy he would have at least reinforced many aspects of Nehru's nationalist thought.

NEHRU'S CONTRIBUTION TO NATION-BUILDING IN INDIA

There were thus positive facets of Nehru's contribution to nation-building in India. But the story does not end there, for Nehruvianism also witnessed certain distortions in India's nation-building process and much of the present day dichotomies in Indian polity are to be found rooted in these distortions. It is important to highlight of these facets of Nehruvism,. But in the process I would hope that my critique of the Nehruvian system does not become confused with the current communalist criticism of Nehruvism. While the sectarian political forces which have unfortunately wrested control of the Indian state take to task the progressive features of Nehruvism, my own critique would rest on the premise that Nehru did not become as progressive as he could have been.

That instead, there were significant gaps between what Nehru preached and what remained the ground reality. The following negative traits in Nehruvian polity can readily be identified: (i) a basic element of continuity with the British style of governance; (ii) the strengthening of the Right in the Congress ; (iii) the establishment of the governmental supremacy over the Party and (iv) the victory of political centralism within Indian federalism.

Continuity between Colonial and Nehruvian Regimes

It can be sensibly argued that despite certain obvious outward changes in forms of governance or employment of new political hyperbolas, the Indian government under Jawaharlal Nehru represented in many respects a continuation of British attitudes both in form and substance. Hamza Alavi has shown that like other post-colonial regimes the Indian state was 'overdeveloped'.. The British Raj had reared a repressive state apparatus which exceeded the needs of an 'underdeveloped and poor post-colonial state'.

The Congress government after 1947 unfortunately chose not to 'develop an alternative State structure', but maintain the police, paramilitary and other civil organisations inherited from the British. Studies by scholars like Betelheim show, the administrative system in independent India 'was renewed without being remodelled, thus retaining many of the colonial system's imperfections'. The Indian people were thus in most cases 'confronted with the same civil servants, the same policemen who treated them with the same scorn and brutality as under British rule'. N.K. Bose, by no means a leftist critic of the Indian polity, thus summarised the situation in the late 1950s:... by virtue of the circumstances of peaceful transfer of power, the Congress inherited an administrative structure which it tried to use for a new purpose. Its idea became, not to disrupt the status quo, but to build up its 'socialistic pattern' of economy on the foundation of the existing order without a violent disturbance. In this prosaic task of reformation, the Congress party... had tried to convert every problem of national reconstruction into an administrative problem... The identification of the Congress with the status quo, even if the ultimate intention may be of using it as a spring-board for reform... has made the organisation unpopular... The loss of ethical quality in the contemporary endeavours of the Congress in the reorganisation of its party machinery, or in the matter of running an old administrative machinery without sufficient proof of desire or capability of reforming the latter, has created a kind of frustration, and even of cynicism amongst those who had made the attainment of political freedom synonymous with the advent of social revolution or moral regeneration. (Bose 1958)

This element of continuity between colonial and immediate post-colonial regimes in India becomes particularly evident from the Nehru-led Congress government's relationship with the police and military. This relationship signified a shift from 'ostensible antagonism until 1947 to increasing interdependence... in the post-colonial period'.. Between 1949 and 1950 the Congress government at Delhi used about 12,000 armed police personnel to curb the Telengana peasant upsurge; in the first decade of independence as many as 800 recorded deaths resulted directly from police actions during the same period; the police expenditure of Indian government increased from Rs.9 million in 1951-52 to Rs.800 million in 1970-71; and the army assisted civil authorities to restore order on 476 occasions between 1947 and 1970 and 350 times between 1980 and 1983.

It can readily be argue that the historical context of this element of continuity between the departing British regime and the new regime under Nehru was created during the working of Congress provincial ministries in the aftermath of the 1936 elections., a period when Nehru with Gandhi's blessings was at the helm of Congress affairs.

Recent studies have demonstrated that the Congress election machinery set up to contest the 1936 legislative elections had a distinct conservative leverage. Candidates were generally selected from local businessmen, contractors and landlords who could not only take care of their own campaigns but also replenish the party's exchequer Defections from non-Congress parties were also encouraged in provinces where the party's organisation was not yet strong. This process 'increased the strength of the conservatives'. and it was this section inside the party which clinched political power when the Congress formed ministries initially in the six provinces of Madras, Bombay, Central Provinces, Orissa, Bihar, United Provinces and later in the North-West Frontier Provinces and Assam.

The rightist orientation of Congress ministers was reflected in similarities between their style of functioning and that of the preceding British officers.. Several members of the I.C.S. noted with relief that 'fire-eating agitators' had turned into 'responsible ministers'. D. Symington, for instance, observed this metamorphosis in Bombay: It was a momentous occasion when, in the month of April, we came under the rule of the party which had been agitating against the British Raj for more than twenty years.

But, if anyone at the time expected dramatic and revolutionary changes, he was in for an anticlimax. Our new Government had enough sense and experience to realise that nine-tenths of its work would lie in the field of day-to-day administration, and that spectacular reform must be a fringe activity.

C.H. Masterman, then a Secretary in the Madras secretariat, had a roughly similar story to tell when he proudly noted: 'He (Rajaji) told me once that he had much greater confidence in the judgement of his British secretaries than in his Indian colleagues'..

This element of permanence between the 1936-37 Congress ministries and their British predecessors could be also felt in respective reactions to various strands of popular protest. By December 1937 the Congress governments were faced with a dilemma: while the Kisan Sabhas - enthused by the formation of 'popular regimes' - pressed for fundamental agrarian reforms, the landlords urged the Congress to contain the 'radical elements'. The Congress choice proved to be more with the latter than the former. In Bihar the 'credibility' of the Tenancy Act was considerably undermined when the Congress submitted to landlord pressures at every stage of the legislation which prompted Sir C.P.N. Sinha to remark appreciatively: the Government in Bihar... were very reasonable and some concessions were secured by zamindars in Bihar which no other Government would have allowed.

In this context Rajendra Prasad's advice to the Bihar peasants is worth quoting: 'The Kisans should maintain those relations with their landlords which were in existence. They should not create any friction with the landlords' Sardar Patel went a step further when he warned in

April 1938: We do not want a Lenin here... Those who preach class hatred are enemies of the country. The Bihar government even imitated the Raj in undertaking a vilification crusade against popular Kisan Sabha activists, and Congressmen in such 'trouble-prone' districts as Saran were instructed to shun all association with the Kisan Sabha. In the United Provinces too there was throughout the 1930s 'a steady movement towards Congress by landlord elements'. The Madras government of Rajagopalachari did not likewise hesitate to prosecute such prominent Socialist leaders as Yusuf Meherally and S.S. Batliwala. Likewise, the Bombay Home Minister K.M. Munshi followed the

British practice of using the Criminal Investigation Department against Communists and other leftist political agitators.

The Ministry era coincided with an upswing of labour militancy: a 158% rise in strikes and lockouts; a 131% increase in the number of strikers; and a 230% upward swing in the curve of mandays lost. The Congress governments, however, sought to tackle this situation not by supporting the labour against capital but 'by a system of government sponsored arbitration', and this strategy found its best reflection in the Bombay government's Industrial Disputes Act of November 1938.

Strikes or demonstrations in Bombay were now met with police brutality. In Madras the government pursued a 'policy of internal settlement', and this meant accommodation with employers' interests.

A case-study of labour dispute in the Tata Iron and Steel Company demonstrates how the Bihar ministry's policy of 'compromise and restraint' remained silent on the 'Company misdeeds' but emphasised 'maintenance of discipline in the works'. The UP government employed the section 144 of the Criminal Procedural Code - the very law introduced by the Raj for counteracting nationalist agitations - to imprison Kanpur labour leaders.

At the behest of the Congress High Command a new organisation - the Hindustan Mazdoor Sabha - was also established in 1938 to counteract non-Congress and Leftist influence within the trade union movement. These moves were intended to assure the indigenous capitalists of protection 'from an assertive labour force'.

R.P. Dutt was not wide off the mark when he remarked: The dominant moderate leadership in effective control of the Congress machinery and of the Ministries was in practice developing an increasing cooperation with imperialism... (and) acting more and more openly in the interests of the upper class landlords and industrialists, and was showing an increasingly marked hostility to all militant expression of forms of mass struggle... Hence a new crisis of national movement began to develop.

Many biographers of Nehru would argue that inside the Congress Jawaharlal privately expressed his unhappiness at the way the Congress governments dealt with popular protest. On 28 April 1938 he wrote to Gandhi: I feel strongly that the Congress ministries are... adapting themselves far too much to the old order and trying to justify it... we are losing the high position that we have built up... in the hearts of the people. We are sinking to the level of ordinary politicians who have no principles to stand by and whose work is governed by a day to day opportunism.

On another occasion Jawaharlal noted: The Congress has now attracted into its fold thousands who are not eager for achieving Swaraj or to join the fight, but are merely seeking personal gains... (The) Congress has lost the... opportunity of action, of fighting imperialism directly and thus of deriving more strength.

Such confessions, however, left little institutional impact on the party since Jawaharlal and his group refused to make public their critique of the Congress governments on the pretext 'We cannot agitate against ourselves'. He even cast aspersions on such Kisan Sabha leaders as Swami Sahajanand Saraswati, remarking: We find today all manner of strange people who have never had anything to do with the peasantry before, talking in terms of programmes of trying in their uncouth way to woo the peasantry. Even political reactionaries of the deepest dye discuss unctuously agrarian programmes.

Attention ought also be drawn to Nehru's reaction to the rising militancy of peasant nationalism in the 1930s: The movement of the peasants no doubt deserves our support; but if peasants' councils mushroom like this here, there, and everywhere, that will harm the freedom movement led by the Congress.

Besides this, Jawaharlal did not dispute the All India Congress Committee resolution of September 1938 which warned those who 'have been found in the name of civil liberty to advocate murder, arson, looting and class war by violent means'. This was presumably done to provide organisational sanction for the use of state force by provincial Congress governments against protest politics. In fact, by 1938 the Right inside the Congress gleefully noted: 'Jawaharlalji has been veering around to our view and the differences which used to be so marked between his viewpoint and ours on many points is less prominent today. Vallabhbhai

Patel was more candid when he wrote to Gandhi: He (Jawaharlal) has done wonderful work, and has been burning the candle at both ends. We found not the slightest difficulty in co-operating with him and adjusting ourselves in co-operating with him and adjusting to his views...'

To Sardar Patel none else but Gandhiji wrote as early as 1934: Jawaharlal's explosion is not as frightening as it seems form the flames. He had a right to let off steam which he has exercised. I think he has calmed down now.

Shortly before independence Gandhi made yet another prophetic remark when he wrote to Nehru: You have no uncertainty about the science of socialism but you do not know in full how you will apply it when you have the power.

The stage was being set for Nehru to became the epitomical figure providing a centrist leadership to a Right dominated post-1947 Indian National Congress.

THE POWER OF THE RIGHT WITHIN THE NEHRUVIAN ASSEMBLY

In all his theoretical exercises Nehru considered socialism as the panacea for India's social and economic distress. To quote him: I am convinced that the only key to the solution of world's problems and India's problems lies in socialism and when I use this word I do not use it in a vague humanitarian way but as a scientific economic doctrine ... I see no way of ending the poverty, the vast unemployment, the degradation and subjection of Indian people except through socialism ... That means ending of private property except in a restricted sense and the replacement of the present profit system by a higher idea of cooperative service. It means ultimately a change in our instincts, habits and desires. In short it means a new civilisation radically different from the present capitalist order.

Commentators have thus drawn attention to Nehru's endeavours in creating the institutional and policy framework to realise his vision of a 'new egalitarian and more prosperous society'. But what was the ground reality? Despite his 'leftist' pretensions, Jawaharlal opted in the Industrial Policy Resolution of 1956 for a 'socialistic' and not a 'socialist' pattern of society. The panacea was found in Five Year Plans and a mixed economy. What actually followed was 'a move towards state capitalism' with considerable participation by the private sector. To the secretary to the Planning Commission Nehru thus once wrote: It should be our endeavour to effect enormous transformation without challenging the existing order. In another context he explicated his stand thus: There is of course no question of doing away with private capital, though it has to be controlled in the interests of the people.

In fact, according to one estimate about nine-tenths of the total domestic product came from the private sector at the close of the Third Plan period while the public sector's share increased by only 4% in the first fifteen years of India's independence. In terms of the relative contribution to the National Income the picture was similar: the private sector's contribution ranged between 90% in 1950-1951 and 85% in 1960-1961, while the public sector's ratio increased from 7.4% in 1950-1951 to only 10.7% in 1960-1961. The few top business houses with a strong communal and regional character - 20 according to the Mahalanobis estimate and 75 according to the Monopolies Inquiry Commission Report of 1965 - retained a controlling voice in the economy; the public sector failed to meet its designated goals of self-sufficiency and balanced economic development. Besides, the foreign capital transactions throughout this period had been considerable: the volume of direct foreign investment rose from Rs.2,176 million in 1948 to Rs.6,185 million in 1964. The share of foreign companies in gross profits of the Indian corporate sector also increased from

29.8% in 1959-60 to 33.3% in 1962-63. Realising the growing importance of private sector in Nehruvian economy the Congress Socialist leader * Jayaprakash Narayan bluntly reminded Nehru:

You want to go towards socialism but you want the capitalists to help you in that. You want to build socialism with the help of capitalism. Yet another perceptible pro-Congress commentator D.R. Gadgil noted in his 1962 Convocation Address at Nagpur University:

The dominance of the rich and the influential in all projects and programmes was a marked feature of the Indian situation. The private sector was expanding with the help of the state, which made no effort to control it. Production before distribution was a plausible thesis, but it was very doubtful if this could late be reversed to secure distributive justice. A group of leading capitalists had virtually taken over the economy, politics and society. The 'ugly businessman' was the major character on the Indian scene, making large profits, promoting corruption, securing the support of officials and manipulating the administrative machinery.

Nehru is supposed to have privately endorse this observation and even admitted that some of his basic social engineering schemes like land reforms had turned out to be a joke. A part of the failure of land reform was Nehru's decision to continue paying privy purses of Rs.5.5 crores to the princes while allowing them to retain their huge estates. In some cases, where surplus land was vested with the government, the quantum of compensation was such that on an average the additional revenue of the state government as a result of the process would be a bare 4.71% of the total compensation paid. This was pointed out by the Congress leader H.D. Malaviya himself. Moreover, by the end of the 1950s the burden of taxes on agriculturists had increased as much as 400% in most areas while the price of primary products had registered a downward trend, further adding to the misery of the rural population.

An important effect of the absence of land reforms was the non-development of an internal market for industrial goods which jeopardised planned industrial growth. The Planning Minister Gulzarlial Nanda in Nehru's cabinet thus made the following significant statement on 12

October 1953: On the one hand, there was the complaint that the country did not produce enough consumption goods. But when they increased production and took credit for it, they were suddenly faced with accumulation of stocks.

Even the otherwise pro-Nehru biographer Gopal acknowledged: the planned development under Nehru's regime did not pave the way for socialism but promoted capitalist enterprise in both industry and agriculture. Significantly enough, state capitalism as it developed in India, received the tacit approval of leading indigenous industrialists. As early as 1944 G.D. Birla, J.R.D. Tata, A.D. Shroff and John Mathai had formulated the Bombay Plan which was not much different from the 1951 draft outline of the First Five Year Plan. The Indian bourgeoisie rapidly curved out its own niche within the Congress. Not surprisingly, subsidies for the party's organisational work were forthcoming from all major business houses. In 1957-58 alone the Tata Electric Company had contributed Rs.300,000 to the Congress party's coffer. The industrialists also liberally supported the Congress in times of national and provincial elections. During the 1962 poll - the last to be held under Nehru's premiership - the three highest declared donations to the Congress were from the Tata and Birla groups (Rs.1.0 million each) and a cement company (Rs.500,000). Financial connections between the Congress and Indian industrialists were such that the latter were not apprehensive of Nehru's socialist jargons and in 1956 Birla is on record as having expressed his agreement with Congress socialist ideals. Six years later and two years before Jawaharlal's death Tulsidas Kilachand, the spokesperson of the Indian bourgeoisie, more confidently announced: The business community is in complete agreement with the socialistic objectives of the government and there are no two opinions on that score. There is no fundamental or ideological difference between the business community and the government.

A number of scholars have opined that conservative sections within the Congress prevented Nehru from pushing through many of his socialistic schemes, but one wonders how far we can push this argument. Rather, it seems that Nehru was more interested in preserving the unity of the party by adopting a centrist posture. After all, the Congress ideology from its inception aimed to harmonise the conflicting interests of classes and groups. An inevitable upshot of such a compromising approach was a substantial rise in the absolute number of people below the poverty line, accompanied by a high degree of concentration of wealth. There are reasons to fear that the size of the poor by the turn of the century will be found to have exceeded the total population of the country at the time of independence. The dreams of better standards of living for the common multitude in independent India are thus far from being fulfilled and Nehru's middle of the path economic policy has much to answer for this discomfiture of the country.

Sustenance of the Conservative Lobby

The sustenance of the conservative lobby within the Congress party during the Nehru years was facilitated by a particular method of decision-making within the Congress. This was the reliance on consensus and it helped the Right to continue its stranglehold on the party. Why? Because there was a 3:1 ratio in favour of the Patel-led conservatives in the Congress Working Committee since the mid-1950s and the modus operandi of consensus proved to be propitious in maintaining the force of the status quo.

What followed was a 'sort of democratic centralism', where the Right-wingers could make their weight felt, while the 'Left' minority had to be satisfied with concessions. Thus, while Nehru adopted an anti-capitalist and anti-landlord stance in his public pronouncements, he refrained from incorporating such sentiments in the party's election manifesto and restricted himself to such vague assurances as lowering of land rents. Similarly, when his eulogy of socialism in election speeches invited the wrath of the business community he hastened to clarify that his mention of socialism was only 'incidental'. Compromise with the Right for the sake of consensus remained the persistent trait in Nehru's political life as the first Prime Minister of free India, and Nehru himself acknowledged: 'My politics had been those of my class, the bourgeoisie'.

Judith Brown contends: By the end of Nehru's life the Congress at its base was no longer an elite, urban party, but reflected the diversity of Indian society, and partly the numerical socio-economic significance of substantial rural caste groups I would, however, go further to argue that a particular shift in power that we notice within the Congress in the Nehruvian period was a shift from urban and intellectual groups to a new rural-urban mix of medium size landowning dominant castes, cultivating owners and superior tenantry, small town middling groups and the upper middle classes in the larger cities, especially the new industrial and commercial classes.

What is important is that this shift helped buttress the influence of conservatives within the Congress party. Apart from this, the hegemony of the Right within the Congress High Command was further guaranteed by a systematic marginalisation of dissent.

The manner in which the Socialists under Acharya Narendra Dev were forced to secede from the parent body in 1948, and certainly not without Nehru's support is a case in point. When in 1948 the Socialists, following their resignations from Congress, surrendered their seats in the UP legislature and sought re-elections, the Congress mobilised its new 'electoral machinery and patronage resources' to defeat all thirteen Socialist candidates and prove the 'political wilderness' of the opposition. This trend of exploiting official power to dismember opposition within the Party was carried to its perfection by none other than Jawaharlal's daughter Mrs. Indira Gandhi, of course, with disastrous consequences for Indian democracy. The Congress no longer symbolised national aspiration in its widest sense but became a party 'representing its members and those who voted for it'.

NEHRU'S LATER NATIONALIST THOUGHT. 1947-1964

One of the most important issues that concerned Nehru was whether or not newly independent India could remain in the Commonwealth as a republic. In Nehru's 1949 speech in the Constituent Assembly in support of his desire that India remain in the Commonwealth, he was able to present a formula for membership which did not infringe India's complete independence or republican status. Nehru stated that "this new Republic of India, completely sovereign and owing no allegiance to the King... will, nevertheless, be a full member of this Commonwealth and it agrees that the King will be recognized as a symbol of this free partnership." It was primarily a decision expressing India's "free will" and demonstrating the removal of the imperial connection that had dominated and tainted Anglo-Indian relations previously. The issue of the Commonwealth was especially pertinent for Nehru because it combined his internationalism, his belief that the freedom to conduct foreign affairs was an integral part of national freedom and his recognition of the link with Britain at the national and personal level. Not only was it in India's own interests to remain in the Commonwealth but Nehru explained that the contacts between India and Britain could not be denied, even Nehru, "A New Type of Association," May 16, 1949, in *Jawaharlal Nehru's Speeches,* vol. 1, 275. The feasibility of such an arrangement was an entirely different matter. For example, Enoch Powell denied the plausibility of a Commonwealth that included an Indian republic.

Here I am the patent example of these contacts, speaking in this Honourable House in the English language. No doubt we are going to change that language for our use, but the fact remains that I am doing so and the fact remains that most members who will speak will also do so. The fact remains that we are functioning here under certain rules and regulations for which the model has been the British Constitution.

In summary Nehru believed that membership of the Commonwealth could be reconciled with an independent and republican India. For Nehru Commonwealth membership recognized the realities through which India had passed prior to independence and it was an expression of India's internationalist foreign policy. Further, India's membership reflected the historical link with Britain and India's desire to maintain free associations with countries to their mutual benefit and the benefit of international relations generally.

In an address at the inauguration of the Indian Council for Cultural Relations in 1950, Nehru outlined the relationship between culture and his nationalist thought. Nehru explained that each nation had "its peculiar idea of culture" that "had its roots in generations hundreds and thousands of years ago." These nations, Nehru believed, were unlikely to be "absolutely pristine, pure and unaffected by any other culture" and were "bound to get a little mixed up, even though the basic element of a particular national culture remains dominant." Nehru proceeded to postulate a direct relationship between the degree of cultural openness and national progress:

My own view of India's history is that we can almost measure the growth and advance of India and the decline of India by relating them to periods when India had her mind open to the outside world and when she wanted to close it up. The more she closed it up, the more static she became. Nehru admitted that the "nations of the East," probably referring to China and India, had suffered from this "sense of superiority" in the past and recently "they have received many knocks on the head and they have been humiliated.' Thus Nehru considered that Indian nationalism had been too narrow in the past and had not been open to potentially beneficial influences from outside and consequently India had suffered. Overall Nehru noted the irony that although nationalism and the national culture were "essentially good" they had the potential to become "evil" if either the national culture became "static" or nationalism was pursued too far and too vigorously. Therefore, Nehru stressed that it was necessary, although very difficult, "to find a balance" between too much and too little nationalism and between a too closed and too open culture. For Nehru finding this balance was "greatest problem today," apart from "the political and economic problems of the age," because "behind it there is a tremendous conflict in the spirit of man." In this speech, given the difficulty of solving this cultural problem, Nehru turned more practically, to the economic problems that must be addressed as a matter of urgency.

Nehru discuss the linguistic aspect of his nationalist thought in a 1955 speech made in southern India. He outlined the position of the various Indian languages under the Constitution and in particular sought to reassure the audience over the propagation of Hindi, which was predominantly and historically a "northern" language, as the official "all-India language" to replace the use of English. Firstly, Nehru explained that although India was a "multilingual country" the various languages were all "fairly intimately connected with one another" and were "in one way or another associated with Sanskrit." This multilingualism was reflected in the Constitution and further Nehru believed that such diversity was a "good" thing. However, Nehru considered that it was necessary to have a single 'all-India' language for communications between the states and between central government and the states and within the armed forces, and further this language should not be English, since it was according to Nehru: "[T]otally unbecoming for us in India to adopt as an official language a foreign language." According to Nehru,

Indian civilization had endured because "it was a dynamic civilization" with the "capacity for synchapter" but it became a static country, "which did not look outside," and it "became weak." It was during this "closed" period that India "developed an exceedingly narrow idea of caste" and "split into innumerable divisions" which began "a period of political, cultural and social degeneration." As a result India became "too weak to absorb" the foreign conquerors and eventually lost political freedom and consequently British influences, of language and modem western civilization had an inordinate impact More recently India had achieved national freedom by uniting under Gandhi's leadership and developing "a new dynamism." However, for Nehru it was crucial that this unity should be maintained and India "should not become parochial, narrow-minded, provincial, communal and caste-minded." What was "required," for Nehru, was "an emotional integration of the Indian people" which would ensure that they "might be welded into one, and made into one strong national unit" and at the same time India's "wonderful diversity" should be maintained. Thus at the end of his life Nehru returned to the causes of India's conquest by Britain and the need to overcome the use of English which was one of the legacies of that conquest. Conclusion

This section has identified a number of British influences on some of the most important aspects of Nehru's nationalist thought. Although Nehru consistently rejected British hegemony in India and sought Indian independence he drew upon a number of positive influences and the negative influence of British imperialism which provided a foil for the development of his nationalist thought. The more positive British influences included the work of Laski, Strachey, Besant, Trevelyan and the L. B. C. and possibly Brailsford. Additionally, Nehru used British sources to alert him to other nationalist struggles from which he drew inspiration and guidance including in particular those in South Africa and Italy.

5

Nehru as Politician

There is a well-nourished legend in India to the effect that the Prime Minister is remote from internal politics and takes little interest in political affairs. It is nourished by many stories and they have also traveled outside of India, giving, as it seems to me, a somewhat erroneous or distorted impression. They make Nehru out to be "above the battle," at least part of the time, as a matter of choice or of temperament, while various developments take place without his knowledge.

Certainly it is true that a prime minister has to devote most of his time to government, and party matters must take second place. The quantity of dispatches Nehru, as Minister of External Affairs, actually reads every day is great, and he is compelled also to spend a good deal of time in parliament. He is consulted by all the administrative departments; a vast number of appointments are referred to him for final settlement; he is the head of the Five Year Plan Commission. The amount of governmental work that devolves upon him is actually much larger than that which falls to most prime ministers.

By choice or by necessity and you will hear both versions he is actively concerned with the business of the whole government. And in addition he has a schedule both of state visits and of public appearances which would discourage many a stalwart. Under these conditions it is obvious that the time he can afford for all the organizational and electoral problems of his own party, the National Congress, is not what it once was. There were long years when, as secretary of the party or as its president, he was immersed not only in the national struggle the fight for freedom but in the entire life of the Congress. He probably knew as many local Congress workers as anybody did except, perhaps, the late Sardar Patel. When he was not in jail he was touring India without respite, and in any given campaign whether electoral or social, such as the work for the farmers of his own province he seemed to be omnipresent. Those days have gone for good. Nobody in his right mind could expect such activity of a prime minister; he has too many other things to do in twenty-four hours. Granted, it is Nehru's nature to do too much: he could scale down some of his work and omit some of the public appearances. To do so, he would have to be a different person, which is not, all things considered, desirable for India. The very critics who think he wastes time on public appearances are well aware that these are a powerful contributory element to the unity of India and the strength of the national government.

The legend of remoteness from politics becomes a charge or an accusation when it is applied to party details. The Congress Party is said to be going to the dogs because Nehru does not pay enough attention to it. Corruption in the party, the jobbing of appointments, various financial peculations and combinations, abuses of political influence all those vices of a party holding exclusive power for a decade are attributed to this cause. If Nehru had more rime to be vigilant such things could not occur, or so the theory goes.

A foreigner has to be extremely cautious about all these accusations of corruption which fill the air in India. You may hear them aired very freely indeed, and you may read them in general terms in the newspapers every day, but when it comes to pinning them down you find them pretty elusive. However, granting that there is a modicum of truth in all of this, and that the Congress Party after its long tenure of power stands in need of something like a Roman censorate, it is beyond reason to demand of Nehru that he assume such a task so long as he has to head the government. What he can do, and does, is act upon the facts when they are presented to him. The Congress Party has lost a number of by-elections in recent years.

Its majority was decreased in the last general election and its popularity in many regions has sharply declined. Whether this can be attributed to the stories about corruption, or whether it is the inevitable reaction against the party in power, nobody can say with authority, but the significant fact is that wherever the Congress loses the Communists usually win. The other parties are weak in the country at large, electing a representative now and then in some local area of special strength.

The Socialists are divided and the Hindu right wing (the Jan Sangh, taking in the old Mahasabha and other Hindu traditionalists) makes little appeal. The Congress had a sweeping victory in the first general elections of India's history, during the winter of 1951-1952 (November to February), when over 160,000,000 men and women went to the polls. Five years later alarming weaknesses had developed in the Congress itself and the results were surprising in many districts.

Congress continues to rule, with a safe majority somewhat reduced; but one whole state, to the astonishment of India, elected a legislature with one more Communist than all the non-Communists put together. This was the new state of Kerala, made up of the old principalities of Travancore and Cochin the beautiful Malabar Coast. In accordance with the Constitution, the Communist Party there proceeded to form a government, responsible to the legislature, which governed for two years and more. So far as I know it is the first time the Communists legally won a free election anywhere, and the first time they undertook to govern constitutionally. The anomaly aroused keen interest, along with anxiety, both in India and abroad.

In both these campaigns Nehru electioneered "with great energy, and whatever caused the decline of the Congress or the emergence of the Communists, it was not lack of speechmaking or travel on his part. Even in a by-election he can be counted on to do his best for his party, and he made a whirlwind tour of Kerala only last spring in the Congress interest. The difficulty lies deeper. Obviously the Communists have been busy building their organization for the past decade, reaching into every village, profiting by every local discontent. When they win, it is not by the votes of Communist Party members, who are nowhere numerous enough to matter.

They win by going out for and getting the votes of people who are displeased with the government, for whatever reason, and thus some weird combinations of local interests have been brought about. So long as these are controlled by the Communist organization their inner discrepancies do not matter to the result. This is how Kerala's Communist government came into being, and how some impressive results were obtained in Bengal and elsewhere. A refugee or a landless peasant needs no great persuasion to vote against the government.

There may also be skullduggery beneath some of the apparent Communist gains: it has certainly been alleged. Voting rolls, residence lists and suchlike papers can be falsified rather easily in a monstrous city like Calcutta, for instance, where a considerable part of the population even in so-called "normal" times is without fixed abode. Now that the city bulges with refugees from East Pakistan and the overcrowding has become a real horror, it would certainly be very easy for a determined Communist organization to roll up fictitious votes. I was told there, on the highest authority, that such had been the case in the last elections, but I have seen no proof brought forward either in the legislature or the courts. It will probably be thought injudicious, for some decades to come, to peer too closely into the electoral processes because a quantity of irregularities would show up on all sides: with over 160,000,000 actual voters, a dubious census system, an overwhelming illiteracy and an inexperienced personnel at the polls, what else could be expected?

What can be said is that the Communist organization, more determined and more unscrupulous than the other parties, is likely to take every advantage of the situation including, it is said, voting dead people and persons who never actually existed. Even allowing for this, the Communists have made a better showing in 1957 and in the by-elections since then than anybody expected. They owe it partly to their own relentless efforts, but also to the growing weakness of the Congress Party. Sometimes it seems that Gandhi's farewell advice, given on the day of his death to Sardar Patel, was the true wisdom. He said that the Congress Party, which had existed to achieve independence, no longer had a reason for existence as a political unit and should confine itself to work for social welfare. The origin of this advice of Gandhi's and indeed of the entire structure of party politics in India is to be sought in the story of the movement toward independence, the national movement, the one thing which has really united Indians in the present century.

Congress was not originally a party of independence far from it; and in sober fact it was not a party at all. It started out to be an annual convention of professional and upper-class Indians and its founder was a Scot named Alan Octavian Hume, a former member of the Indian Civil Service, who thought of the meeting as a way of bringing out Indian opinion. The absolute rule of the Viceroy in Council, plus the unlimited autocracy of the Indian princes in their own separate states, had robbed the educated and thinking tenth of the population of any way to express themselves. The All-India National Congress was a harmless, gentle way of supplying this lack. The year was 1885 and the place was Bombay. We read that the proceedings began with "three times three" cheers for the Queen-Empress, Victoria. From that polite beginning the Congress evolved into a full-fledged nationalist movement, stage by stage and year by year, until only a few decades later it was threatening the foundations of the British Empire. By 1929 (forty-four years after the foundation) it was declaring the independence of India.

To this development many astute and devoted men contributed, most of them Hindus, to be sure, but among them a good many Muslims. One thinks of B. G. Tilak, the intrepid publicist and speaker who aroused his own native Maharashthra (in the west, that is) but also the whole of Bengal in the extreme east of India. Tilak believed in violence. So did Aurobindo Ghose, that wonderful phenomenon of the Indian consciousness who afterward became the silent, remote sage of Pondicherry. This was the period when bomb-throwing was not only frequent but was actually approved by the intelligent elders. They, like the Irish, did not seem to have perceived that woeful wrong, and wrongful woe, do not bring happiness. This period was 1906- 1914.

The situation of Indian nationalism, its aims and methods, its ways of using brain and heart, altered from the time when Mahatma Gandhi returned to his own country from a long sojourn in South Africa. This was 1914. At first he did not take any part in public life or least of all in politics, but the country was already extremely aware of him because of his struggles in behalf of the unfortunate Indian laborers in Africa. He set up his colony or retreat near Ahmedabad and began to preach his gospel, on a small scale, to those willing to listen. His "political guru" G. K. Gokhale, had advised him to be quiet, and as silent as possible, until he could get used to his native land again.

We sometimes wonder at the strange antithesis between Tilak and Gokhale in those days which have begun to seem so incredibly far off. Tilak was all fire and fury. He is a sympathetic character, really, and one understands his impatience. At the same time his nationalism passed all bounds. He published an edition of the Bhagavad Gita in which he made the most extravagant claims for its antiquity, purely on nationalist grounds. So unassailable an authority as Professor Radhakrishnan, now Vice-President of India, has put the Gita at about 300 B.C., later than the whole body of the Mahabharata. Tilak wanted it to have the authority of immense age and proceeded to bestow this regardless.

In the same way he welcomed imprisonment and exile (or "internment" in the Andaman Islands) for his "sedition." He was probably a necessary, and certainly a comprehensible, flame of life in the awakening Indian nationalism. Even today some of his words strike off flashes when we read them, He loved mightily, was ready to strike and also to die. Every nationalism must have, it seems, some such paladin. But Gokhale was astute, thoughtful, cautious, fond of silence and meditation. He lived in the middle of the rising nationalist turmoil (he and Tilak were rivals for control of the Congress) but he knew how to shut it out of his mind. It was Gokhale who most deeply impressed Mahatma Gandhi on his return from Africa in the early part of this century, and it is Gokhale alone, who died in 1915, to whom Gandhi applies the term "my political gum."

To put it in other language, one might say that Tilak placed the Mahabharata in 3,000 B.C., for no reason at all, whereas Gokhale, if he had been asked, would have truthfully said that he did not know. And it was Gokhale that Mahatma Gandhi chose to follow.

But the Congress to which Gandhi and Nehru came as members and ineluctable leaders was a very different body, just the same, from that which they made out of it. Gandhi was horrified at the sanitary arrangements when he first went to one of the annual conventions, and he spent most of his time digging latrines, with such aid as he could obtain. He was also shocked at the fact that nobody spoke any Indian language everything was in English and at the general comfortable, satisfied attitude of the members. The combination of frock coats, striped trousers and bad sanitation seems to have been enough to keep Gandhi out of Congress politics for several years. Nehru had some of the same dissatisfactions but he does not seem to have voiced them. His own father was by this time so important a member of the Congress (and several times its President) that he could not have done so with much decorum. We do know from his autobiography that these middle-class gatherings of lawyers and doctors were not to his taste. We also know that on his first view of Gandhi, at such a meeting (1916), he found him "remote" and established no bond. We are perhaps better situated, at this distance in time, to understand what ailed them.

What both of them wanted, of course, was to make the All- India Congress into some kind of mass movement or mass party for the liberation of India. Neither Gandhi nor Nehru stated any such aim until much later but it must have been in heart and soul even during the First World War. When the opportunities arose (1918-1920) neither was slow to seize them. Gandhi and the two Nehrus found the Congress an annual convention of arrives in American, stuffed shirts and turned it into a national mass movement. The actual instrument, the National Congress, was an assembly of imitation Englishmen. What Gandhi did was to make Indians out of them, with the most enthusiastic cooperation of the two Nehrus, father and son. Specifically what started the national movement off in its final, or Gandhian, phase was the Rowlatt Act, a piece of repressive legislation at the end of the First World War which violated the ordinary civil rights of Indians, or other British subjects. Against this legislation Mr. Gandhi declared a hartal, or day of mourning, day of the cessation of all activity something with the effect of a general strike.

It worked with the most astonishing completeness and the world saw for the first time how one little man, simply by prayer, fasting and a word of advice, could paralyze an empire. It went on from there, ever wider and deeper, year after year, until the liberation of India from imperial rule became, in 1930 and after, a matter chiefly of time and method. In the process Gandhi made an enormous expansion of the original Congress Party. Instead of an annual palaver of Anglicized Indians in frock coats it became a mass movement with its roots in the villages, with a network of organized workers, a religious and philosophical coloration suited to the Indian tradition, an irresistible appeal to youth and a power of unity based upon collaboration between Hindu and Muslim. This honeymoon of the Hindus and Muslims in the 1920's was due mainly to a British error, the destruction of the caliphate in Constantinople. Actually the British could have waited a short while and Mustapha Kemal Pasha would have done it for them. Gandhi became an advocate of the caliphate of Islam and brought into the Congress fold a great Muslim mass which had never been there before.

Gandhi's own social and economic innovations, the revival of the spinning wheel, the boycott of foreign cloth, the emphasis on asceticism and ethics, did not always convince every Indian of their necessity; Nehru rebelled in his mind more than once, and sometimes in public.

The Mahatma's prolonged fasts and his way of calling off any public activity if it were marred by violence his deeply religious nature, his "inner voice," his day of silence, his iron rules for his own immediate followers all this made his personality distinct from that of any other leader of the century. He was, indeed, saint rather than politician, and we have amply stated that this is not Nehru's nature.

The reverence with which he was regarded made his course successful in at least one of its aims, the liberation of India, and this alone, his constant rightness of judgment when seen by the results, was enough to give him dominion over those who might otherwise have doubted.

But the point is, on the subject which here concerns us, that it did not create a political party. In the decade of the 1920-8 Gandhi's unique personality impressed itself on the Congress in ways almost without number: the effect persists today. The wearing of homespun garments and the white cap, the "Gandhi cap," became universal among nationalists, and there were few among them who could not recite some of the main verses from the second chapter of the Bhagavad Gita. Dietary rules, pledges of behavior, "disciplinary resolutions" and the like became very common throughout the movement; fasting was prevalent, especially when the Mahatma himself was fasting.

All these manifestations gave evidence of Gandhi's immense power over the Indian mind, but they were not, in any practical sense but one, classifiable as "politics." The one political aim and result was, of course, independence. In all the realms of thought and desire aside from India's freedom, the Congress was not a coherent political entity. It contained conservatives, liberals and radicals all at once; the two Socialist groups were "within it also; the Communists generally supported it and in the 1930's were even members of it, as a part of the world-wide tactical arrangement called the "Popular Front." In short, the Congress 'was India, in a good many ways, and had every right to speak for India as a whole, but it was far too comprehensive, too universal, for party politics.

It came near to fulfilling George Washington's prescription for the newborn American Republic: Washington said, "If parties exist we must reconcile them." This unwieldy and cumbersome universality of the Congress heritage its catch-all and carry-all quality has to be borne in mind even today when we wish to apprehend the peculiar characteristics, the individuality, of Indian political life.

There were wide extremes within the Congress at die moment of independence and they still exist. Sardar Patel and Pundit Nehru, at the moment of Gandhi's death, differed widely on important political problems. Nehru's triumph in a doctrinal sense has been fairly complete, and since 1955 the Congress has been pledged to "a socialist pattern of society," but you find Congress members who interpret this pledge in widely different ways. One fact stands out above all others in the Congress, which is its control of the central and state governments, its power over appointments, its hold on the purse strings, during more than a decade of independence and another decade of regional autonomy before that. It has been in power for a long time. Many intelligent men in India think that what it needs most of all is an opposition, some kind of political party which would keep it from lapsing into complacency and staleness.

The Communist Party, although alert and noisy enough in parliament, does not qualify as a democratic opposition because its allegiance is too obviously elsewhere it obeys external directives. And the Socialists, in spite of some admirable leaders (Jayaprakash Narayan first of all), have not developed as once was hoped. For some reason, possibly in their own party organization, the Socialists do not make a strong electoral appeal, even in areas such as Bombay where they once seemed likely to prevail. No foreigner could make a safe guess about the outcome of the present disquiet in the Congress itself, its misgivings about its future, or the criticism to which it is constantly subjected.

About a decade ago my guess would have been that a split in the Congress ranks was likely, with the conservative and liberal elements going their separate ways; and such a guess would have been wrong.

When Sardar Patel died the chief conservative leader was gone and Pundit Nehru's sovereign personality had full sway. The emphasis upon the "welfare state" and the "socialist pattern of society," to which he has persuaded the whole Congress, right, left and centre, is essentially a program of the moderate left, and in some of the Congress membership it gets only lukewarm support at best. A movement of division in the Congress between right and left, the two clearly perceptible tendencies, may still be possible, but nobody now considers it probable so long as Nehru remains at the helm.

He knows all this better than anybody else could, and although he may not have as much time for party politics as before, it is also true that he does not need it. His comprehension is wide and deep; in five minutes he can take in a local party situation and, if it is necessary, deal with it. He has had too much experience to need maps and compasses in such matters. My own feeling is that what his Indian critics call "remoteness" from politics is not that at all, but the inevitable result of the priority he gives and must give to government, foreign affairs, high policy.

Certainly when he goes at it he is not only the best electioneer in India and the most indefatigable speaker, but a skillful organization man as well. If he cannot be all these things at once, twenty-four hours a day, it is because in the just balance of time first things must come first. Speaking of the Congress Party's monopoly of central and state governments up to 1957 Nehru said to me, with a wry smile, "We were becoming almost monolithic." I could not quite decide whether he regretted the monolith or deplored it. Anyhow, for better or for worse, the Congress control is monolithic no longer. The principal rift is down in Kerala, where a state government with a tiny Communist plurality (one, subsequently two and then three votes) ruled after April, 1957.

This was the most striking upset in the elections of 1957, but was abetted by Communist gains in the lower house of the central parliament as well as in a number of state legislatures. The opposition that has come into being in these two years is therefore not a "loyal" opposition, in the old parliamentary sense, such as might have evolved if the Congress had divided into two parts. It is an opposition which is plainly aiming at what Communists everywhere want, a party dictatorship called of the proletariat." The Indian Communists naturally put the soft pedal on all ultimate aims, since they are trying, in the present phase, to win non- Communist votes from any convenient discontented element. At the same time no Indian Communist could disavow the ultimate aims and still remain a Communist.

So we get a rather intricate tactical pattern in Communist activity, and contradictions which are only apparent and temporary are permitted to flourish, evidently with Moscow's approval. The Communist state government in Kerala was bound by the Constitution of India, for instance, and could not hold office otherwise, although that constitution is incompatible with Communist doctrine. The main consideration of the Communists in the present stage of their being is what will or will not bring them most votes which seems remarkably like the thought of politicians everywhere. In Kerala they want to be reflected in 1962; in other states they want to gain more seats in the legislature, as they do also in the central parliament.

Their leadership has confidently predicted Communist majorities in two more states, Andhra and West Bengal, in the next elections; sometimes they claim even more. For these objectives to be attained they must go through some temporary and apparent compromises with democracy, at least on the surface, while their party organization assiduously cultivates the combinations and bargains which, at the village level, may deliver them the votes. The victory they won in Kerala was perhaps a pattern for those they hope to win afterward. They spread their net in the villages and plantations, among the untouchables and a special Kerala caste which is close to the untouchables; they combined with this some middle-class elements (even among the ancient Hindu clan of the Nayars) who were at odds with the Congress; they went into the fields to organize the landless and the most underprivileged. In public speeches and appeals to the general electorate and the educated, who in Kerala are more numerous than elsewhere in India they never ceased attacking the Congress state government for corruption, malfeasance and promises betrayed.

A considerable vote in cities like Travancore and Cochin came from educated, middle-class men and women who were very dissatisfied with the Congress and registered their protest in this manner; I have spoken with some of them and know they voted for "good government" rather than for Communist government. Most of them were as surprised as possible when the votes were counted; so, I am assured, were the Communists themselves. They found themselves pledged, at least on the surface, to "good government" rather than to Communist government, which, under the Constitution, was not possible anyhow.

In their two years of power they did not make great changes, but they exerted themselves to disseminate this impression of "goodness." Certain gestures of austerity such as not using state motor cars marked their early weeks and months.

A year later they were being accused of using too many state automobiles for their work I remember the debate in the legislature when I was there although the detail seemed faintly irrelevant. They preach against corruption but it has not saved them from being accused of some curious transactions, such as a deal with the Birla interests in Bombay for industrial development. Their main clash with the central government was on a constitutional issue: whether they had the right to bring all private, parochial and church schools under some degree of state control in appointment of teachers, maintenance of standards, etc.

Since the state pays heavily in grants for all these schools it did not seem strange to an American that they should want some control, but they were obliged in the end to modify their stand. On taxation their position has been more orthodox. I was in Travancore when the budget of 1958-1959 was presented, and was struck by the fact that the new taxes proposed would fall most heavily on the poor (public bus fares, for instance). The Minister of Finance explained that he had no choice in the matter because direct taxation was reserved for the central government under the Constitution. On some occasions not when I was there public order has been endangered by clashes between demonstrators and the police.

The Catholics, Protestants, Muslims and even the Nayars have private schools subsisting largely on state grants, and they resented the Education Bill to the point of public demonstrations; the police are accused of considerable brutality. Misuse of the state police for Communist Party purposes is also charged in other connections and in both ways i.e., permitting Communist street shows while suppressing others. And, of course, efforts to favor Communists in the state in all sorts of minor ways might be expected of a Communist administration. They have, it seems, occurred, especially in villages.

On the surface, just the same, nothing in Kerala seems to indicate a regime different from the rest of India. Travancore, by the sea, is the state capital, a beautiful city open for centuries to a variety of cultures. There is even some hint of Chinese (tilted roofs) in its special architecture. The high level of literacy here came originally from its accessibility to foreign missionaries, who long ago set up central schools and colleges in the city. The rulers were mostly beneficent; public works flourished; there are roads, schools and cheap electricity here and all the way up the Malabar Coast. Food is a perpetual problem to any administration because it must be imported in quantity from other states.

The level in clothing and cleanliness often seems higher in the Malabar villages than elsewhere, although I saw little of the untouchable and the landless. The greatest medical center in India, one of the largest and most modern anywhere, has sprung into being during the past few years outside of Travancore. One would think the whole state of Kerala, Travancore and Cochin alike, to be better off than a good many other districts that come to mind. Even so, it is here that the Communists were able to win their first electoral victory of any importance in the world.

Mr. Namboodiripad, the Chief Minister of the state, was frank to tell me he was surprised at the elections. "We thought we might win," is the way he put it, "but we did not expect it." He also was perfectly candid about the inability of his administration to operate on a Communist basis so long as it was obliged to keep within the Constitution of India. He thought the discontented agricultural workers provided the bulk of his vote in 1957 and looked forward to being reflected, mainly, I gathered, on the basis of having provided "good" government in this period of trial. No doubt his government would never pass up a chance to strengthen the Communist organization from the roots up, but he did not say so: he took a straightforward constitutional position for the moment without giving up any of his long-term Communist aims or beliefs. It is a strange position indeed, and without access to the secrets of the Communist Party organization or any other, it seemed by common sense to be untenable for long at a time.

I remarked something of the kind and Namboodiripad laughed in a way which indicated agreement. When I assumed (fishing for response) that he and his colleagues had never had any of the conspiratorial, underground experience of their coreligionists in Europe he laughed again, this time uproariously. He started counting up the number of years he had spent underground and the number in jail; they seemed to come out about even. "But I was in jail more often as a Congress Party worker than as a Communist," he added with glee. Such are the anomalies in the lives and minds of these "constitutional" Communists, a new breed in politics.

They do not, and cannot, believe in what they are doing but evidently think it might lead to what they do believe in. The spectacle must induce a rare state of confusion among their voters, mostly non- Communists, and no doubt that is one of the things they want. The clear-headed nucleus of the organization, by taking advantage of the caste system and other misfortunes, can bring out a combination of the muddle-headed in their support. Namboodiripad is a Brahmin of the highest rank known in those regions but has gone to great lengths in his efforts to use the lowest castes and the out-castes for his purposes. It is a little strange, too, that nobody seems to have foreseen, up until these past five years or so, what an instrument the Communists would find in the manipulation of caste grievances. By bringing backward castes forward and combining them, under a system of universal suffrage, it is possible to get a disparate "protest vote" big enough to become a majority. So far as I remember nobody took this possibility into consideration until it was proved in Kerala.

The whole world became aware of the problems presented by the State of Kerala during the summer of 1959, particularly during the seven weeks which preceded the final assumption of authority there by the central government on August first. The world misunderstood completely, utterly, thoroughly, as almost never before. It was assumed through the greater part of the world that some kind of "Communist revolution" was going on in Kerala, and headlines to that effect appeared in even the most reputable newspapers. It was hardly possible for the voice of sanity to be heard in the uproar of journalistic nonsense.

We who were in India at the time looked on in utter bewilderment while the outside world manufactured a revolution which had never existed. Any fledgling journalist who could find blood on an old woman's sari was convinced that this was Armageddon. It was, in fact, almost precisely the contrary to what the outside world supposed and proclaimed. That is, there was no

"Communist revolution" in Kerala. The legally elected Communist government had so alienated a good part of public opinion that it was opposed by strongly entrenched and organized bodies such as the Roman Catholic Church, the Nayars, the Muslims and the disgruntled Congress Party. Deplorably enough, these forces, professing their faith in democracy, endeavored to overthrow their legally elected government by street demonstrations, without any legal process whatsoever. It is one of Gandhi's precepts, as it was Abraham Lincoln's, that the people have the right to "dismember and overthrow" a government they do not like. Only a few weeks ago a member of the central parliament in Delhi said that the right of the people to indulge in civil disobedience" (or passive resistance or whatever it may be called) was sacrosanct in India because it came from Gandhi and would never be forgotten or surrendered.

In my own opinion, and I am far from a novice in such matters, the Communist government of the Kerala state could have gone on for a long time at least until the next general elections without arousing any wholesale popular protest if it had not been for external events.

That is, the Communist administration in the state was hamstrung, as I have explained several times, by the Constitution of India, under which it could not introduce any specifically Communist legislation of any kind. Its innovations were devious or invisible (favoritism to Communist puppetry in villages, etc.) except on the rarest occasions when police action was employed for partisan purposes. It was about as harmless as any Communist administration could possibly be merely, of course, because it had no power to be anything else. It could do nothing about taxes, property or the judiciary, little about the police, less than nothing about civil liberties or the free press; it was forbidden to touch anything fundamental, with one exception, which was education. Education is a state prerogative or responsibility, as it is in the United States.

The Kerala Communists produced an education bill which would have brought the entire conglomerate school system of that state under some degree of central control. In effect it would have established the principle that where the state pays the bills the state must have the right to choose teachers, audit the accounts and supervise the curriculum. This is very old hat to Americans or English or French people. We went through all that a century ago and more, and we do not call ourselves Communists.

However, state control of the churchly schools was immediately and bitterly opposed in Kerala that is, a year and a half ago and more, when the proposed law was first introduced. (It has never been put into effect, by the way another thing the outside world omitted to notice.) Emotion is the determinant in mass movements, of course, and some emotion might be generated by the idea of state control of the subsidized schools. Some. Not, in my opinion, enough to explain the outburst of anti-Communist feeling in Kerala. I traveled all over the state a year before and discussed the education bill with all sorts of persons: many were against it. I never met anybody who wanted to make a "revolution" about it. Well, what happened? What was new in the summer of 1959? What made men, women and children go out into the streets and lie down in front of buses and tram cars, or defy the police by forbidden demonstrations, or offer themselves for punishment in other ways? Merely because of the schools?

I think not. I am convinced that it would not have been possible to arouse the anti-Communist ardor of so many ordinary human beings in Kerala by the education bill (which is, in itself, fairly reasonable) or by anything else the Communist administration has tried to do since 1957. The ardor of the anti-Communist population was aroused, not by anything the Communist administration did or omitted to do, but simply by the fury of indignation which shook all India after March, 1959, when the Chinese Communists absorbed the autonomous country of Tibet. All India was enraged and still is enraged; sometimes it seems to me that India's anger is deeper and bitterer than that of any other country, partly, I suppose, because it is materially impotent. No Indian of my acquaintance is the same today as he was before March, 1959.

Now, if this wave has swept the whole country, as I am quite certain it has, what do you suppose an Indian who is a citizen of Kerala, living under a Communist administration, must have felt? He, and he alone, is governed by those whom he now considers to be his country's enemies.

His anger and his bitterness are immensely multiplied by the fact that right there, in his own home state, the devil's henchmen are in power. So, being an Indian and steeped in the Gandhian tradition, he joins organizations of protest, offers himself in voluntary sacrifice, parades in the streets, makes up slogans and defies the police. These are the methods Gandhi used to obtain freedom from the British, and they were used in 1959 to overthrow the elected (Communist) administration of the State of Kerala. By the end of July it was apparent that public order could no longer be maintained under these conditions, and the central government took over the state administration pending new elections.

Mr. Nehru came to this decision reluctantly, since the precedent thus established is dangerous to the democratic principle. If a legal government can be overthrown at any time by organized demonstrations in the streets, the theory and practice of elective representation are gravely weakened. What is more, the Communist Party of India has thus had presented to it, on a silver platter, a perfect technique for their own purposes: they can use the same methods against legal governments elsewhere, and have already tried them in Bengal. If they had more adherents, or enough adherents to put up a simulacrum of mass movement, they could be toppling over their democratic opponents in one state after another if, that is, Kerala is to be a precedent. However, the Communist Party of India is itself in the doldrums just now, so far as any extension in the masses is concerned.

The C.P.I, contains some brilliant intellectuals, and some of its representatives in the central parliament are skillful to a degree, but the anger which India as a whole feels about events in Tibet and relations with Communist China cannot be overcome by clever argument. The entire C.P.L, and the Communist administration of the State of Kerala in particular, have paid dearly for the aggrandizement of China. As the summer turned into autumn it became evident, indeed, that relations between the governments at Delhi and Peking were getting worse every day. Mr. Nehru steadfastly maintained and maintains his desire for peace and for friendly communications with all powers. He can do no other: it is his basic principle.

Yet even his heroic determination has been sorely tried by the stubborn arrogance of Chinese claims. Perhaps the worst thing he has had to bear is the contempt with which the Peking doctrinaires receive representations from the Government of India. Sometimes these representations are not even acknowledged; often they are acknowledged without being really answered; generally they are contested as being untrue or unfounded. It may be said that nothing but the patience of a saint could endure the kind of humiliating and vexatious treatment to which Mr. Nehru has been subjected from Peking since March, 1959. Mr. Nehru is not a saint, of course, and his patience is not inexhaustible. If worst came to the worst he would defend the frontiers of India by any and all means in his reach: anybody who thinks otherwise knows nothing about him.

The Tibetan nationalist rebellion against Chinese military occupation (March, 1959) was followed by the romantic escape of the young Dalai Lama, the "god-king" as the newspapers call him, from his Himalayan fastnesses. When the Dalai Lama reached safety in India, he was of course made welcome by Nehru no other course would have been consistent with Jawaharlal's principles and has been protected ever since. The Peking regime declared promptly that the Dalai Lama was "under duress," and that the national rebellion had been contrived by foreign imperialists and "Indian interventionists." Chauvinism and xenophobia are easily aroused in China indeed the ordinary Chinese character meaning "foreigner" contains within it the symbol of a devil: we are all "foreign devils" to the Sons of Han.

And yet nobody on earth has tried harder to make friends with the Chinese than Jawaharlal has. Even when his doubts were strong he still tried, in accordance with Gandhi's principle. "If a man betrays you, trust him again," said the Mahatma, "and if he betrays you again, trust him again." This was perhaps a little easier for Mahatma than it is for other human beings. At all events the People's Republic of China has become increasingly rude, crude and insolent with respect to India all through 1959, and incidents on those icy frontiers of the High Himalaya have shown that it respects no boundaries.

When you add to this the incessant attack on Indian trade with Tibet, Indian traders, Indian currency (all guaranteed by treaty); when you consider further that public insult has become a settled part of Peking policy; and when you perceive that the Himalayan principalities of Nepal, Sikkim and Bhutan are actually threatened with military aggression at every moment, it becomes nothing short of wonderful that any semblance of diplomatic civility can still exist between India and China.

If things go on like this, a severance of diplomatic relations can hardly be avoided. Now, of course, all this has been deeply offensive to Indians of all parties, classes and races.

A bitterness has been created which obliterates other distinctions and unites those who otherwise have few points of agreement. Jawaharlal's incredible skill, his immense prestige and the love the people bear him have all been hard pressed these last months because he alone, very often, seems to stand for peace with China at almost any cost. When he is forced to speak out against the pretensions of Peking (particularly on boundaries) he is cheered to the echo; and when he advises moderation, patience and restraint, his own followers are restive and ill at ease. It has been a development fraught with misery, and the end is not yet. Politically speaking, the India-China relationship of the late summer and autumn of 1959 seems very nearly to dominate the mind of India. It certainly dominates every other consideration in foreign affairs.

With Indian friends I have often noted a tendency to blame Jawaharlal at each step in the development, without any compensating suggestion of an alternative. Sometimes I have asked point-blank: "What do you want him to do? Do you want war?" Oh, no, of course not: nobody wants war! Well, what is there, short of war, which will contain the expansive megalomania of the Communist Chinese? And, supposing war comes, what are the respective strengths of China and India? These are stark, grim matters. China has at least eight million men under arms, thus, in numbers only, being sixteen times as strong as India. Angry and bitter as the Indians may be, they have to remember such unpleasant facts.

So, as to the State of Kerala and the activities of the C.P.L, as to foreign affairs in general and a considerable number of internal matters, the passionate resentment against China which inhabits the very air of India today is a political reality of the greatest importance. It flows in upon almost every other consideration, even the most distant; it pervades the intellectual and emotional climate of the hour. It has required every resource of Nehru's personal supremacy to ride out this storm "without disaster, and it casts the chilliest and most somber fog over the future. Nehru's attitude toward the Communists of India has always been clear enough. They are a legal party; all parties and shades of opinion are legal.

If they win enough votes they are elected. But whenever they threaten public order, the laws, the Constitution or the public interest in such matters as food supply or communications, he comes down upon them with severity. He accepts their interruptions and attacks in the central parliament as part of the day's work, and has developed a considerable resistance to those personal slings and arrows with which they assail him. This is all part of his deep belief in parliamentary democracy. What threatens the food or life of the people is a different matter. The Communists, through their influence in the railway unions influence, not membership made a disruptive effort of some gravity in 1949-1950. If they had carried out their intentions there might have been a strike which imperiled the food supply of some provinces (now states) which are always running short. Reserves of food are permanently very low, often for no more than about three weeks in advance, in many parts of India.

At that period and for some time thereafter a large number of Communists went to jail under the Preventive Detention Acts. The figures were not published in detail but I was told there were about 12,000 of them in prison in 1950. In certain states, from time to time, Communists throw their organizational weight in favor of some disruptive movement which is not Communist, or even not political, in any intelligible sense. They do it for the sake of disruption and disorder, to increase a climate in which they hope to flourish. Such a movement was rife in the country districts of Hyderabad just after India took over; there was a lawless agrarianism akin to banditry, and the Communists saw advantages in giving it leadership. There were public disorders in Maharashtra not long ago when the same thing happened. The quarrels were over language, essentially, which has nothing to do with Communist doctrine, but it was a chance to make trouble and it was taken.

Generally speaking, direct action by the police maintains public order and the Detention Acts are a powerful weapon against those who would upset it. The law provides punishments for infringements after they have occurred;

the Detention Acts prevent their occurring by incarceration of the ringleaders. There is no use denying that preventive detention offends most of our democratic principles and there are few observers, Indian or foreign, who take kindly to such methods.

Those directly involved in the maintenance of public order think differently. They believe that a country in the making, a country new to self-government and unity, needs special defenses against those who would disrupt and destroy it. The Chief Minister of Hyderabad had just signed four preventive detention orders when I went to see him one day last year. They were against four known Razakars (remnants of the Muslim guerrilla bands which had terrorized the state before integration). "I am not ashamed of it and I do it when necessary," he said. He was young, incisive, sure of himself. "I know that if they had their way and went free there would be destruction and deaths."

In this same way and in this same spirit the governors and chief ministers of the Indian states have sent thousands of Communists to prison not as Communists, but as menaces to the public order. I do not myself like this way of dealing with their activity, but when asked point-blank what else to do, I have no practical reply. Obviously there are a good many cases in India in which the full application of all the civil liberties known in England and the United States would endanger the life and livelihood of the people. In our countries we do not have famines, and there they do: that is enough to make the critic think twice.

Preventive detention orders are not absolute, of course. The state government has to "show cause" within thirteen days, but it usually can do so. A trial is entailed, dependent upon the law's delays, but often the persons detained in prison are released by executive order before any trial takes place. The judicial branch often has no chance to pronounce. This is not at all appetizing to those who believe in the separate and independent powers of executive and judiciary in a democratic system. I know that Jawaharlal Nehru does not like the method any more than I do. He uses it or avails himself of it because the emergencies of a nation aborning are so great, the stresses and strains are so violent, the necessity for union so imperative. Under the federative system of India these special powers belong to the separate states, but obviously the Prime Minister could encourage or discourage their use: his wishes generally prevail when he chooses to express them. He has not discouraged preventive detention.

All this indicates one way, maybe the chief way, in which the Communists are kept in order or at least from revolution in parts of India. The method is arbitrary but reposes upon the supposition that the chief ministers of the states, who use it, and the magistrates, who keep an eye upon it, are honorable men with a just view of the state's necessities.

They have to judge, sometimes within a microscopic measure of time, when the activities of known rebels will be disruptive to the state, and then to put those known rebels into jail with all celerity. They must do so without arousing too much protest, either, since, as these decades have more than proved, Indian opinion can get extremely vociferous when it is aroused. These procedures may be distasteful to persons born in Illinois or California (or, for that matter, Devonshire or Normandy).

However, it is not our problem. As observers we can see that the procedure works without any real disturbance to the ordinary population and without a sense of tyrannical excess. It has nothing to do with the Gestapo or Cheka method we have known elsewhere, which strikes in the dark and has no issue. Here all is open and known and, in fact, temporary. The governor of the state usually regrets having to use these emergency powers (invented by the British) and would curtail the detention, or soften it, whenever possible. Often the dependents of the detained person are allotted sustenance. Sooner or later the detained person is released, none the worse for wear, to resume his former activities or to refrain from them as the case may be. There is no secrecy about any of it and no human being simply vanishes without a trace, as they did so very often in Hitler's Germany and Stalin's Russia. Communists, being by definition hard-boiled, do not make much fuss about these procedures which often confine thousands of them to jail.

They know they will get out again. They also know, without a doubt, that these methods are very gentle and soft as compared to the methods they would use if they ever attained the supreme power. When it comes to foreign affairs they are at a great disadvantage with Nehru, because he always speaks for the national interests of India and they too obviously cannot (unless, that is, you concede that the national interests of India are those of Communists everywhere, including the Soviet Union, Red China, etc., etc. a nonsensical proposition on the face of it). Their internal argument has force with unhappy and underprivileged people: in effect they say, What has the Congress government done to destroy poverty? Where is that chicken in every pot on Sunday?

The government can reply that poverty is immense, that it takes a long time to abolish it, and that great steps have already been made in that direction; but such responses do not always counteract the easy yell of protest. In foreign affairs the Communists do not have much to offer, aside from pointing to the material achievements of the Soviet Union, along with stereotyped or mimeographed diatribes against the "imperialism" of the

Americans. They can oppose the British or any connection with the British: this has gained them some votes, no doubt. Nobody knows very much about the Americans and the hullabaloo the Communists make against "American imperialism" does not signify a great deal to the people. (To the present day, travelers in out-of-the-way places in India, if they happen to be Americans, face the problem of explaining what that means: most Indians take them to be British.)

But there are numerous questions on which the Communists are at a great disadvantage in foreign affairs. They cannot possibly condemn anything done by the Communist governments of Russia, China and the satellite states. Many of the things so done are repugnant to Indian feeling, especially when wholesale brutality and violence are concerned. Russian actions in Hungary in 1956-1957 were a terrible shock to Indian opinion worse by far, I think, than the shock given by the Anglo-French expedition to Suez. Worst of all, naturally, is the "rape of Tibet," as the Hindustan Times called it (March, 1959).

The Chinese invasion of Tibet in 1950 had aroused strong protest, which went into abeyance afterward with the "Five Principles" and the Chinese promise to respect the autonomy and customs of the Himalayan theocracy. When, in 1959, all pretense vanished and the Chinese troops undertook to conquer the entire Tibetan territory, Indian opinion was on fire.

Mr. Nehru tried to calm it down, of course, since nothing could be done to eradicate the cause, but he also expressed the natural concern of India at the course of events. He furthermore welcomed the Dalai Lama not as a refugee, but as an honored guest of India.

The Communists in this juncture behaved in accordance with their overall directives and ultimate aims: that is, they hailed the action of their coreligionists in China and attacked Nehru. He replied with energy, and in terms which may cost the Communists a good deal in the coming years. He said they were "not Indians." He did not know what they were; they had non-Indian superiors and mentors; they sought non-Indian purposes. It was enough for him to say that they were "not Indians."

Episodes of a similar character have occurred before, naturally, and with all his desire to respect every shade of opinion Nehru has been forced to flame out at them. Once during the election campaign of 1952 they paraded in front of him with an array of red banners bearing the hammer and sickle. "Why don't you go and live in the country whose flag you are carrying?" he shouted at them. "Why don't you go to New York and live with the Wall Street imperialists?" they shouted back. Since Nehru has not the faintest desire to live anywhere but in India, or to be anything but Indian, these taunts are meaningless. When he, on the other hand, says the Indian Communists are "not Indian," there is not a peasant in the country who will not ponder his words. He has behind him a lifetime of devotion to the country's interests, and his independence toward "the Wall Street imperialists" has been proved as often as his independence toward London and Moscow.

When the Communists attack him, at any rate in foreign affairs, they are beating against an impregnable wall. They are not at all independent and he is. Strange to relate of a country so largely illiterate, this is well known in all parts of India. When I am told that Nehru is "remote from politics" in the sense of internal party squabbles, I think of a long series of episodes in the past twelve years in which the contrary has been proved to me. He no longer has the time he once had for party matters I have nagged on that point because it is all-important but his interest never fails. He watches every by-election and every regional or provincial fight. They are many.

His sense of communion with and responsibility for the Congress Party is greater today, I think, than it was about twenty years ago. He electioneers with fury and at times yields to the dominion of his party against his own wish, instinct and judgment. Such a case occurred in the spring of 1958 when he wished to resign his office for a trial period a period of thought and refreshment while others tried their hand without him.

The uproar in the country and even abroad was great; it looked as if everybody thought the entire machine depended on Jawaharlal. He thought this exaggerated and persisted in his intention. (I think he was supremely right.) The parliamentary party, which means the Congress Party representatives in the central parliament, held a meeting in the courtyard there and sought to dissuade him by every argument they could bring forward: duty, honour, country, of course, but underlying all this and added to it was the concept of party loyalty. The truth is that the party was frightened at the thought of having to get along without Nehru even for a trifle of time (three months had been mentioned).

I was not at the parliamentary party meeting because I was waiting at the Prime Minister's House for Mr. Nehru. His daughter Indira, Mrs. Feroze Gandhi, who has the beauty and intelligence so lavishly bestowed on that family, whiled away the time with me; we talked of remote parts of India which each of us had visited. The Prime Minster eventually came in, not from the ceremonial entrance which most of us use, but from the other side, and I could tell at a glance that he was spiritually and perhaps physically exhausted. No doubt he had totally forgotten that I was waiting for him, but it came back to him the moment he saw me (he never really forgets anything), and he began to speak to me of a book containing his remarks about democracy. "Is it any good?" I asked.

"That is not for me to say," the Prime Minister answered in a tired and rather ironical manner. "It does contain everything I have ever said on the subject. He has put it together." He did not tell me a word about the grueling meeting from which he had just come.

I learned it an hour or so later from the press representatives who had been present. But I really did not need to be told: I knew from his manner and his words that he had again, as in so many other cases, yielded to the wishes of the majority. He has done this a large number of times for a very simple reason, because he believes in it. He shares this political simplicity with Abraham Lincoln and Winston Churchill, both of whom used their authority to the utmost but at the same time were willing to give in when a majority had spoken.

In this I do find one overwhelming difference between Mahatma Gandhi and Mr. Nehru: the Mahatma would rather retire, fast, pray, take care of lepers and educate children, than go along with a majority opinion in which he could not concur. He did so often. In a sense, he did not believe in democracy: he believed in the good and the true, with far behind the beautiful, which he could understand only as a function of the good and the true. If his "inner voice" had informed him that such-and such was the good and the true, all the hundreds of millions in India could never dissuade him.

Rather he hoped, by God's aid, to persuade them to his view. Franklin Roosevelt was also one who yielded to the majority, as we saw in the case of the Supreme Court. These are believers in democracy, persons who believe that sovereignty resides in the people and that the majority of the people might, conceivably, be wrong, but must eventually come right, in the fullness of time, with the working out of the consequences. A faith in the people is probably the indispensable mainspring of political action among men who have governed great democratic states: even when they disagree with the majority's errors they will accept and serve them in the hope of ultimate correction. Even if a corrected course should never come, the believer in democracy yields just the same because he thinks that this course is far preferable to the evils of its opposite coercion, dictatorship, tyranny.

Nehru has yielded to the majority of his party and of the country (more or less the same thing) in the same way and for the same reasons. For example, the question of languages and of linguistic states caused him much suffering some years ago, because it seemed a disruptive tendency, something inimical to the unity of India which he holds so dear. It was what the Mahatma would have called "fissiparous," using that word which, rare in the English-speaking' world at large, is quite common in India. Mahatma did not live to see the demand for separate linguistic states or its fulfilment. Nehru lived through it, did not like it, and yielded to it simply because it was the wish of the majority of the people.

To see India all chopped up in accordance with the linguistic differences was to postpone for a century, or perhaps more, that ideal communion which might come through a national language. And yet Nehru yielded. One could name many other instances. He has campaigned against popular causes, such as cow protection, with vehemence, and acknowledged defeat without changing his own views. "Cow protection" is the name given in India to the laws under which, in certain provinces, the diseased and starving cows, many of them belonging to nobody, are allowed to roam at will on the ground that they are sacred. It is forbidden to slaughter them but it is not forbidden to starve and maltreat them. Jawaharlal's method of cow protection would be to round them all up and let the fittest survive, as has been done in the state of Bombay; he is interested in the improvement of breeding; he knows what can be done if science has its way. He would breed more and better cows and give the cities milk; but he has had to yield on this, hoping for a better time. (It should be explained that such questions are for the separate states, not All-India, and the campaign in which Nehru opposed the majority was in his own state of Uttar Pradesh, the former United Provinces.)

It is well known in India that some hideous villains, guilty of the exploitation of child labour and all labour, as well as unavowable transactions on the stock market and in politics, have gained merit in the eyes of an illiterate Hindu public by cow protection. It should also be noted that no reasonable human being could object to the ancient thought, deep in Hinduism, that the cow as the "foster mother of the human race" is worthy of all respect and should be cherished. The cow may even be sacred if one wishes to consider it so. However, to regard it as sacred and then leave it to decay of famine and all maladies, infecting human beings as well, is sheer nonsense and Nehru has said so. The Swami Vivekananda, apostle of Hinduism to the West and founder of the Ramakrishna Mission, agreed with him completely sixty years and more ago, although I do not know if Nehru, so penetrated by Western culture, has been aware of it.

The Prime Minister respects all the beliefs of all of the people, whether they are religious, political or social. He has no patience with superstition and has had to gulp hard many, many times when he faces it. When he went to Kerala last spring he was perfectly courteous to the Chief Minister there, Mr. Namboodiripad, the Communist leader responsible for many of the worst attacks on Nehru and his government.

It must be said that at least Nehru knows what the Communists are doing and what they are after: they do not mystify him. There are elements in Indian life, which means also politics, that do mystify him and there is nothing he does in public life which arouses my admiration more than the way he deals with them. Whether it is Hindu, Muslim, Buddhist, Christian or pagan, he sees the belief and takes it for what it is, a social reality indeed, a political reality. Such things are eminently consequential in India. On one occasion he took me with him to Calcutta (spring, 1949) to receive the relics of the beloved disciples of the Lord Gautama Buddha. These two young men, Mogallana and Sariputta, followed the Lord Buddha in his old age and what he said to them, as well as what they said afterward, is deep in Buddhist lore.

Some small bones of the young disciples were preserved in the ancient Buddhist stupa at Sanchi, in the principality of Baroda, where they were discovered by Sir John Cunningham in the early part of the last century and removed to the Royal Albert Museum in London. On the archaeological evidence about Sanchi, which had not been disturbed until Cunningham got there, these are almost certainly the oldest relics in the world. After the liberation of India it occurred to the British Government, headed by Clement Attlee and Staiford Cripps, to send the relics back to India in the battleship called the India, which was to be given as flagship to the Indian Navy. It was an astute combination of material generosity and spiritual comprehension, for, as a matter of fact, the transfer of the relics caused a wave of intense emotion throughout the Buddhist world.

They remained for an entire year in Ceylon, being venerated by the populace, and paused also for acts of worship in Siam and Burma. They were ceremonially received at Calcutta by Jawaharlal Nehru, transferred by him after three days to a Buddhist monastery, and eventually restored to the depths of the great stupa at Sanchi, where they will remain an object of pilgrimage while mankind endures. The entire Buddhist world, which means most of East Asia, was represented at these ceremonies. For two days the relics were exposed in the throne room of Government House at Calcutta, not far from the imposing, oversize portraits of King George V and Queen Mary, and just underneath the golden throne. When I got a chance I used to sit there and watch the Buddhist princes, monks and politicians at their worship. There was an atmosphere of utter sincerity. I remember well the Maharaj Kumar of Sikkim (an Oxford man) and the incommunicable devotion in his eyes as he gazed upon the small reliquary. He and the other Himalayan princes not the Dalai Lama: he was not there were the ones I recall best because of their worshipful submission.

The monks, some of them mere children, who had come from Ceylon, Siam and Burma to sit there in attendance, had not anything like the same concentration. The political representatives cabinet ministers and the like came and went more briskly. But Jawaharlal Nehru was the phenomenon of the occasion to me. He had a schedule which began at seven each morning and ended each night with some sort of official dinner ambassadors, governors, cabinet ministers. That dinner might end when it ended, not late, of course, but long after my own poor old bones were longing for bed. During die day the string of motorcars would start out at seven or shortly afterward; there were speeches, dedications, ceremonies; we were back at Government House for lunch but then started out again. The crowds in the streets and for miles outside of Calcutta were suffocating.

Even though the police stood arm to arm along the way, the mobs often broke through them in the hope of touching Jawaharlal or seeing him close. Sometimes I was actually frightened, not for me of course but for him, at these tumultuous demonstrations. I was generally placed in the car immediately following him, with the security officers and the aides-de-camp, and there were many times when the crowds had broken through with such insistence that we could make no progress at all and almost lost him. And yet he would be standing up in the open motorcar waving his hands at them or making namasthe, the prayerlike greeting with two hands joined. It was during these days that I decided he was to the Indian crowds what Antaeus was to the earth the native son deriving strength from contact with the mother. These were public and political things, of course. There was the mass meeting in the Maidan of Calcutta, half a million people perhaps, when representatives of all the free Buddhist nations spoke and Nehru finished. There were also more private and strictly religious ceremonies.

The one of these which will remain in my memory forever is the scene in the small Buddhist monastery where Nehru consigned the relics to the monks. There were not a dozen persons present. It was cool and dark. The Prime Minister sat on the floor in the middle and half a dozen monks in saffron robes encircled him. The relics were brought; he presented them; the monks prostrated themselves before them. There were some brief chants and prayers and it was over. We had come into this place, up some stairs, from the streets boiling with an almost uncontrollable affluence of people. I had been actually dragged through the mob by the security officers in the wake of Jawaharlal. The silence and serenity of that monastic room were a startling interlude. His behavior both in public and in private during this episode was marked by an instinctive elegance and delicacy which few men can attain when they are in touch with the intimate beliefs of others. Nehru has no attraction to relics; he is not a Buddhist; he is not given to forms and ceremonies. I think I take to all these things more naturally and easily than he does, by which I mean that I feel them without thinking, without questioning. Jawaharlal feels them humanly, that is, with relation to those other persons there present, so that he cannot be indifferent to their beliefs or hopes, but must share them for the moment. He is sympathetic not to the august tradition here worshiped, but to the human beings who feel, worship and love. He would never say one word or do one thing to injure that exquisite integument between a man and his god, whoever the man or whatever the god.

Let us be plain about this: the Prime Minister is a thoroughly rational human being. The relics of the disciples Mogallana and Sariputta no doubt meant to him precisely what they meant to me: the oldest relics on earth, venerated by some hundreds of millions of human beings. He was well aware of the importance of this occasion to India and to the Buddhist world, which means a large part of Asia. That to which he paid reverence, and to which he bowed very deeply (although he never prostrated himself), was the faith of mankind, not the occasion of its faith. No doctrinaire could behave as Nehru does in such contingencies. The particular occasion was rare; it will never occur again; but it indicates the soul of the man. He certainly knew the political advantages of his course with regard to the Buddhists. This may even have had some weight in his decision to go to Calcutta and receive the relics with such reverence. But once he got into the thing his responses were all true, unsought and unthought, the instinctive answer of a son of Asia to one of Asia's greatest sons. Buddhism makes a distinct appeal to Nehru, of course, as it did to Gandhi not the Buddhism of the innumerable sects, but the Lord Buddha himself and his pure doctrine, or what is left of it.

Many are the Indians who have regretted the conquest of Buddhism by Brahmanism centuries ago. But in contemporary fact Nehru has had more occasion to champion the Muslims and has done so than the Buddhists. There are few Buddhists in India now, and what he does with respect to their towering faith must affect persons outside of India more than his own people. But the Muslims are a huge part of the population. There may be fifty-five millions of them by now. They regard Nehru with trust, affection and a species of awe. He has been their friend all their lives and they cannot think what it would be like to get along without him. They know perfectly well that he does not share their beliefs but they realize that he would go to any length to protect their right to believe as they do. He has constantly struggled for them and his most fundamental statement about India the "secular state" reposes upon his confidence in them. He will protect their festivals, their ceremonies and their mosques, wherever the civil power is competent to do so, and they know it.

I remember Nehru's house and garden in York Road, in New Delhi, in the bad days of 1947-1948, when horror was abroad. Even in New Delhi, usually more or less like Washington, which it physically resembles, there was fear everywhere and there had been murders in the streets. In Old Delhi, too dense with humanity, the situation was much worse. Nehru's house and garden were crammed with persons taking asylum. Every inch of the garden was occupied.

He had made the army put up tents for the people who came to him; they mushroomed all over the grass. In his own house he had many. Every room was filled and they put army cots in the corridors. These were fugitives from every sort of outrage the time provided. I know that some of them were Hindus from the Punjab. I also know (and every Muslim knows) that many were Muslims from Delhi itself. Furthermore, even in Pakistan it is understood that Nehru has befriended the Muslims whenever and wherever it was possible. They may say he does it for political reasons (I have heard brash young Pakistani say so), implying thereby that it is insincere action.

I have seen enough of politics to realize that combinations of motives occur oftener than not; and I do not think any the less of Nehru's natural, instinctive and lifelong friendship for the Muslims because it also happens to be good politics. But the point is, so far as the subject of the present chapter is concerned, that it is good politics. It is a kind of good politics that the Communists cannot begin to touch, because it concerns a realm of being which they are, for doctrinaire reasons, obliged to treat with a contempt they can scarcely disguise. The Muslims of India support Nehru, by and large, although communism is said to have made some inroads among their university students. The Muslims of Pakistan tend, on the whole, to put more trust in him than in other Indian leaders. These two things are vast political realities in the most practical domain; not in "religion" but in common sense.

A Pathan on the Northwest Frontier, a great bearded primitive who leaned his rifle against the wall of the house while he noisily inhaled his tea, said to me in the spring of 1948, "Tell Jawaharlal that if he is in any danger we will send Pathans to Delhi to protect him." It was supposed to be a joke, of course, especially since the struggle in Kashmir was then going on between the Pathans and the Indian Army; but it was one of those jokes which point to an underlying element of truth. The Pathans would never send riflemen to Delhi, and could not if they tried; but they would want to do so. They may not precisely like "Hindu Raj," as they call it, but they regard Nehru as its least objectionable feature.

These, mind you, are primitives of the Northwest Frontier, culturally akin to Bedawin of the desert and Professor Toynbee even calls them savages. How much more appreciative of Nehru are the city Muslims, the educated and the middle class, who have had occasion to know his concern for their welfare!

Among them I doubt if he fails to win every election, although the majority may vary in their voting according to the local candidate, local situations, etc., etc. They are a very significant part of the electorate, roughly an eighth or ninth, which, however vastly outnumbered, must always make itself felt.

So far as Buddhism is concerned the political advantages of Nehru's course are not to be counted in votes inside the Indian Union; there are few Buddhists left in the land of the Buddha. But outside of India the echoes are great. They count in the Buddhist countries all around India to the north and east, especially in the Himalayan kingdoms, in Tibet and in Burma. Even as far off as Japan Nehru is regarded as one who understands and protects the Buddhist faith. This, on the rebound, has considerable effect among religious Hindus, who, without abandoning Brahmanism, have long revered the Lord Buddha and often have devoted study to his doctrine. Here it behooves us to make another contrast between Gandhi and Nehru, who have done so many of the same things for such different reasons.

Gandhi was profoundly sympathetic to Buddhists, Muslims and Christians because to a very considerable extent he, like other Hindu sages, participated in their beliefs. Many Buddhists think of him as a Buddhist, and actually once on the American radio I was trapped into an unfortunate argument with a missionary who contended that Gandhi was a Christian.

The Muslims do not go so far as to believe he was one of them, but they have revered him for decades in all parts of the world. You would have found some kind of fly-specked photograph of Gandhi, generally in color, in almost any rebel nest of Muslim Asia during this century, whether it was the Algerian mountains or the mud huts of Kurdistan. Gandhi's death brought forth religious commemorations of a mass character in the Buddhist countries of Asia. He had earned this regard because he was Buddhist, Muslim and Christian, as well as being supremely Hindu.

He could rationalize all of this: he had read the scriptures of all the religions and in each one he found his own beliefs reflected, boldly and beautifully stated for other peoples in other lands. Thus the Beatitudes, in the Sermon on the Mount, became a part of his nature; the resolute equality of all men before God was what he found in the Koran, and he could not even reject the doctrine of "holy war" as it was austerely expressed by the Prophet Mohammed (Upon Whom Be Peace!) As he pointed out, "holy war" was a last resort, the result of much fasting, prayer and meditation, and was historically extremely rare.

As for Buddhist doctrine (that part of it which we can be fairly sure of), it was more or less what he had believed all his life anyhow. Gandhi's religious attitude toward these psychological realities in the world was essentially different from Nehru's. Nehru respects all the beliefs without, as it seems to me, sharing them. He is aware of their separate merits and their decisive part in the evolution of human history, but I doubt if he has ever had time to read their scriptures with care or to contemplate their several truths. There is, as in everything he does, an element of sheer good manners, something of taste and breeding, something of grand seigneur, about the reverence he pays to the gods of others. And a very lucky thing it is for India, I should say! Returning, then, to this alleged "remoteness from politics," I should say that it does not exist and that those who bring the charge are in reality thinking of something else. After watching Nehru from near and far for the past twelve years and more, it would seem to me that he possesses real political genius.

This does not consist merely in a grasp of his own party organization, although he has it when he needs it. It consists in a grasp of all the political realities, including a very considerable number which are beyond the comprehension of the party hacks. He believes in democracy and yields to it when he cannot persuade; he is quite capable of the necessary compromises between irreconcilables; he even makes appointments on a purely political basis when necessary. Nothing could exceed the respect and decorum he displays in the parliament, toward its members and toward the Speaker of the House. "Sir, if I may say so... !"

How often have we heard him preface a remark with this bow to the Speaker! He endures interruptions and attacks in the House, even of the most personal nature, with a demeanour which seldom reveals the resentment or anger he must often experience. And, finally, toward the new problem presented by the Communist successes in 1957, as course is quite clear: they are on the same basis as any other legal party up to the point where they may endanger the security of the country, its constitution and its laws. When they do that, as they sometimes have done, they go to jail.

Aside from party matters, elections, parliamentary procedures and all the rest, Nehru's political power in the country really does transcend electoral democracy. It comes from dozens of extraparrisan matters which I have attempted to indicate. It comes also from plain and simple popularity, which never has been a party matter in any country.

The man appeals to the people and what is more, he fascinates them. They would all rather talk about him than almost any other subject. The delicate adjustments I have mentioned, as with Muslims, are in a different category from this simple, straightforward popularity. Whenever he shows himself, which is often, we see the evidence. I think he has been in more parts of India (meaning, in the past, undivided India) than anybody else except probably Gandhi. With a smile and a wave of the hand he can throw oceanic crowds into wild enthusiasm. Last year I sat with him at the folk dancing in the big National Stadium (formerly the Irwin Stadium) and he explained some of the dances to me. This festival is now an annual part of the celebration of Republic Week (the week around January 26). He seemed familiar with the choral dances of the villagers from every part of India. I wondered aloud: "Have you been everywhere in India?" He considered the question with a thoughtful smile.

"Depends what you mean by everywhere," he said. "If you mean every village, certainly not. No life would be long enough. But if you mean distinctive parts, areas, regions, I should think I had probably visited them all at some time or other." Anybody who does not regard popularity of the simplest kind as a power in politics has forgotten Roosevelt, Churchill and dozens of other democratic exemplars.

It may be a natural phenomenon, but it takes hard work to attain and retain. We see it at its purest form with children, soldiers, sailors, villagers, the nonpolitical, the prepolitical and the apolitical. With all of these Jawaharlal has a magic touch; I have seen it many times. Take, for an example, the children. One of the commonplaces of campaigning in all democracies is the attention the candidates pay to children, the "baby-kissing," as we call it in America. It has become a more or less routine joke at election time; we had a thorough exhibition of it during the New York elections of 1958 when Mr. Harriman and Mr. Rockefeller were opposing candidates.

This kind of thing is simple nature to Nehru. He loves children and always has done so; they bring forth his friendliest smile; he notices them before anything or anybody, wherever he is. By instinct he wants to pat them on the head and say "hello." If they give him namasthe, the greeting with hands joined before the face, he solemnly gives it back to them, and if they say "Jai Hind!" he says it back to them again. I have watched him a considerable number of times with children so young that they could not possibly know who he was. It is quite extraordinary how they smile and beam at him. I have never seen a child who showed the slightest sign of fear before him. He has some knack of making them all, singly and collectively, accept him instantly as a friend. Once in Calcutta we went to a school for girl refugees, not, let us say, a very happy gathering by definition, but the same thing happened at once. His affection for children has made him yield, on their account, to one or two things which are against his own rather fastidious rules.

He does not like to see his own name plastered over public monuments, streets, institutions and the like. He refuses permission. Otherwise, I suppose, there would be as many streets and buildings called Nehru as there now are called Gandhi. There are two exceptions which I have seen, one in Madras and one in Kashmir, and both are playgrounds for children. In the same way the public insistence on making a national festival out of his birthday used to worry him; he has solved the problem by appointing that day (November 14th) as "Children's Day," which is now celebrated throughout India. Say what you like, such things are immensely popular, and although they are not politics they affect politics deeply. Some of Nehru's political critics in Delhi who say he wastes time on children's art exhibits or children's hospitals or children's parties when he might be attending to the cesspools of party politics are ignoring the facts.

Nehru's personal popularity is the leading political fact of contemporary India. His party profits by it exceedingly, and ought to have sense enough to realize that it transcends the party system. With soldiers and sailors, who are as a rule not interested in politics at all, Mr. Nehru has the same personal power. They beam upon him; they love to talk about him; they listen to him with rapt attention. Once in a while they may yell "Hear, hear, sir!" in the best accents of Sandwich, but that is the only breach in their eager silence. The Indian Army and Navy are not ascetic any more than they are political. I heard a very high officer once, long ago, refer to some Congress Party ministers as "chaps in white caps." Prohibition, for example, is not applied to the armed services, and religious distinctions, although scrupulously honored, do not have the same acuity as in civil life.

All things considered, one might not expect Nehru to make the same appeal to officers and men of the armed services as he does to civilian India. He, too, is a "chap in a white cap," which nowadays means mainly the Congress Party, although it once meant nationalism. Although he is not ascetic or religious, Mr. Nehru does not drink alcohol or eat meat, out of deference to Hindu feelings in these matters. He is a cabinet minister something which most soldiers and sailors everywhere regard as a deadly bore and a politician. What, then, is the secret of the magic he holds for Army and Navy?

To me it appears that it comes from one very broad, deep layer of his being, which is nationalism. It is not his highest level but it is very strong, strong enough to support all the rest. The soldiers and sailors feel it, and since he, like St. Paul, is all things to all men, it is from this level of being that he speaks to them. Instinct, intuition, call it what you please: he communicates with these men on the electric channel of their unifying faith, which is in India and the future of India.

Once in the Punjab I was present at an army dinner (a regimental mess and an anniversary) when all these things were vividly apparent. After dinner he spoke at considerable length, improvising as usual reminiscing in a rambling manner about his attitude toward the Army from his earliest days; recalling his father and what his father had said to him. "One day, you must always remember," Motilal had said, "it will be our Army, even though it may be British today." The sense of the Army as India's shield was put forward in these unprepared, easy, somewhat disconnected remarks more cogently than could have been done by any prepared oratory. I saw tears glistening in some very martial eyes.

To these men and their like since then, Nehru's word is the law and the prophets. Again it is one of those nonpolitical facts which are stronger than politics. To sum the whole matter up, Nehru may be somewhat less of a politician than the late Sardar Patel, who held the nationwide party organization in the palm of his hand. And yet even Patel knew the facts: "They come for Jawahar, not for me," he said of the immense crowds once in his own Bombay. It is also true that Nehru does not have time any more for the details of party work every day. But by and large there is no man in India with a keener political sense, as he has repeatedly shown in emergencies, or with a deeper sense of responsibility toward his own party in the democracy. If he finds wider and deeper sources than the party machine for his own strength, it is because his nature, and the people's, would have it thus: such sources are older than parties and will outlast them. In turn he supports his own party with all the energy thus acquired, and it has every reason to be grateful to him. What may happen in his absence is another matter, but so long as he is there the political equilibrium will be maintained.

ORIGIN OF NON-ALIGNMENT MOVEMENT: COLONIAL EXPERIENCE

Nonalignment had its origins in India's colonial experience and the nonviolent Indian independence struggle led by the Congress, which left India determined to be the master of its fate in an international system dominated politically by Cold War alliances and economically by Western capitalism. The principles of nonalignment, as articulated by Nehru and his successors, were preservation of India's freedom of action internationally through refusal to align India with any bloc or alliance, particularly those led by the United States or the Soviet Union; nonviolence and international cooperation as a means of settling international disputes. Nonalignment was a consistent feature of Indian foreign policy by the late 1940s and enjoyed strong, almost unquestioning support among the Indian elite.

The term "Non-Alignment" itself was coined by Indian Prime Minister Jawaharlal Nehru during his speech in 1954 in Colombo, Sri Lanka. In this speech, Nehru described the five pillars to be used as a guide for Sino-Indian relations, which were first put forth by Chinese Premier Zhou Enlai. Called

Panchsheel (five restraints), these principles would later serve as the basis of the Non-Aligned Movement. The five principles were:

1. *Mutual respect for each other's territorial integrity and sovereignty*
2. *Mutual non-aggression*
3. *Mutual non-interference in domestic affairs*
4. *Equality and mutual benefit*
5. *Peaceful co-existence*

Jawaharlal Nehru's concept of nonalignment brought India considerable international prestige among newly independent states that shared India's concerns about the military confrontation between the superpowers and the influence of the former colonial powers. New Delhi used nonalignment to establish a significant role for itself as a leader of the Third World in such multilateral organizations as the United Nations (UN) and the Nonaligned Movement. The signing of the Treaty of Peace, Friendship, and Cooperation between India and the Soviet Union in 1971 and India's involvement in the internal affairs of its smaller neighbours in the 1970s and 1980s tarnished New Delhi's image as a nonaligned nation and led some observers to note that in practice, nonalignment applied only to India's relations with countries outside South Asia.

Early Developments

The movement had its origins in the 1947 Asian Relations Meeting in New Delhi and the 1955 Asian-African Conference in Bandung, Indonesia. India also participated in the 1961 Belgrade Conference that officially established the Nonaligned Movement, but Jawaharlal Nehru's declining prestige limited his influence. In the 1960s and 1970s, New Delhi concentrated on internal problems and bilateral relations, yet retained membership in an increasingly factionalized and radicalized movement. During the contentious 1979 Havana summit, India worked with moderate nations to reject Cuban president Fidel Castro's proposition that "socialism" (that is, the Soviet Union) was the "natural ally" of nonalignment.

In 1980s

Under Indira Gandhi in the early 1980s, India attempted to reassert its prominent role in the Nonaligned Movement by focusing on the relationship between disarmament and economic development. By appealing to the economic grievances of developing countries, Indira Gandhi and her successors exercised a moderating influence on the Nonaligned Movement, diverting it from some of the Cold War issues that marred the controversial 1979 Havana meeting. Although hosting the 1983 summit boosted Indian prestige within the movement, its close relations with the Soviet Union and its pro-Soviet positions on Afghanistan and Cambodia limited its influence.

The end of the Cold War left the Nonaligned Movement without its original raison d'être, and its membership became deeply divided over international disputes, strategy, and organization. During the 1992 Jakarta summit, India took a middle position between countries favoring confrontation with developed nations on international economic issues, such as Malaysia, and those that favoured a more cooperative approach, such as Indonesia. Although New Delhi played a minor role compared with Kuala Lumpur and Jakarta on most issues facing the summit, India formulated the Nonaligned Movement position opposing developed countries' linkage of foreign aid to human rights criteria.

Consequences

The early 1990s demise of the bipolar world system, which had existed since the end of World War II, shook the underpinnings of India's foreign policy. The Cold War system of alliances had been rendered meaningless by the collapse of the East European communist states, the dissolution of the Warsaw Treaty Organization (Warsaw Pact), and the demise of the Soviet Union. In the early 1990s, most colonies had become independent, and apartheid in South Africa was being dismantled, diminishing the value of anticolonialism and making it impossible for antiracism to serve as a rallying point for international political action (India and South Africa restored full diplomatic relations in 1993 after a thirty nine year lapse).

The Panchsheel (Panch Shila), peaceful resolution of international disputes, and international cooperation to spur economic development which was being enhanced by domestic economic reforms were broad objectives in a changing world. Thus, the 1990s saw India redefining nonalignment and the view of India's place in the world.

India also is a founding member of the Group of fifteen, a group of developing nations established at the ninth Nonaligned Movement summit in Belgrade in 1989 to facilitate dialogue with the industrialized countries. India played host to the fourth Group of Fifteen summit in March 1994. At the summit, Prime Minister Narsimha Rao and other leaders expressed concern over new trade barriers being raised by the industrialized countries despite the conclusion of a new world trade agreement.

POLITICAL THOUGHT OF NEHRU

Nehru was the first Prime Minister of India from 1947 until his death in 1964 and founder of the Nehru-Gandhi dynasty. His life was full of apparent contradictions. He was one of the most passionate opponents of British rule in India but was educated almost wholly in the British style, including Harrow and Cambridge, and subsequently at the Bar. Further, he was also a passionate democrat and became the leader of the world's most populous democracy, but at times advocated a brand of socialism, and sometimes Marxism, which owed much to Soviet influences.

It was Nehru's years in captivity that provided him the opportunity to write and his books were very popular in Britain. There is a vast body of literature on Nehru which examines all aspects of his life and work which can also usefully be divided into the biographical, topical and ideological. There are several biographical works by compatriots. The definitive work in the field, is the three volume study by Sarvepelli Gopal, *Jawaharlal Nehru: A Biography* (1975).

Another thorough biography is B. N. Pandey's *Nehru* (1976). A popular recent work is M. J. Akbar's *Nehru: The Making of India* (1988). There are also a number of works by British authors. Among the most thorough early works are those by Michael Brecher and Michael Edwardes that share the same title, *Nehru: A Political Biography,* the former published in 1959 and the latter in 1971. A succinct recent work is that by the British historian Dennis Judd, *Jawaharlal Nehru* (1993). Finally, Judith Brown's *Nehru* (1999), a biographical sketch for the Longman 'Profiles in Power' series, is an objective recent account of Nehru's life and work.

The wealth of biographical material identifies the various international connections and influences on Nehru's life and work and, in particular, his British connection. English speaking was enforced at home by Nehru's very westernized and anglicized father, Motilal. Motilal employed tutors who instructed Nehru in the British style prior to his formal schooling. Nehru was then educated at the quintessential British public school, Harrow, between 1905 and 1907 and studied at Trinity College, Cambridge between 1907 and 1910. At Cambridge, although Nehru took the natural science Tripos, he noted that the people he met all "talked learnedly about books and literature and history and politics and economics."

After Cambridge he studied law at the Inner Temple and was called to the Bar in 1912. Nehru read widely whilst at university and in London, for example, Edwardes, states that whilst at Cambridge Nehru "began to read widely in other fields, in literature, Greek poetry, politics, history and economics." Of Nehru's early years, Pandey, concludes: "He had been brought up in the best of both Indian and English cultures, had learnt to be at home in but not committed to either." Following this education it is hardly surprising that Nehru explained in his autobiography that all his "predilections (apart from the political plane) are in favour of England." Nehru made several other trips to Europe, and in particular Britain, in later life.

The trip to Europe in 1926-1927 is widely held to be an important landmark in Nehru's life and especially his political thinking. The primary reason of the trip was to enable his wife to recuperate in Switzerland.

Whilst based in Switzerland he was able to visit many countries in Europe including several trips to Britain, including London and Derbyshire at the time of the general strike. During this visit he attended the International Congress against Colonial Oppression and Imperialism, as the representative of the Indian National Congress, in Brussels in February 1927.

Nehru made further trips to Europe, including Britain, in 1935,1936 and again during the Spanish civil war and the eve of the second world war, in 1938. Another striking feature of Nehru's life is the extent to which he moved, intellectually at least, in British socialist circles. For example, J. K. Galbraith, in recalling his association with Nehru in the 1950s and a meeting in 1961, confirmed the influence of Laski, Tawney, Bernard Shaw, the Webbs and the early Labour Party on Nehru."

Whilst this feature is often mentioned it has not been thoroughly explored in connection with his political thought.

There are a number of studies works which can be considered as topical, in that they discuss certain aspects of Nehru's life and work. B. R. Nanda's *The Nehrus* (1962) examines the first forty years of Nehru's life as well as that of his anglicized, father Motilal. There is also a relatively short, but insightful, study of Nehru and his most characteristic policies, such as economic planning, by Hiren Mukerjee, *The Gentle Colussus: A Study ofJawaharlal Nehru* (1964).

This study stands out as a fair and balanced assessment of Nehru's life and work despite the author often finding himself in opposition to Nehru, a member of the Communist Party. There are then some collections which place Nehru's life and work in the wider international context, for example, A. B. Shah's *Jawaharlal Nehru: A Critical Tribute* (1965) and Milton Israel's *Nehru and the Twentieth Century* (1991). Another interesting work which falls into the 'topical' category is Tibor Mende's *Conversations with Mr. Nehru* (1956).

This series of interviews that Nehru gave with the author during the 1950s contain valuable insight on current issues combined with recollections of early influences. Finally, B. R. Nanda's *Jawaharlal Nehru: Rebel and Statesman* (1995) contains a collection of essays which discuss various aspects of Nehru's life and work. Of particular relevance are chapters on Nehru's writings, his relationship with Britain and the British and his economic policies. The 'topical' literature illustrates clearly the range of British influences that impacted in Nehru and also the rather contradictory nature of his political thought.

The current material highlights very well the contrast between Nehru's long struggle against the British authorities in India prior to independence and his British connection. Nehru became increasingly involved in Congress politics and the non-cooperation movement in the early 1920s which eventually placed him before a magistrate where he delivered one of his first important statements. Whilst the statement confirmed Nehru's nationalist orientation it also revealed an interesting facet of his background:

Less than ten years ago I returned from England after a lengthy stay there... I had imbibed most of the prejudices of Harrow and Cambridge, and in my likes and dislikes I was perhaps more an Englishman than an Indian.... And so I returned to India as much prejudiced in favour of England and the English as it was possible for an Indian to be.

Moraes relates a poignant example of this which took place in London during the Commonwealth conference in 1952. Moraes noted that "Nehru attended the Old Harrovian dinner and took an impish delight in singing the school song "Forty Years On" in the company of another Old Harrovian, also a Prime Minister, Winston Churchill." After independence these two adversaries were reconciled and in a letter Churchill wrote to Nehru in 1955 he confessed that, "one of the most agreeable memories of my last years in office is our association." This relationship, between British conservative and Indian nationalist, demonstrates well the contradictions within Nehru.

The ideological work on Nehru provides evidence of considerable western and particularly British influences on his political thought. A good general study is M. N. Das's *The Political Philosophy of Jawaharlal Nehru* (1961) which identifies influences of Gandhi, Russian communism, Marxism and British parliamentary democracy as being of most importance. In the preface to the collection *Studies on Nehru* (1987), V. T. Patil observed that: "The core of his political thought was based on his compact adherence to democracy, individual freedom and socialism."

Perhaps reflecting this potentially contradictory 'core' the more specific 'ideological' material divides broadly between studies of Nehru's socialism and studies of his liberal and democratic ideas. Pratibha Kagalkar's *Nehru - A Study in Indian Socialism* (1992) identifies the Russian and Marxist influences but notes that: "His attachment to individualism and liberalism reinforced by the influence of Gandhi, prevented him from becoming a total convert to Marx."

In the preface to his study, *Socialism of Jawaharlal Nehru* (1981), R. C. Dutt observed that "there is no systematic study of Nehru in his various phases in terms of his socialist thinking." Neelam Mishra's *The Socialist Orientation of Jawaharlal Nehru* (1989), also identified vacillations in Nehru's political thought which reflected the influences of liberalism and socialism to which he was exposed.

Neeraj's *Nehru and Democracy in India* (1972) also identifies phases in his socialism, which reached a zenith in the early 1930s: "This may be regarded as a period when Nehru's intellectual adherence and emotional attachment to socialism was at its peak." Donald Smith's *Nehru and Democracy: The Political Thought of an Asian Democrat* (1958), stated that "his thinking is steeped in Western democratic traditions."

Ganesh Prashad in his study, *Nehru: A Study in Colonial Liberalism* (1976), believes that Nehru's political thought was in essence the manifestation of the British liberal tradition, amended by the Fabians, and adapted to suit the Indian situation.

As such, for Prashad, it reflects the fact that Nehru had "imbibed the values and ideals of the British humanist liberal tradition" The ideological work discusses the distinguishing features of Nehru's political thought as well as influences which included the British liberal tradition, Gandhi, Russian communism and Marxism. In addition to these are Nehru's own ideas which often attempted to blend the early liberal and the later socialist influences, explaining why Dutt considered he was "a man who defied classification into an accepted category, such as Fabian Socialist, Social Democrat, Marxist, or Humanist."

Kagalkar believed that: "Fabian methods of reformism, gradual progress and constitutionalism had a permanent impact on Nehru's thought and action" and his "receptive mind imbibed the very spirit of the British liberal tradition."

Dutt noted at an essential characteristic of Nehru's thought by referring to its "various phases" of more and less moderate socialism over Nehru's career. According to Dutt, Nehru saw no conflict between socialism and liberalism and in fact believed that "civil liberty could hardly co-exist with gross economic inequality."

Smith also identified Nehru's British education, his trip to Europe in 1926-1927 and Gandhi's influence, especially in the 1920s, as crucial periods in the development of his political thought. Whilst a number of British influences are mentioned in the 'ideological' literature, the extent of Nehru's British connection suggests further influences may be uncovered by a more systematic analysis.

Have identified some of the influences and sources of Nehru's thought the latter itself may now be examined. Whilst there is much available material from which to discover Nehru's political thought it does not all lend itself to analysis. For example, although the *Selected Works of Jawaharlal Nehru* (1984-

1994) currently available only cover the period from September 1946 to October 1951 they run to sixteen volumes.

Similarly the *Letters to Chief Ministers 1947-1964* (1985-1989) fill five volumes which elucidate Nehru's years as Prime Minister. However, it is often in Nehru's speeches, and especially his addresses to the Indian National Congress, that his political thought can be found and there are several volumes of speeches which are most helpful in this regard. The first of these was edited by Jagat Bright *Important Speeches of Jawaharlal Nehru,* which contain numerous speeches from his involvement in the nationalist movement between 1922 and 1946. A second is *Indian Independence and Social Revolution* (1984) which contains several of Nehru's most important Presidential Addresses to the Indian National Congress. Finally, the three volume *Jawaharlal Nehru's Speeches* (1949-1958) covers the period from 1946 to 1957.

Nehru was also a prolific and widely read author prior to Indian independence when prolonged periods of captivity provided ample opportunity for writing. Das describes Nehru's three most important books that contain his "deeper political ideas" as essentially three histories: one of the world, one of India and one of himself."

Interestingly they were all written whilst Nehru was imprisoned by the Government of India. The first of these, his history of the world *Glimpses of World History* (1934-1935), is a series of letters that Nehru wrote to his daughter Indira from prison. Dutt considered that *Glimpses of World History* "was not the work of a professional scholar" but "threw so much light on his contemporary thinking."

In particular, Smith noted that it "reflected very clearly his political thinking during the period 1930-1933." Nehru's history of himself, his *Autobiography* (1936), was written whilst he was in prison between June 1934 and February 1935. Judd shares the view that much of Nehru's political thought is rather vague and commenting on his *Autobiography* states: "The book is no closely-argued political tract. Rather it reflects the self-doubt, confusion and philosophical uncertainty that characterized much of Jawaharlal's thinking." Nehru's history of India, *The Discovery of India* (1946), contains a lengthy critique of the period of British rule which is placed in the context of Indian history.

As well as these books there are several collections of essays writings and speeches which help to develop Nehru's political thought. *The Unity of India* (1948) covers the period between 1934 and 1940. Another collection *Whither India* (1933) contains other work, his famous essay of that name and represents an important source of his thought at that time. Pandey believed that this essay "came near to being" Nehru's "political manifesto." Another collection,

India and the World, (1936), contains further writings and speeches of that important period.

An excellent two volume compilation with a helpful commentary which covers the period up to 1950 is Dorothy Norman's *Nehru: The First Sixty Years* (1965). This study, containing excerpts of much of Nehru's work, is interspersed with interviews and other biographical material and was compiled with access to many varied sources.

Of particular relevance to this chapter, Gopal, who edited a *Jawaharlal Nehru: An Anthology* (1983), notes in the preface that "it was primarily in English that his thoughts were formulated and expressed." Nehru's correspondence is also a valuable source and there are several important volumes.

Two of these are devoted to the correspondence between Nehru and his daughter Indira Gandhi, and were both edited by her daughter in law, Sonia Gandhi. The first, *Freedom's Daughter* (1989) covers the period between 1922 and 1939 and the second, *Two Alone, Two Together* (1992) covers the period between 1940 and 1964. Finally, there is one volume of miscellaneous correspondence, A *Bunch of Old Letters* (1958) which ranges over his life and includes letters to and from Bernard Shaw and Harold Laski.

Nehru's life and work has been variously assessed. Thus it may be asked as Smith did in 1958: "Nehru is a politician and is it possible to determine what a politician really believes about anything?" Smith observed that: "Some of Nehru's election campaign speeches contain obvious exaggerations, and may be taken with the proverbial grain of salt." The implication here is the importance of gauging if Nehru's political thought was more profound than mere rhetoric. However, Smith concluded that it was possible to separate Nehru's role as a politician from his role as a thinker because his statements were often backed by action, he exhibited consistency and frankness, and he avoided expediency. Further, it is possible that a number of British influences have been overlooked as Nehru's thought has been dismissed especially in the many studies that have focused on his record as Prime Minister.

Nehru's height as a philosopher-statesman and role as bridge traditional and modern, western and particularly British ideas has been variously interpreted. For Arnold Toynbee Nehru was "unquestionably" a great statesman.

For Das a special quality of Nehru was that: "Combined thought and action helped him in formulating his ideas and, in a sense, his political philosophy became embodied in his practical experiments." But for M. N. Roy: "Personal attachment to Gandhi precluded his moving in the direction of genuine political greatness and creative leadership." These variations have been attributed, by Patil, to the fact that: "Nehru was a highly complex individual and that explains why different scholars have either showered wholesome praise on his contribution or have criticised him in uncertain terms."

Neeraj, also draws attention to Nehru's dual role, as philosopher and politician, and observes that Nehru was "a man who was not primarily a political thinker or a philosopher, but a practical statesman and an administrator." Although Nehru might not have been a political philosopher, and did not consider himself as such, for Gopal he "was one of the most articulate of modern statesman." In an interview in 1956, Nehru insisted that he was "not a professional philosopher."

This view is shared by Das, who contends that though Nehru was "not a political philosopher in the conventional sense" he did distinguish himself "more or less as a philosopher-politician." Kagalkar describes Nehru as "not a systematic thinker, but an intellectual eclectic."

However, for Kagalkar this eclecticism was a strength: "Nehru's greatest achievement was his adaptation of the western ideas of Socialism to the Indian context." This view is echoed by Smith who concludes: "His political theory is essentially eclectic, drawn from diverse intellectual currents of the nineteenth and twentieth centuries." Whilst acknowledging Nehru's significant contribution to the nationalist movement, Brecher also identifies Nehru's eclecticism but believes it prevented him from making a "systematic effort to integrate them into a consistent personal and political philosophy." In more general terms, Norman concludes that, "Nehru emerges as both an outstanding literary figure of our epoch, and as an important political force." For Judith Brown, Nehru was "one of the most influential Asian political figures of the twentieth century."

Nehru, more than Gandhi and Sun, had the chance following his emergence as Indian Prime Minister at independence, to implement his ideas. Ironically, in light of the recognition that he was primarily a statesman, many of the criticisms of Nehru concern his failure to fully implement his ideas. For example Prashad concludes that Nehru, "had the vision, but without the ruthlessness to implement it."

This belief in Nehru's lack of ruthlessness is shared by Mukerjee who concludes that Nehru's "historic failure" was "the failure to achieve change for fear of the price that might have had to be paid." Brecher concluded his biography by noting that, "one of Nehru's weaknesses as a political leader" was that "the gap between words and deeds was often wide." The American author John Gunter summarised Nehru's weakness as a statesman as being because he was "too decent, too honourable to be a good politician. He is a gentleman. Worse, he is an English gentleman." Interestingly, J. K. Galbraith recalled that Nehru had once quipped, that he was "the last Englishman to rule in India." In terms of his personal and mass appeal the testimony is predominantly positive. Brecher remarked of Nehru in 1959: "For twenty-five years or more he has been the idol of the Indian masses, second only to Gandhi. They literally adore him, with a vivid affection and hero-worship." Pandey observed that in assessing Nehru's place in history, statesmen and historians have been influenced more by the personality of Nehru - his ideas, vision and humanity -than by the impact he made on the course of history.

This brief survey of some assessments of Nehru reveals an interesting contradiction. Nehru was both a philosopher and a statesman, but whilst not primarily a philosopher he was thwarted as a statesman in the implementation of his ideas. N. D. Palmer concluded his assessment as follows: "He deserves the major credit for the success of the new Indian state in preserving and operating the system of Parliamentary democracy which was established upon Independence." Similarly, Judd concluded that, "Nehru can be credited with the establishment of a strong democratic tradition in India." Brecher also concedes that, despite Nehru's failures in the practical sphere, his contributions to the nationalist movement "form an impressive record, perhaps without peer among political revolutionaries of this century." On this more general level Smith concluded that: "Jawaharlal Nehru may justly be regarded as the foremost interpreter of liberal democracy that Asia has produced." It is evident that Nehru's interpretation of democracy, which was in part shaped by British influences, has been subject to much debate. The further elaboration of British influences on Nehru will help to provide a better assessment of Nehru and his political thought.

The above survey of the lives and works of Sun, Gandhi and Nehru has revealed several similarities. Firstly, they each possessed a substantial British connection. Second, they were all in favour of democracy, albeit to varying extents and in different guises. Thirdly, they all played crucial, transitional and guiding roles in the nationalist and independence movement. Fourthly, they can all be considered as political thinkers *and* nationalist leaders, if not philosopher-statesmen, and their stature as such has been variously assessed from the hagiographic to the blatantly critical and dismissive. These similarities make the three of them eminently comparable in terms of the nature and extent of British influences on their political thought.

NEHRU POLICY OF CHINA

In the late autumn of 1962, there was a short, intense border war between India and China. It resulted in the complete rout of an underprepared and poorly led Indian Army. The battle was seen in national, civilizational, and ideological terms. India became free of British rule in 1947; China was united under Communist auspices in 1949. These two nations were, or at least saw themselves as, carriers of ancient civilizations that had produced great literature, philosophy, architecture, science, and much else, but whose further evolution had been rudely interrupted by Western imperialists. The recovery of their national independence was seen as the prelude to the re-emergence of China and India as major forces in the world.

The defeat of 1962 was thus at once a defeat of the Indian Army at the hands of its Chinese counterpart, a defeat of democracy by Communism, a defeat of one large new nation by another, a defeat of one ancient civilization at the hands of another. In India, the defeat was also interpreted in personal terms, as the defeat of Jawaharlal Nehru, who had held the offices of Prime Minister and Foreign Minister continuously since independence in 1947.

That disaster at the hands of China still hangs as a huge cloud over Nehru's reputation. There is an intriguing comparison to be made here with with his fellow Harrovian, Winston Churchill. Robert Rhodes James once wrote a book called *Churchill: A Study in Failure,* whose narrative stopped in 1940. It excavated, perhaps in excessive detail, its subject's erratic and undistinguished career before that date. But of course, all Churchill's failures were redeemed by his great and heroic leadership in World War II. It is tempting to see Nehru's career as being Churchill's in reverse, insofar it was marked for many decades by achievement and success, these nullified by the one humiliating failure, with regard to China, which broke his nation's morale and broke his own spirit and body. The war was fought in October-November 1962; a year-and-a-half later, Nehru was dead.

The four towering figures of 20 century India were Rabindranath Tagore, Mohandas K. Gandhi, Jawaharlal Nehru, and B. R. Ambedkar. All four had a close connection with England, a country they each spent extended periods in, and whose literature and politics they were influenced by. But all also had a long engagement with a second foreign country. In the case of Tagore, this was Japan, which he visited on four separate occasions, and whose culture and art he greatly admired. In the case of Gandhi, this second country was South Africa, where he spent two decades working as a lawyer, community organiser, and activist. In the case of Ambedkar it was the United States, where he studied, and by whose democratic traditions he was deeply influenced.

As for Nehru, other than India and England, the country that interested him most was China. His first major book, *Glimpses of World History,* published in 1935, has as many as 134 index references to China. These refer to, among other things, different dynasties (the Tang, Han, Ch'in, etc.), corruption, communism, civil war, agriculture, and banditry. Already, the pairing of China and India was strongly imprinted in Nehru's framework. Thus China is referred to as 'the other great country of Asia', and as 'India's old-time friend.' There was a manifest sympathy with its troubles at the hands of foreigners. The British were savaged for forcing both humiliating treaties and opium down the throats of the Chinese, this being an illustration of the „growing arrogance and interference by the western Powers.

Additional notable, perhaps, was the chastisement of the Japanese, which „not only followed Europe in industrial methods, but, at least with regard to China, „also in imperialist aggression. Speaking of the wars between the two nations in the 1890s, Nehru writes that „no scruple had ever troubled China in the pursuit of her imperial policy. She grabbed openly, not caring even to cover her designs with a veil. Nehru also judged Japan harshly with regard to the war with China that took place at the time of the book s writing. Thus, when Japan met with resistance from Chinese nationalists, it „tried to break it by vast and horrible massacres from the air and other methods of unbelievable barbarity. But, continued Nehru, „in this fiery ordeal a new nation was forged in China, and the old lethargy of the Chinese people dropped away from them. ... The sympathy of the people of India was naturally with the Chinese people, as it also was with the Spanish Republic, and in India and America and elsewhere great movements for the boycott of Japanese goods grew.

The understanding of this particular Indian manifested itself in a trip he made to China in August 1939. The visit was cut short by the outbreak of hostilities in Europe, which forced Nehru to come home to discuss with his nationalist colleagues the impact of the War on their movement. Even so, the two weeks he spent in China were, wrote Nehru, „memorable ones both personally for me and for the future relations of India and China. I found, to my joy, that my desire that China and India should draw ever closer to each other was fully reciprocated by China s leaders.... ... I returned to India an even greater admirer of China and the Chinese people than I had been previously, and I could not imagine that any adverse fate could break the spirit of these ancient people, who had grown so young again. Soon after writing these words, Nehru was jailed by the British. While in prison for the next three years, he composed *Discovery of India,* a brilliant and idiosyncratic work that mixes autobiography with history, and cultural analysis with political prophecy. One important strand in the book relates to relations between the two great Asiatic civilizations. Nehru speaks of the exchange of ideas and artefacts carried on down the centuries by pilgrims, mystics, scholars, travellers, and diplomats. „During the thousand years and more of intercourse between India and China, he writes, „each country learnt something from the other, not only in the regions of thought and philosophy, but also in the arts and sciences of life. Probably China was more influenced by India than India by China, which is a pity, for India could well have received, with profit to herself, some of the sound commonsense of the Chinese, and with aid checked her own extravagant fancies.

In the *Discovery of India*, Nehru again compares China favourably with Japan, observing that the former s struggle for national dignity attracted „much sympathy in India, in contrast to „a certain antipathy for the latter. The Chinese leader Chiang Kai-shek had visited India during the War; although the British did not allow him to meet Indian politicians or mix freely with the Indian people, the presence of the Generalissimo and his wife, thought Nehru, „and their manifest sympathy for India s freedom, helped to bring India out of her national shell and increased her awareness of the international issues at stake. The bonds that tied India and China grew stronger, and so did the desire to line up with China and other nations against the common adversary (namely, fascism and imperialism).

Writing at the conclusion of the Second World War, Nehru could clearly see the decline of Great Britain, and the emergence of the United States and Soviet Russia as the two major powers. This bipolar world would, in time, become a multi-polar world. Nehru thought that „China and India are potentially capable of joining that group. Each of them is compact and homogeneous and full of natural wealth, man-power and human skill and capacity.... No other country, taken singly, apart from these four, is actually or potentially in such a position'. 'It is possible of course', wrote Nehru presciently, 'that large federations of groups of nations may emerge in Europe or elsewhere and form huge multinational States.'

In his pre-1947 writings, Nehru saw China from the lens of a progressive anti-imperialist, from which perspective India and China were akin and alike, simultaneously fighting Western control as well as feudal remnants in their own society. Chiang and company, like Nehru and company, were at once freedom-fighters, national unifiers, and social modernizers. It stood to reason that, when finally free of foreign domination, the two neighbours would be friends and partners.

NEHRU'S ATTITUDE OF CHINA

Jawaharlal Nehru's attitude to China as Prime Minister and Foreign Minister. The bridge between these two periods, pre-and-post Indian independence, is provided by the Asian Relations Conference, held in New

Delhi in March-April 1947. In his speech to the Conference, Nehru called China 'that great country to which Asia owes so much and from which so much is expected'. The Conference itself he characterized as 'an expression of that deeper urge of the mind and spirit of Asia which has persisted in spite of the isolationism which grew up during the years of European domination. As that domination goes, the walls that surrounded us fall down and we look at one another again and meet as old friends long parted.'

The Chinese delegation to this Conference represented Chiang Kaishek's Guomindang Party; there was also a separate delegation from Tibet. Two years later the Communists took power in China. The Indian Ambassador to China, K. M. Panikkar, was greatly impressed by the new ruler of China. He compared Mao Zedong to his own boss, Nehru, writing that „both are men of action with dreamy, idealistic temperaments, both „humanists in the broadest sense of the term.

One do not know what Nehru complete of this comparison. But an Indian who had a different and more realistic view of Mao and his comrades was the Home Minister, Vallabhbhai Patel. When China invaded Tibet in October 1950, Patel wrote to Nehru that „communism is no shield against imperialism and that the Communists are as good or as bad imperialists as any other. Chinese ambitions in this respect not only cover the Himalayan slopes on our side but also include important parts of Assam... Chinese irredentism and Communist imperialism are different from the expansionism or imperialism of the Western Powers. The former has a cloak of ideology which makes it ten times more dangerous. In the guise of ideological expansion lies concealed racial, national or historical claims. The Prime Minister, however, continued to give the Chinese the benefit of doubt, Speaking in the Indian Parliament in December 1950, he said: Some hon. Members seem to think that I should issue an ultimatum to China, that I should warn them not to do this or that or that I should send them a letter saying that it is foolish to follow the doctrine of communism. I do not see how it is going to help anybody if I act in this way.

Through the first half of the 1950s, Nehru continued to see China as a kindred soul. Like India, it had embarked on an ambitious and autonomous programme of economic and social development, albeit under communist auspices. One more the two great civilizations could interact with and learn from each other. As Nehru wrote to his Chief Ministers in June 1952: „[A] variety of circumstances pull India and China towards each other, in spite of differences of forms of government. This is the long pull of geography and history and, if I may add, of the future.' Later the same year, after a visit to India's northeast, Nehru insisted that was not 'the slightest reason to expect any aggression on our northeastern frontier. A little clear thinking will show that it is a frightfully difficult task for any army to cross Tibet and the Himalayas and invade India. Tibet is one of the most difficult and inhospitable of countries. An army may possibly cross it, but the problem of logistics and feeding it becomes increasingly difficult. The climate is itself an enemy of any large-scale movement. Apart from this, there was no particular reason why China should think of aggression in this direction.' Nehru even thought 'there is a definite feeling of friendliness towards India in China.'

In June 1954, Zhou-en-lai visited New Delhi. In a letter to his Chief Ministers written immediately afterwards, Nehru reported that the Chinese Prime Minister 'was particularly anxious, of course, for the friendship and co-operation of India.... His talk was wholly different from the normal approach of the average Communist, which is full of certain slogans and cliches. He hardly mentioned communism or the Soviet Union or European politics.' Nehru then reported his own talk: 'I spoke to him at some length about our peaceful struggle for independence under Gandhiji's leadership and how this had conditioned us. Our policies had developed from that struggle and we proposed to follow them.'

Nehru's made a return visit to China in October 1954. His reception there was described by his security officer, KF Rustamji. In Beijing, a million people lined the roads to greet and cheer Nehru and Zhou as they drove in an open car from the airport to the city. 'All along the route', observed Rustamji, 'not a single police in uniform was visible'. Then he visited Canton, Dairen, Nanking, and 'at each place the cheers became louder, the clapping more vigorous. At each place we felt that nothing could be better than the reception given there. Then we moved on and found that there was something better —Shanghai. There the airport was a mass of people waving gladioli flowers —there were so many flowers that they seemed to change the colour of the airport.

This reception must certainly have flattered Nehru. But it seems also to have convinced him of the depth of popular support for the regime (with not a policeman in sight), and of the desire for friendship with India. As he wrote to his closest friend, Edwina Mountbatten, „I had a welcome in China, such as I have in the big cities of India, and that is saying something. ... The welcome given to me was official and popular. ... One million took part on the day of arrival in Peking. It was not the numbers but their obvious enthusiasm. There appeared to be something emotional to it.

In a correspondence to his Chief Ministers, Nehru likewise insisted that „this welcome represented something more than political exigency. It was almost an emotional upheaval representing the basic urges of the people for friendship with India. He had „no doubt at all that the Government and people of China desire peace and want to concentrate on building up their country during the next decade or so.

Towards the end of 1956, Zhou-en-Lai visited India again. The Dalai Lama was also in his party. The Tibetan leader briefly escaped his Chinese minders, and told Nehru that conditions were so harsh in his country that he wished to flee to India. Nehru advised him to return. In 1958, the Indian Prime Minister asked to visit Tibet, but was refused permission. Now the first seeds of doubt, or at least confusion, were planted in his mind —perhaps the Chinese were not as straightforward, or indeed as progressive, as he had supposed.

In July 1958, a map was printed in Beijing which showed large parts of India as Chinese territory. It was also revealed that the Chinese had built a road linking Xinjiang to Tibet, which passed through an uninhabited, and scarcely visited stretch of the Indian district of Ladakh. There were protests from New Delhi, whereupon Zhou-en-Lai wrote back saying that the McMahon Line, marking the border between India and China, was a legacy of British imperialism and hence not 'legal'. The Chinese leader suggested that both sides retain control of the territory they currently occupied, pending a final settlement.

Meanwhile, a revolt broke out in Tibet. It was put down, and in March 1959 the Dalai Lama fled into India. That he was given refuge, and that Indian political parties rushed to his defence, enraged the Chinese. The war of words escalated. That autumn there were sporadic clashes between Indian and Chinese troops on the border. In October 1959, Nehru wrote to his Chief Ministers that 'this tension that has arisen between India and China is, of course, of great concern to us. That does not mean that we should get alarmed in the present or fear any serious consequences. I do not think any such development is likely in the foreseeable future. But the basic fact remains that India and China have fallen out and, even though relative peace may continue at the frontier, it is some kind of an armed peace, and the future appears to be one of continuing tension.'

'Behind all this Frontier Trouble', Nehru Continued, there appears to me to be a basic problem of a strong and united Chinese State, expansive and pushing out in various directions and full of pride in its growing strength. In Chinese history, this kind of thing has happened on several occasions. Communism as such is only an added element; the real reason should be found to lie deeper in history and in national characteristic. But it is true that never before have these two great countries, India and China, come face to face in some kind of a conflict. By virtue of their very size and their actual or potential strength, there is danger in this situation, not danger in the present, but rather in the future. That danger may be minimized by other developments and by the world moving gradually towards peace. But the danger will still remain, partly because of the tremendous rate of increase of the population of the Chinese State. Apart from population, there has been and is a certain homogeneity among the Chinese people which probably we lack. I have no doubt, however, that in the face of danger there will be much greater cohesion in India than we have at present. Perhaps, that may be one of the good effects of this new and unfortunate development.

By now, Nehru appeared to have come around, at least in part, to the point of view articulated by Vallabhbhai Patel in 1950. The Chinese state was more nationalist than communist. Still, he felt that there was no chance of a full-fledged war between the two countries. To protect India's interests, Nehru now sanctioned a policy of 'forward posts', whereby detachments were camped in areas along the border claimed by both sides. This was a preemptive measure, designed to deter the Chinese from advancing beyond the McMahon Line.

In 1960, Zhou-en-Lai came to New Delhi in an attempt to find a settlement. India's case was stronger in the Western sector, where Chinese interests were greater. Here lay the access road linking the two troublesome provinces of Tibet and Xinjiang, a road that passed through territory claimed by India. On the other hand, in the Eastern sector, where Chinese claims were more robust, their strategic interests were minimal.

Zhou offered a *quid pro quo.* The Chinese would not challenge Indian control of the eastern sector, so long as the Indians in turn winked at their incursions in the west. It was a practical, and in terms of *realpolitik,* a reasonable proposal. Nehru himself was open to considering it favourably. But by this time knowledge of the road in Ladakh had become public, and there was an outcry in Parliament and the press. The border clashes and the flight of the Dalai Lama had further inflamed public opinion. Opposition politicians accused Nehru of betraying the national interest by talking to the Chinese. Not an inch of Indian territory, they said, could or should be ceded to the Chinese. In the prevailing climate, Nehru chose not to pursue the idea of a settlement.

6

Foreign Policy of Nehru

Nehru saw war and violent insurgency from very close quarters as a freedom fighter, and he believed in neither. In his foreign policies, Nehru tried to guide India in such a way, so as to steer clear from any form of violence and militarism. He rightly believed that a newly decolonized nation must invest all its economic and logistic resources towards development and not defense and armament. Just like his economic policies, which were non-committal towards any ideological position, Nehru wanted to bring in a healthy level of pragmatism in his dealings of India's foreign affairs as well. He understood that overt commitment to any of the two major power blocs to emerge in the aftermath of World War II, would not serve India's path. He therefore wanted to tread a third path, which was not necessarily the middle path.

It should be remembered that this dogged non-commitment of Nehru was not seen sympathetically by any of the super powers of either East or West at its initial stage. It was frequently termed as a kind of international opportunism and was accused of 'neutralism'-a stance reckoned to be not only dangerous but also equally immoral in the world of International politics. However, the increasing popularity of NAM among various Asian and African countries and Nehru's growing stature as a statesman situation changed their views. India too benefited from this position, as it managed to secure rebuilding grants from member countries of either bloc. After Nehru's successful mediation in the Korean War and the Congo problem, putting an end to a long and violent struggle, his status as a commendable and efficient statesman reached new heights. Jawaharlal Nehru's theory of ideological non-commitment in a world that was rendered dangerous by the Cold War was appreciated by one and all.

Nehru and the Non-Alignment Movement: The greatest success of Jawaharlal Nehru's non-committal international politics was the formation of the Non-Alignment Movement (NAM). Nehru found allies in Tito, Nasser,

Soekarno, U Nu and Nkrumah at a later stage in his formation of this new alliance. An alliance of newly independent and long colonized nations was not taken seriously in the beginning, either by the Eastern or the Western bloc. However, the importance of the alliance was soon felt, and initially led to a great degree of international pressure from both parts of the globe. However, Nehru proceeded with his mission undaunted. It was great test for his courage and it was soon found out that the NAM was not merely a passive platform of neutral and inactive nations.

It had clear objectives that included the gradual decolonization of the world, and a strong statement that the member countries were not party to the ever escalating tension of the Cold War. The favored process of decolonization as adopted by the NAM member countries was one of discussion and peaceful agreement.

On many occasions, NAM met with success, often under the leadership of Nehru. Whoever supported its cause was an ally and a friend. Nehru preached a policy of issue based alliance and not one based on political and economic dogmas. He was proud of being an Asian, and wanted Asian nations to be the primary determinants of their political fate, not always guided by Western forces.

Nehru's unshaken belief in the force of international brotherhood was attested with his decision to continue with India's Commonwealth status. He was made subject to much criticism back home because of the support he extended towards the Commonwealth, particularly after the complication of the independence issue by the British government in the post World War II years, leading to the unwanted partition. However Nehru, always the believer in peaceful alliances and solution of international affairs based on discussions, went on with his ideals.

Nehru and the Kashmir Problem: Nehru's Foreign policies did not augur well when it came to deal with the neighbors. Kashmir was a perpetual problem, and he failed to reach any successful negotiation regarding Kashmir with the neighbor Pakistan. Nehru had an innate belief in honest fellow-feeling and political generosity. He tried to force a negotiation with the Pakistani government through the United Nations. But the Pakistani military rulers denied any peaceful agreement. The offer of a possible plebiscite was also taken off in 1950. After India's dogged denial of the two-nation theory, a result in favor of Kashmir in the Muslim dominated Kashmir would be a strategic disaster for India. The Kashmir problem remained unresolved, and not even Nehru's diplomatic expertise could give any positive direction to the problem. It still continues to be the one of the key international problems in South Asia.

Nehru and the China Crisis: Nehru's foreign policies concerning China have been made subject to much criticism. However, even in this case, it was Nehru's faith in transparency in the handling of International relations that is seen to be the root of all problems.

Nehru was intent on a very warm and mutually beneficial relationship between India and China. The five-point agreement or the Panchsheel between New Delhi and Peking initiated in 1954 was a result of these negotiations. However, China started patrolling certain parts of the Indian border from 1955 onwards.

Delhi started negotiations to solve the problem in a peaceful way. India, under the leadership of Nehru wanted to take one issue at a time and begin the discussions. The Chinese government, under Chou En-lai wanted to treat the border issue in its entirety at one go. It was gross violation of the five-point agreement. The Chinese denial for the arbitration from the International Court of Justice complicated the problem.

Amidst such tensions, the Chinese suddenly started a full-scale invasion in 1962. It was a rude shock, not only to Nehru, but to the entire international society. The Indian military was unprepared and also unequipped. Both USA and the Soviet extended token help. Soviet was quite busy with the Cuban crisis, however soon after the problem subsided, President Kruschev did extend some help.

American help was minimum, compared to the massive military help that was extended to Pakistan in 1954. On top of that, the Sandys-Rusk team visited India to hold talks in order to make India concede certain areas of Kashmir to Pakistan, a claim that was squarely denied. Nehru stood firm with this faith in the five-point principle.

The international community stood by him, as China withdrew under growing international pressure, fearing isolation and global antagonism. Nehru played his last masterstroke in international policy, as he turned the military defeat in a moral victory for India.

The Chinese invasion had far reaching effects on India's foreign policy. It forced Nehru to change his stance on international affairs. He realized that unmitigated goodwill was not necessary the way the business of foreign affairs was conducted. Nehru's dreams were more or less shattered. It was also a great eye-opener. It made India to see that it is important to strengthen one's military strength and not overtly depend on peaceful negotiations in matters of international affairs. The Chinese invasion was a shock to Nehru, almost shaking his idealistic foundation to the very base. Domestic problems also kept escalating, putting a great degree of mental and physical stress on Nehru.

NEHRU'S BUNGLING FOREIGN POLICY

In one of the most incisive books written about the Tibetan situation, "The Fate of Tibet: When big insects eat small insects" by Claude Arpi, Mr. Arpi shows that not only did the Nehru government betray Tibet, but it also severely destabilized India's national security. In 1947, India had special rights in Tibet, a legacy of the British Raj. In 1949, though clearly aware of China's strategic interests in Tibet, Nehru failed to get any assurance from China that it would not invade the region. However, what is worse is the fact that he did nothing to prevent China from committing blatant aggression against a weak and peace loving Tibet, in 1950. Mr. Arpi provides proof in his book that argument that India was not in a position to halt Chinese aggression in Tibet in 1950 is erroneous and misleading. India had three trade agencies with military escorts within Tibet and with the support and help of the democratic world could have checked the communist aggression. Paying more attention to the Korean War than the happenings in Tibet, Nehru gave an open and clear invitation to China that she could unhesitatingly conquer the poor and helpless nation. In one stroke, Nehru's government was single-handedly responsible for converting the Indo-Tibet border into the Indo-China border. Nehru's reaction was expressed merely in words saying that the "Indian government was perplexed and disappointed by the Chinese Government's action".

Once Tibet was occupied, China undertook a gigantic road-building program between 1951-52. In 1959, Nehru said that it had taken his government over 2 years to notice that the Chinese had been building a road on the barren heights of Aksai-Chin plateau in Ladhak. In his book Mr. Arpi shows that Nehru and his associate Krishna Menon were fully aware of the Chinese encroachment in Aksai-Chin. In 1955, an English Mountaineer named Sydney Wignall deputed by General Thimayya verified reports that the Chinese were building a road through Aksai-Chin. This basically shows that government did know about the encroachment but did nothing about it.

After the Chinese invasion, the Indian government was expected to spring to its feet and make an attempt to consolidate its borders with China. Instead Pandit Nehru started an era of false and pretentious friendship with the Chinese, which culminated in the famous Hindi-Chini-Bhai-Bhai campaign. The Chinese for one, never considered India as any friend, instead cleverly used Nehru's stupidity to further their interests. After having "gifted" Tibet to China, the fictitious fraternization concluded in the so-called "Panch-Sheel" Treaty. Prime Minister Nehru and the Chinese counter part, Chou-En-Lai, signed this treaty on April 29, 1954. "Panch Sheel" literally meant five norms of good conduct, viz. mutual respect for each other's territorial integrity and sovereignty, mutual non- aggression, mutual non-interference in each other's internal affairs, equality and mutual benefit and peaceful co-existence. China very diplomatically signed the treaty but was never intent on following its norms. The treaty was aptly described in the Indian Parliament by the Late Acharaya J.B. Kripalani, a former President of the ruling Congress Party, as "born in sin".

NEHRU AND INDIA'S FOREIGN POLICY

Jawaharlal Nehru, the first Prime Minister of India, has been under criticism from different quarters all through. The reasons of this have been diverse for different political streams. Currently a section of intellectuals is blaming him for forcing India into Socialist Russia's camp. Their argument comes in the backdrop of Left's pressure not to sign the nuclear deal with U.S. One of the inherent arguments of critics of left and others is that not signing it will keep us away from the deeper friendship of U.S., the land of wealth and prosperity, whose alliance will benefit us a lot. In the complex scenario, which our world is, to support or oppose a political line is not easy enough. Also the left while opposing the nuclear deal has an attitude towards nuclear power, energy itself, which is not acceptable to most peace workers. While one will like that the left takes a stand which is totally against the nuclear energy and weapons, this is not the case. The major built in argument in their current stance in opposing the nuclear deal with U.S., is that this will push us in the camp of America, as its satellite ally and that will be the doom of India's foreign policy, which has been that of non alignment. There is a criticism that in the name of non-alignment India was tilted towards the Soviet block of yesteryears. Some also pose the question, is it possible in today's post 'Soviet regime' era to remain non-aligned, not to toe the singular pole of global power, America?

Critics of Nehru's foreign policy undermine the fact that India's foreign policy was aimed at minimizing the domination of imperial powers in the World in general and India in particular. Though U.S. and USSR both were the superpowers, there was some difference in their attitude. While opposing the concept of global poles, one also recognizes that most of the countries which were coming out from the slavery of colonial powers needed to develop their industrial infrastructure. U.S. and U.K. were not for helping these countries with the technological support for this infrastructure while USSR partly helped India in building the foundation of industries, which in turn laid the base for the major industrial growth in times to come.

The contrast is most visible, when India is compared to its major neighbor Pakistan, which allied with America, and the difference in the in the trajectory of two nations is there for all to see. Pakistan, happy with the short cut of supply of industrial goods, as a US ally, free market, no license permit raj, a free economy to begin with landed up as a puppet economy in due course. India seeing that the industrialists here cannot set up the base of industrial growth on their own opted for the mixed economy, public sector, many of which were supported by the USSR, for heavy industries and private sector for the rest. The public sector was labeled as Socialist by all and sundry, without givingmuch thought to the concept of socialism, and was strongly opposed by the right wing economists, communalists and western imperialist powers. U.S. pursued its policies of supporting its minor allies by giving them weapons and ready made goods in return for various things including their loyalty to its global designs.

This struggle between capitalist and socialist model was in turn also a shadow boxing between the upcoming economies in the third world countries and the domination of western ex-colonial powers. U.S. and its allies, with their economic interests being jeopardized by the independent attitude and policies of the third world nations, the success of Soviet block in various fields, stepped up their ideological campaign against socialist ideology. What the Western powers wanted was that the third world should not set up their own industrial base and shouldremain dependent on the U.S. and its allies. The socialist policies in India meant essentially a public sector which will provide the base for growth of theindustries in general and lift up India's level from an economically dominated colony towards the possibility of an strong economy with own say. Interestingly as India began to chart its course after getting independence, the thinking of the big industrialists, which got reflected in the Bombay plan, and Nehru's fascination for growth model of the countries like USSR, which helped them come out fromthe clutches of feudal economic system, matched wellat this point of time. Industrialists did want the state to set up infrastructure industries. Here centralized planning and its accompaniments, which later became frozen and were unable to change with times and led to the demise of Soviet socialist economies.

India's charting independent path with the help of others, more particularly with USSR, in setting up theinfrastructure, helped it stand on its feet, while most of the countries which became independent at that time and opted for pro U.S. policies eventually marched towards banana republics, without the core, the base for their social and economic systems. Parallel to this economic path, India took the road of non alignment. The major opposition to the nonalignment policy came from the BJP and its predecessor Bharatiya Jansangh, who have always advocated thick relations with U.S. Politically their ideologueGolwalkar had listed communists as a threat to Hindu nation. So far the policies of RSS-BJP had always been in parallel to those of US. In late 1940s America was following MaCarthism and hunting communists. Around that time in the aftermath of Gandhi murder, Golwalkar was writing to the Sardar Patel that RSS workers should be released from jails and in turn they will help the government to contain communists. And today when U.S. is leading the global anti Muslim tirade, RSS is the lead organization spreading anti Muslim venom here in India.

USSR had no problems with the this non alignment course in foreign policy so it not only endorsed it but also kept giving core support to India for its indigenous growth. US annoyed with India's not accepting US patronage branded India's policies andnon alignment in general as the decoy for being proUSSR. India did keep supporting the national liberation struggles in Vietnam and many other nations to the annoyance of US. Today with the changed of World scenario, US is keen that India does not formanother block away from U.S., that's why its tilt towards India, away from its nurturing of Pakistan till date.

The basic dilemma which countries like India faced was weather to have 'ready made goods' or to produce the same the hard way. US wanted India to go on this readymade path, while India defied it and pursued independent path. The same got reflected in the foreign policy and attempt to stay clear of US-USSRblocks. It's another matter that USSR for its own strategic reasons was supportive of the non alignment. This had reflection in India's policy vis a vis Israel-Palestine. Israel, the hub of US interests, hand in glove with Western powers, dominated theregion, led to the exile of lakhs of Palestinians and installed an authoritarian state. Palestinians has been struggling for years to get back their own land. Here the aggressor-victim duel was clear and India did opt to keep away from Israel and kept supporting the cause of Palestine. US designs in the region wereprompted by the lust for oil, its policy is hegemonic, it theme, 'Oil is too important to be left to the Arabs'.

In this direction it overthrew the Government of Mossadeq in 1953, installed Raza Shah Pehlvi who in turn brought in superficial westernization notbothering to develop the country's infrastructure. The political rebellion against him was given a religious turn and so came in Ayatollah Khomeini. And with this began another chapter in World history. US projected it as signaling the rise of Islam as the 'new threat'to freedom and democracy and this slogan has been serving it in all its aggressions in the Middle East.

While condemning the foreign policy charted out by the builder of Modern India, Nehru, these ideologuesconveniently forget that it is important for the Worldas a whole to promote democratization amongst nationsand democratization within nations. The attempt tokeep India out of the stifling patronage of US is of paramount importance to ensure the building of democracy amongst nations, away from the hegemony of global bully. The current hegemonic, bullying policies of US, which are the major cause of violence in theworld, aggression on Afghanistan and Iraq was preceded by promotion of terrorist outfits, Al Qaeda and its clones, to fight Soviet occupation of Afghanistan. These need to be understood in their proper perspective. We do have to keep the goal that the world marches towards peace and harmony amongstnations and amongst people.

In the contemporary scenario it is easy and also fashionable enough to criticize Nehru's economic-foreign policy. It is difficult to see todaythat it is precisely these policies of public sectorand non alignment which resulted in India charting the course of democracy and economic growth. One is not saying that what has been achieved is satisfactory. The point is this was the comparatively better option, which did help us go some distance in the direction of industrialization-education in the givencircumstances. World is essentially global, how westrike a balance between external support and internal growth is a million rupee question. Blindly submittingto the wishes of super power number one, may land us up in the direction of many a banana republics or leadto the fate which our neighbor is seeing due toembracing the Uncle Sam. Time that we build the non aligned movement again, time that we promote regional alliances, time that we see the vision of Nehru in its perspective of indigenous growth and global democracy away from thedomination of one or the other superpower. *India Foreign Relations*

BILATERAL AND REGIONAL RELATIONS

Neighbours

Afghanistan: Bilateral relations between India and Afghanistan have been traditionally strong and friendly. While India was the only South Asian country to recognize the Soviet-backed Democratic Republic of Afghanistan in the 1980s, its relations were diminished during the Afghan civil wars and the rule of the Islamist Taliban in the 1990s. India aided the overthrow of the Taliban and became the largest regional provider of humanitarian and reconstruction aid.

The new democratically-elected Afghan government strengthened its ties with India in wake of persisting tensions and problems with Pakistan, which was suspected of continuing to shelter and support the Taliban. India pursues a policy of close cooperation in order to bolster its standing as a regional power and contain its rival Pakistan, which it maintains is supporting Islamic militants in Kashmir and other parts of India. India is the largest regional investor in Afghanistan, having committed more than US$2.2 billion for reconstruction purposes.

Bangladesh: Both states are part of the Indian subcontinent and have had a long common cultural, economic and political history. India played a crucial part in Bangladesh's breakaway from Pakistan. The people of the two countries are indistinguishable to most outsiders. The cultures of the two countries are similar; in particular India's West Bengal and Tripura states and Bangladesh are all Bengali speaking regions. India gave large amounts of aid to Bangladesh. In recent years India provides co-operation and assistance during annual natural calamities. India is a supplier of staple foods such as rice and live animals which helps keep their prices affordable for the masses of Bangladesh. Most of differences are of sharing water resources between the two countries. Also Bangladesh has been accused of providing shelter to militants.

Bhutan: Historically, ties with India have been close. Both countries signed a Friendship treaty in 1949, where India would assist Bhutan in foreign relations. On February 8, 2007, the Indo-Bhutan Friendship Treaty was substantially revised under the Bhutanese King, Jigme Khesar Namgyel Wangchuck. Whereas in the Treaty of 1949 Article 2 read as "The Government of India undertakes to exercise no interference in the internal administration of Bhutan. On its part the Government of Bhutan agrees to be guided by the advice of the Government of India in regard to its external relations." ashton

In the revised treaty it now reads as, "In keeping with the abiding ties of close friendship and cooperation between Bhutan and India, the Government of the Kingdom of Bhutan and the Government of the Republic of India shall cooperate closely with each other on issues relating to their national interests. Neither government shall allow the use of its territory for activities harmful to the national security and interest of the other." The revised treaty also includes in it the preamble "Reaffirming their respect for each other's independence, sovereignty and territorial integrity", an element that was absent in the earlier version. The Indo-Bhutan Friendship Treaty of 2007 strengthens Bhutan's status as an independent and sovereign nation.

Tata Power, is building a hydro-electric dam. This dam, will greatly develop the Bhutanese economy, by providing employment, and by selling electricity, to India, to fulfil India's burgeoning energy needs. Due to this dam, Bhutan, grew at 20+%, the second highest growth rate in the world.

Burma: India was one of the leading supporters of Burmese independence and established diplomatic relations after Burma's independence from Great Britain in 1948. For many years, Indo-Burmese relations were strong due to cultural links, flourishing commerce, common interests in regional affairs and the presence of a significant Indian community in Burma. India provided considerable support when Burma struggled with regional insurgencies. However, the overthrow of the democratic government by the Military of Burma led to strains in ties. Along with much of the world, India condemned the suppression of democracy and Burma ordered the expulsion of the Burmese Indian community, increasing its own isolation from the world. Only China maintained close links with Burma while India supported the pro-democracy movement.

However, due to geo-political concerns, India revived its relations and recognised the new name of Myanmar in 1993 overcoming strains over drug trafficking, the suppression of democracy and the rule of the military junta in Burma. Burma is situated to the south of the states of Mizoram, Manipur, Nagaland and Arunachal Pradesh in Northeast India. and the proximity of the People's Republic of China gives strategic importance to Indo-Burmese relations. The Indo-Burmese border stretches over 1,600 miles and some insurgents in North-east India seek refuge in Myanmar. Consequently, India has been keen on increasing military cooperation with Myanmar in its counter-insurgency activities. In 2001, the Indian Army completed the construction of a major road along its border with Myanmar. India has also been building major roads, highways, ports and pipelines within Myanmar in an attempt to increase its strategic influence in the region and also to counter China's growing strides in the Indochina peninsula. Indian companies have also sought active participation in oil and natural gas exploration in Myanmar.

India is a major customer of Myanmarese oil and gas. In 2007, Indian exports to Myanmar totaled US$185 million, while its imports from Myanmar were valued at around US$810 million, comprising mostly of oil and gas. India has granted US$100 million credit to fund highway infrastructure projects in Myanmar, while US$ 57 million has been offered to upgrade Myanmarese railways. A further US$27 million in grants has been pledged for road and rail projects. India is one of the few countries that has provided military assistance to the Myanmarese junta. However, there has been increasing pressure on India to cut some of its military supplies to Myanmar. Relations between the two remain close which was evident in the aftermath of Cyclone Nargis, when India was one of the few countries whose relief and rescue aid proposals were accepted by Myanmar's ruling junta.

Maldives: India enjoys a considerable influence over Maldives' foreign policy and provides extensive security co-operation especially after Operation Cactus in 1988 during which India repelled Tamil mercenaries who invaded the country. As founder member in 1985 of the South Asian Association for Regional Cooperation, SAARC, which brings together Afghanistan, Bangladesh, Bhutan, India, Maldives, Nepal, Pakistan and Sri Lanka, the country plays a very active role in SAARC. The Maldives has taken the lead in calling for a South Asian Free Trade Agreement, the formulation of a Social Charter, the initiation of informal political consultations in SAARC forums, the lobbying for greater action on environmental issues, the proposal of numerous human rights measures such as the regional convention on child rights and for setting up a SAARC Human Rights Resource Centre. The Maldives is also an advocate of greater international profile for SAARC such as through formulating common positions at the UN. But the Maldives claims the Indian-administered territory of Minicoy as part of its country, that is inhabitanted by Muslims.

Nepal: Relations between India and Nepal are close yet fraught with difficulties stemming from geography, economics, the problems inherent in big power-small power relations, and common ethnic and linguistic identities that overlap the two countries' borders. In 1950 New Delhi and Kathmandu initiated their intertwined relationship with the Treaty of Peace and Friendship and accompanying letters that defined security relations between the two countries, and an agreement governing both bilateral trade and trade transiting Indian soil. The 1950 treaty and letters stated that "neither government shall tolerate any threat to the security of the other by a foreign aggressor" and obligated both sides "to inform each other of any serious friction or misunderstanding with any neighboring state likely to cause any breach in the friendly relations subsisting between the two governments." These accords cemented a "special relationship" between India and Nepal that granted Nepal preferential economic treatment and provided Nepalese in India the same economic and educational opportunities as Indian citizens.

Pakistan: Despite historical and cultural links, relations between India and Pakistan have been plagued by years of mistrust and suspicion ever since the partition of India in 1947. The principal source of contention between India and its western neighbour has been the Kashmir conflict. After an invasion by Pashtun tribesmen and Pakistani paramilitary forces, the Hindu Maharaja of the Dogra Kingdom of Jammu and Kashmir, Hari Singh, and its Muslim Prime Minister, Sheikh Abdullah, signed an Instrument of Accession with New Delhi making the state an integral part of the Union of India. The First Kashmir War started after the Indian Army entered Srinagar, the capital of the state, to secure the area from the invading forces. The war ended in December 1948 with the Line of Control dividing the erstwhile princely state into territories administered by Pakistan (northern and western areas) and India (southern, central and northeastern areas). Pakistan contested the legality of the Instrument of Accession since the Dogra Kingdom has signed a standstill agreement with it. The Indo-Pakistani War of 1965 started following the failure of Pakistan's Operation Gibraltar, which was designed to infiltrate forces into Jammu and Kashmir to precipitate an insurgency against rule by India. The five-week war caused thousands of casualties on both sides. It ended in a United Nations (UN) mandated ceasefire and the subsequent issuance of the Tashkent Declaration. India and Pakistan went to war again in 1971, however this time the conflict was over East Pakistan rather than Kashmir. Due to the large-scale atrocities committed by the Pakistan army, millions of Bengali refugees poured over into India. India, along with Mukti Bahini, defeated Pakistan and the Pakistani forces surrendered on the eastern front. The war resulted in the creation of Bangladesh.

In 1998, India carried out the Pokhran-II nuclear tests which was followed by Pakistan's Chagai-I tests. Following the Lahore Declaration in February 1999, relations briefly improved. However, few months later, Kashmiri insurgents and Pakistani paramilitary forces, backed by Pakistani Army, infiltrated in large numbers into the Kargil district of Indian Kashmir. This initiated the Kargil conflict after India moved in thousands of troops to successfully flush out the infiltrators. Though the conflict did not result in a full-scale war between India and Pakistan, relations between the two reached all-time low which worsened even further following Pakistan's alleged involvement in the hijacking of the Indian Airlines IC814 plane in December 1999. Attempts to normalize relations, such as the Agra summit held in July 2001, failed. Following the attack on the Indian Parliament in December 2001, which too was blamed on Pakistan, there was a standoff between the two countries which lasted for nearly a year raising fears of a nuclear conflict. However, a peace process, initiated in 2003, led to improved relations in the last few years.

Since the initiation of peace process, several confidence-building-measures (CBMs) between India and Pakistan have taken shape. The Samjhauta Express and Delhi–Lahore Bus service are one of these successful measures which have played a crucial role in expanding people to people contact between the two countries. The initiation of Srinagar–Muzaffarabad Bus service in 2005 and opening of a historic trade route across the Line of Control in 2008 further reflects increasing eagerness among the two sides to improve relations. Though bilateral trade between India and Pakistan was a modest US$1.7 billion in March 2007, it is expected to cross US$10 billion by 2010.

The recent terror attacks in Mumbai, however, have seriously undermined the relations between the two countries. India is alleging Pakistan of harboring militants on their soil, while Pakistan vehemently denies such claims. The Pakistani Prime Minister Yousuf Raza Gilani, President Asif Zardari, Foreign Minister Shah Mehmood Qureshi and the Pakistani consulate in India have been at the fore-front of these denials. Relations are currently hampered since

India has sent a list of 40 alleged fugitive in various terror strikes to Pakistan, expecting the handover of the said 40 people to the Indian Government. Pakistan, on the other hand, has openly declared to be having no intentions whatsoever of doing the above said extradition.

Sri Lanka: Bilateral relations between Sri Lanka and India have been generally friendly, but were controversially affected by the on-going Sri Lankan civil war and by the failure of Indian intervention during the Sri Lankan civil war. India is the only neighbor of Sri Lanka, separated by the Palk Strait; both nations occupy a strategic position in South Asia and have sought to build a common security umbrella in the Indian Ocean.

India-Sri Lanka relations have undergone a qualitative and quantitative transformation in the recent past. Political relations are close, trade and investments have increased dramatically, infrastructural linkages are constantly being augmented, defence collaboration has increased and there is a general, broad-based improvement across all sectors of bilateral cooperation. India was the first country to respond to Sri Lanka's request for assistance after the tsunami in December 2004. In July 2006, India evacuated 430 Sri Lankan nationals from Lebanon, first to Cyprus by Indian Navy ships and then to Delhi & Colombo by special Air India flights.

There exists a broad consensus within the Sri Lankan polity on the primacy of India in Sri Lanka's external relations matrix. Both the major political parties in Sri Lanka, viz., the Sri Lanka Freedom Party and the United Nationalist Party have contributed to the rapid development of bilateral relations in the last ten years. Sri Lanka has supported India's candidature to the permanent membership of the UN Security Council.

INDIA & THE US-A DIALOGUE BETWEEN TWO GREAT DEMOCRACIES

India values its bilateral relations with the US. As democracies, both countries have many shared ideals. Relations have also continued to grow with the 15 countries of the European Union, and with Japan. These countries are important economic partners of India, especially in the wake of our economic reforms. However, in pursuing bilateral relations, we have sought to preserve the independence of our viewpoint and protect our national interests from the pressures of conformity. Our relations with Russia have grown over the years to constitute an important foreign policy priority for both countries. There is a recognition in both counties to the strategic dimension of our multifaceted ties. The considerable goodwill for India in Russia has been further cemented in recent years.

Economic diplomacy has been a key component of India's foreign policy. Apart from long established Divisions in the Ministry to deal with economic issues, an Investment Publicity Unit (IPU) was specifically set up in 1990 with a view to disseminating economic information and coordinating the economic and commercial activities of Indian Missions abroad in the light of the recent economic reforms underway in the country. One aspect of economic diplomacy has been the promotion of South-South Cooperation. The Indian Economic and Technical Cooperation (ITEC) Program was established in 1964. Today it extends to 110 countries in Asia, East Europe, Africa and Latin America and facilitates the training of as many as 1000 foreign candidates in Indian institutions each year.

As many as 20 million people of Indian origin live and work abroad and constitute an important link with the mother country. An important role of India's foreign policy has been to ensure their welfare and well being within the framework of the laws of the country where they live.

The strength of any foreign policy depends also on the professional abilities of those who implement it, both at Headquarters and in the field. With a view to ensuring this, the Foreign Service Institute was established to undertake specialist training for entrants into the Indian Foreign Service, and conduct several other specialist courses for Indian and foreign diplomats.

INDO-PAK RELATIONS IN NEHRU ERA: PRAGMATISM ON KASHMIR

Though its use in development of WMD is terrible, science has delivered uncountable comforts to mankind. No only that, it is a great social equalizer also. It has helped the humanity to break the millennia old chained social connections. No individual is superior now on the basis of race, religion and region. Whosoever excels in knowledge can enter into the world of his choice. It was not possible earlier because differentiation and its worst forms such as apartheid, caste system and slavery were being practiced puritanically. The science-induced civility has influenced the psyche of nations also. Hence, assimilation or annihilation of small nations is no more possible. Subjugation, however, still continues, and the poverty of knowledge is the only reason behind it. The victims instead of learning and improving their economies are engaged in confrontation from within and without. Who are to be blamed more, literate outsiders or indifferent insiders?

Chances to bring about change inside are always there, and chances to end external confrontation also appear quite often, but they are not availed due to the indecisiveness of leadership. Though the repeated indecisiveness of small nations usually makes them lose more, it does not spare the big nations either? After WW II, the Soviets should have gone for revision of their stagnant system; fifties was the proper time: they wanted to do it, but didn't, and when they did it, they were too late; and eventually the break-up of the Soviet Union was the only remedy left with them.

The situation in the Indian subcontinent is not so grim, so far. But, given the faulty perceptions and indecisiveness of its rulers, it is likely to become so. The concept that militancy in Kashmir is keeping the Kashmir issue alive, and it is bleeding the Indians, is simplistic, cruel, retaliatory, and self-destructive: In this age of enlightenment it is not possible to assimilate or annihilate small nations.

So, until Kashmiris are satisfied, their peaceful struggle too will create an impact, which would not be negative as created by the militancy. It would be humane and reconciliatory, and hence positive. As far as Pakistan is concerned, it has become totally dependent economically, as its strategy of bleeding India has backfired. Accordingly India too has failed. Its militarism, even if in retaliation to militancy, has made it lose much; if not technically, on moral front certainly. What is needed is immediate end to confrontation and start of positive engagement. Both activities should start simultaneously. It is a difficult decision but it must be taken.

Leadership of Indian subcontinent took many bold and timely decisions in the past. It arrived at a consensus plan to divide India. Afterwards the Liaqat-Nehru Pact on the question of refugees saved Pakistan from unthinkable miseries. Similarly the most difficult of all the questions, the question of lifeline, the water dispute, was resolved through Indus Basin Treaty. But all the good that happened between India and Pakistan is neither discussed nor appreciated in both the countries. However not everything that happened between the two was good. There were grey areas as well, such as wars of 1948, 1965 and 1971, and warlike clashes in Khem Karn, Siachin and Kargil. Alongside these open examples of extreme confrontation, both countries subtly attempted to increase the intensity of each other's internal and external conflicts. Pakistan supported Sikh and Kashmiri struggles and India attempted to fuel the ethnic tension in Sindh.

Why did the good and bad strategies run side by side in Indo-Pak relationship is a very complicated question. However, if answer is to be summarized in one sentence then it can be said with clarity that the fears created problems, and commonness and commonsense led to solution of some of them and those, which remained unresolved remained so mostly due to indecisiveness of the leadership who had faulty perceptions about the ground realities. Any way the prevailing situation demands complete halt to the confrontation, militancy and militarism, because it has already done a lot of damage, and its continuity would inflict more, and that may eventually lead to irreversibility.

It is widely believed that the source that created tension and ills in the subcontinent is issue of Kashmir. Though it is not even the half-truth, let us take it as such. Again the key to solution of Kashmir issue lies with the leadership of India and Pakistan, and not with the Kashmiris. If India could surrender twenty percent of Kashmir to China in Aksi Chin, if Pakistan could settle Kashmir border issue with China—on Chinese terms, and if India and Pakistan could decide the fate of three rivers of Kashmir, then what does stop them from solving the issue in totality?

However, to find an achievable and acceptable solution is not that easy. The process would first require that the parties involved must turn to acceptance of existing realties and try to know how they were shaped. Kashmir was a part of undivided India, though with a status of princely state. Couple this sub-continental status with enormous confronting diversities that are located and locked in a complex and economically unviable geography of Kashmir, no one can and will take the Kashmiris as a separate nation in totality, no matter what they do, and how they fight; and the earlier this is understood, by the Kashmiris of valley, the better. Allow me to elaborate the argument. Kashmir cannot become independent – though in future it may get a special status under the joint Indo-Pak protection – because of its geography and small resources, and also due to the fact that there is a terrible division among the Kashmiris themselves that has basis in religion, ethnicity, geography and desires. The Gilgatis and Baltis do not count themselves as Kashmiris, and they will prefer that their area should become a province of Pakistan at the earliest. The people of Jammu and Ladakh will be happier if their areas are given separate status of states within the Indian Union. The Azad Kashmiris have socially and economically merged themselves with the Pakistanis and it won't make any difference to them if the status of Azad Kashmir is changed to a province of Pakistan.

Accordingly, whether India is in Kashmir due to inhuman Instrument of Accession (designed jointly by the Muslim League and the Congress; on the insistence of the former) and muscle power, or Pakistan has annexed a part of Kashmir through war and support of Kashmiris, the fact remains that both have attained some kind of legitimacy and fifty-six years of occupation has further entrenched their claims. But Indians' legitimacy is, surely, under constant question in the valley of Kashmir. Though it has roots in the concept that divided India, the politico-economic mismanagement by the Indians played a bigger part. And the rest was done by the Pakistan backed resistance, though at a colossal cost that has brought destruction to everything – to life, to soul, to spirit, to intellect and even to the environment. Probable reconciliation between India and Pakistan would save the Kashmiris of valley from further destruction and recover the paradise lost, we can only hope and pray for that. But what is almost certain is that both countries will again be on the right road that was jointly built by their leadership through Liaqat-Nehru Pact, Indus Basin Treaty, Tashkent Declaration, Shimla Accord and Lahore Declaration. Now, once they are on the road, they should remain on it.

FOREIGN RELATIONS AND TRADITIONAL POLICY

India's Foreign Relations reflect a traditional policy of nonalignment (see Glossary), the exigencies of domestic economic reform and development, and the changing post-Cold War international environment. India's relations with the world have evolved considerably since the British colonial period (1757-1947), when a foreign power monopolized external relations and defense relations.

On independence in 1947, few Indians had experience in making or conducting foreign policy. However, the country's oldest political party, the Indian National Congress (the Congress—see Glossary), had established a small foreign department in 1925 to make overseas contacts and to publicize its freedom struggle. From the late 1920s on, Jawaharlal Nehru, who had the most long-standing interest in world affairs among independence leaders, formulated the Congress stance on international issues. As a member of the interim government in 1946, Nehru articulated India's approach to the world.

During Nehru's tenure as prime minister (1947-64), he achieved a domestic consensus on the definition of Indian national interests and foreign policy goals—building a unified and integrated nation-state based on secular, democratic principles; defending Indian territory and protecting its security interests; guaranteeing India's independence internationally through nonalignment; and promoting national economic development unencumbered by overreliance on any country or group of countries. These objectives were closely related to the determinants of India's foreign relations: the historical legacy of South Asia; India's geopolitical position and security requirements; and India's economic needs as a large developing nation. From 1947 until the late 1980s, New Delhi's foreign policy goals enabled it to achieve some successes in carving out an independent international role. Regionally, India was the predominant power because of its size, its population (the world's second-largest after China), and its growing military strength. However, relations with its neighbors, Pakistan in particular, were often tense and fraught with conflict. In addition, globally India's nonaligned stance was not a viable substitute for the political and economic role it wished to play.

India's international influence varied over the years after independence. Indian prestige and moral authority were high in the 1950s and facilitated the acquisition of developmental assistance from both East and West. Although the prestige stemmed from India's nonaligned stance, the nation was unable to prevent Cold War politics from becoming intertwined with interstate relations in South Asia. In the 1960s and 1970s, New Delhi's international position among developed and developing countries faded in the course of wars with China and Pakistan, disputes with other countries in South Asia, and India's attempt to balance Pakistan's support from the United States and China by signing the Treaty of Peace, Friendship, and Cooperation with the Soviet Union in August 1971. Although India obtained substantial Soviet military and economic aid, which helped to strengthen the nation, India's influence was undercut regionally and internationally by the perception that its friendship with the Soviet Union prevented a more forthright condemnation of the Soviet presence in Afghanistan. In the 1980s, New Delhi improved relations with the United States, other developed countries, and China while continuing close ties with the Soviet Union. Relations with its South Asian neighbors, especially Pakistan, Sri Lanka, and Nepal, occupied much of the energies of the Ministry of External Affairs.

In the 1990s, India's economic problems and the demise of the bipolar world political system have forced New Delhi to reassess its foreign policy and to adjust its foreign relations. Previous policies proved inadequate to cope with the serious domestic and international problems facing India. The end of the Cold War gutted the core meaning of nonalignment and left Indian foreign policy without significant direction. The hard, pragmatic considerations of the early 1990s were still viewed within thc nonaligned framework of the past, but the disintegration of the Soviet Union removed much of India's international leverage, for which relations with Russia and the other post-Soviet states could not compensate.

Pragmatic security, economic considerations, and domestic political influences have reinforced New Delhi's reliance on the United States and other developed countries; caused New Delhi to abandon its anti-Israeli policy in the Middle East; and resulted in the courtship of the Central Asian republics and the newly industrializing economies of East and Southeast Asia. Although India shares the concerns of Russia, China, and many members of the Nonaligned Movement (see Glossary) about the preeminent position of the United States and other developed countries, different national interests and perceptions make it improbable that India can turn cooperation with these countries to its advantage on most international issues. Furthermore, although Cold War politics have ceased to be a factor in South Asia, the most intractable problems in India's relations with Pakistan—conflict over Kashmir, support for separatists, and nuclear and ballistic missile programs—still face the two countries.

COMMUNICATION POLICIES IN THE NEHRU ERA

The modernization paradigms pertaining to mass media were crystalised in communication scholarship emanating particularly from the US. The modernization label ascribed to Nehru has spawned many debates in analysing his policies with regard to the onerous and unenviable task of nation building. Nehru's views towards the press is framed in oft repeated references to the fact that he believed in retaining the contours of freedom of expression subsumed in the freedom of the press as is normally suggested and argued. For Nehru, "freedom of expression was an inalienable human right. He was for criticism of persons in authority and a free press.

A free press for him was an essential attribute of the democratic process. He would rather have a free press with all its attendant ills than a suppressed or regulated press." Nehru also believed in regular interaction with the press. His press conferences have been described as one of the instruments for promoting democracy:

"The Nehru era, it is perhaps needless to add, was the journalists` delight. Jawaharlal Nehru was rigorously regular in holding press conferences—as a rule once a month—because he considered the press conference as one of the instruments for promoting democracy. Of course, the numbers were small then and there was no television. A commission room in Vigyan Bhavan and, before it was built, a committee room in Parliament House could accommodate us all. Mercifully, security was also minimal. On the dot at the appointed time, Nehru would take his seat at the dais and start the proceedings. He had devised an excellent system of inviting the Press to mention the broad topics it wanted to discuss. He would then jot them down, have his say on a subject, allow any number of supplementary questions on it, and then move on to the next topic. The verbal feast usually lasted 90 minutes."

The Nehruvian era was marked by an overwhelming belief in mass media and its perceived role in development and nation building. While it is difficult and perhaps ambitious to comment on the general trends in social sciences at that time it can be safely said that the power of media was assumed to be very high supported by successes in especially war and conflict contexts. Terms and concepts such as publicity, propaganda and public opinion were freely used with implied caution about its impact under Fascist dispensations. Advocacy for mass media, especially broadcasting, was very high and at the same time it was also recognized that relegating entertainment and upholding development and nation building was perhaps more viable to a leadership that had established modernization as an underlying framework for its policies and programmes.

The modernization paradigms pertaining to mass media were crystalised in communication scholarship emanating particularly from the US. The passing of the traditional society, mass media and national development, mass media and political development and diffusion studies pertaining to health and agriculture were the main drivers in upholding the argument for the development of mass media in developing nations. "In the years subsequent to independence, India had ventured out to become progressive and industrialized in keeping with the west-inspired dominant paradigm of development of the 1950s through 1970s. Mass media were seen as instruments to change the mind-set of the people and to create a climate for modernization and development through centralized economic planning, large-scale industrialization and the expansion of basic communication infrastructure (Lerner, 1958; Schramm, 1964; Rogers, 1976)."

On this front ideological differences and the camps we wanted to be in did not matter, as belief in mass media was overwhelming. For example, erstwhile Soviet Union and Mao's beliefs and practices endorse the overall belief in communications for achieving national integration. These were sufficient counters to override any opposition on this score. While socialist oriented philosophy guided the approach to broadcasting in the formative years the press seemed to have inherited and promoted capitalism and consumerism since Independence. Specifically with regard to Press, Robin Jeffrey has noted that the formation of Audit Bureau of Circulation, The Registrar of Newspapers in India and National Readership surveys "refract both the efforts of government and the forces of capitalism."

The Nehruvian approach towards institutionalising the Planning Commission and the centralized approach towards development coincided with his belief that plans and programmes have to be carried and communicated to the people. His letter to the Chief Ministers of various states in the early fifties symbolizes the need for creating awareness and the importance of information. His belief in press freedom perhaps withheld his otherwise persuasive abilities to seek their cooperation in his modernization efforts. He addressed his concerns to the press by asking them to cooperate. The press, based on its experience during the nationalist and Independence struggle, had perceived an adversarial role for itself. Further, the elite bias towards the English language press to some extent alienated the administration from people's problems. For example, circulation of English dailies was higher than Hindi dailies and this is evident from the annual reports of the Registrar of newspapers for the Nehruvian era. The inherited legacy of the Indian press had strong association with British and American conceptions of freedom and democracy and the role of the press.

The limited access to press by the government for propagating its development programmes led to a default faith in broadcasting which had safely passed into the hands of the Central Government. Much has been said and written about broadcasting initially by retired senior administrative and programming staff and later by others. While bureaucratic intervention and snippets of policy history are evident in these writings-political, economic and sociological perspectives are the subject matter of contemporary scholarship. The Nehruvian era of broadcasting inherited the Reithean legacy where AIR set out after independence to 'improve' the masses by giving them not "what they sought to hear but what they ought to hear". "The objectives of broadcasting in India sought to provide information, education and wholesome entertainment, keeping in view the motto, Bahujan Hitaya; Bahujan Sukhaya i.e. the benefit and happiness of large sections of the people, and strive to produce and transit varied programmes designed to awaken, inform, enlighten, educate, entertain and enrich all sections of the people, with due regard to the fact that the national broadcast audience consists of a whole series of public"

Nehru's tenure as Prime Minister was marked by at least two powerful ministers of information and broadcasting, Patel and Keskar. In the initial phase, with Sardar Vallabhai Patel, the first and ostensibly the most influential Minister for Information & Broadcasting, at the helm of affairs, a scheme to build up 'pilot' stations with one KW medium wave transmitters was taken up to expand radio broadcasting infrastructure in state capitals and in border areas and to include the linguistic and cultural areas that had remained uncovered. The re-modeling of programmes towards a "nationalist image, a countrywide broadcast of national programmes and the promotion of Hindi as the national language" became a guiding principle. Subsequently, it also saw an unusual but short-lived experiment in the use of folk media for social communication.

B.V. Keskar, perhaps the longest serving minister (for 10 years) of information and broadcasting patronized classical and folk music. His aversion to 'cheap and vulgar' film music and the concomitant rise of Radio Ceylon's commercial service is well known. The inevitable launch of Vividh Bharati is regarded as a response to stem the rising popularity of Radio Ceylon. Critics of Keskar's policies have other theories including his strong roots in one form of Maharastrian culture that disdained particular varieties of music. Nehru's tenure was also marked by the unsavory episode pertaining to the Voice of America offer for setting up a transmitter in the wake of set backs during the conflict with China. This episode in a way also indicts the Nehruvian era for not building and cultivating a communications infrastructure that could reach out to the people in such crises. Apart from lapses in foreign policy, which have been analysed extensively, the role of the then media set up deserves closer scrutiny by scholars. Critique of Nehru approaches to modernization and its top down and trickle down ideas has been the subject matter of past and contemporary scholarship. The ideas are reflective of the overall concern about the failure of certain development options worked out and implemented in the first two decades of our independence. To some extent the faith in broadcasting was overwhelming but in a way it had not translated into any significant allocation for development of broadcasting in India. The number of radio sets (to some extent reliable as we had the licence raj then) was around 50 plus Lakhs. It had grown from around 5.5 Lakhs at the time of Independence to nearly 55 Lakhs by 1965-the end of the Nehruvian era.

A realistic assessment that individual ownership of radio sets was perhaps beyond the means of the intended listeners led to the formulation of a scheme for community listening. It has been observed that by 1965 the number of community listening sets had escalated to 150,000 and the scheme did not thrive due to replacement of batteries and maintenance problems.

On television, clearly there was considerable resistance and perception that it was luxury that India could not afford. It was also based on the already clear impact of the medium in other countries. The limited transmission and launch of television albeit on an experimental basis in 1959 could very well be considered token and reflective of the radio establishment's enthusiasm rather than any Nehru diktat. Scholars may like to pore over his pronouncements to argue the contrary but clearly the medium was not on the nation's agenda. However, the Chanda Committee in it chapter on television does note the pro and con arguments regarding the medium which was reflective of the thought processes during Nehru's tenure.

The philosophy of broadcasting and its use for development was premised on providing exogenous expert inputs. The role of radio in green revolution has been acknowledged so much that a rice variety propagated through radio came to be known as radio rice. The foundations for Science and Technology that Nehru laid and the creation of the Department of Atomic Energy and its subsequent diversification to space programme has one significant contribution through the ideas of Vikram Sarabhai and his team. It was also the formative years of satellite development internationally and there was a slow but deliberate movement towards capitalizing on certain civilian spin offs that certain military/defense technologies offered. Space technology was one of them and communication satellites were the frontier products. It has already been mentioned that resource allocation for broadcasting sector did not necessarily match its perceived importance. Justifiably there were other competing priorities.

What satellite technology in due course promised was a choice between terrestrial based expansion versus satellite technology. This choice was more relevant for television and clearly there was a conflict between the arguments contained in the Master plan of AIR and the leapfrog potential that satellite technology promised for introducing and expanding television in India. The satellite technology brigade was led by Sarabhai and crystalised by his thoughts on television and development. A NAMEDIA document subsequently labelled this enterprise as the Nehru-Sarabhai approach to communication and development.

The Sarabhai approach advocated the use of satellite and satellite based communication technologies for telecom, meteorology and broadcasting. The arguments for broadcasting, particularly, television are crystalised in the text book case of the Satellite Instructional Television Experiment (1975-76) which essentially reversed the logic of broadcast development as a spread phenomenon from the urban to rural areas to rural first and that too in the most backward districts of six states. Nostalgically it can be argued that the villagers in the backward districts of Karnataka, Andhra Pradesh etc had experienced direct reception of television programmes much earlier than the urbanites. Community listening earlier and community viewing through SITE had certain egalitarian social objectives and to some extent had overcome certain social dynamics in a village context. However, its instruction overload negated the good intentions and laid the foundations for fulfilling their nascent appetite for entertainment. What followed after SITE and Mrs. Gandhi's desire in centralized communication system firmly entrenched broadcasting as an important media unit of the Ministry of Information and Broadcasting. Her detractors in the euphoria after winning elections in 1977 did very little to restore the credibility of the media.

The Nehruvian faith in the so-called BBC model of broadcasting has many admirers but few practitioners. The structure of Prasar Bharati occasionally reminds us of its so-called autonomous structure. The Supreme Court's intervention has no doubt de monopolized broadcasting albeit in a very narrow sense.

The proliferation of television channels, the commercial expansion of the FM radio sector and ferment in the print media sector frequently raise questions about media and its role in social sector communication. The struggle for community broadcasting is currently locked in the so called GoM reference and may well come after the commercial players have earmarked territories and drafted their binding conditions for such stations. Seminarians never forget to recall the Nehruvian concern for creating awareness through communication media. His faith in a free press and a promised ideal towards a BBC like broadcasting set up are often hailed. A significant contribution that in a way had an induction effect was Nehru's avowed policy of non-alignment. Although in his lifetime the ideas never got articulated in communication related issues. The call for a New World Information and Communication Order in 1980s refers to certain basics that echo the ideas of Nehru. Since his death the paradigms have been revised and we have new paradigms that talk about participation and horizontal communication structures. It may well be an interesting topic for scholars to thread and link the foundations of modernization and its link to communication policies in the Nehruvian era.

INDIA'S NON-ALIGNMENT DOCTRINE

India's Non-alignment Doctrine as a foreign policy precept was formulated by India's first Prime Minister Jawaharlal Nehru. He continued as India's Prime Minister from its independence in 1947 until his death in 1964, a long spell of seventeen long years. He dominated India's political scene as the indisputable leader of the ruling Congress Party and in the process established India's ruling political dynasty which extends till today. The aura which he acquired as the more visible face of the Congress freedom struggle led to the endowment of a political charisma on him as the Prime Minister of the Congress Party which began governing India in 1947. As a consequence his political decisions became unquestionable including those in the foreign policy field. Foreign policy formulation became personalized in the person of the Prime Minister, Jawaharlal Nehru and continued as such even in the tenures of his dynastic successors, namely his daughter Indira Gandhi and his grandson, Rajiv Gandhi.

India's Non-alignment Doctrine was formulated by Nehru as the touchstone of new India's foreign policy and Nehru steered India in the international community accordingly. Nehru's passionate obsession to non-alignment led him to establish the Non-Alignment Movement (NAM) which he did in the company of leaders like President Tito of Yugoslavia, President Nasser of Egypt, President Sukarno of Indonesia and President Nkrumah of Ghana. They all were leaders of newly independent countries that emerged in the wake of the end of the Second World War and the shake–off of colonial rule of the European powers. But this did not deflect the first major criticism of international observers, and especially Western leaders that Nehru as a highly professed democrat had to rely on the dubious company of military dictators and civil autocrats as founding fathers of the NAM. This criticism grew over the years as NAM expanded and most of the members that were added to ultimately reach a figure of over seventy had similar backgrounds, more or less. It also included countries that were openly allied with the Soviet bloc like Cuba.

Nehru, it seems was attempting to craft a Third World Bloc in the bipolar structure of the Cold War era with idealistic hopes that the newly independent under-developed countries as a bloc could emerge as a ginger group in international affairs and extract maximum concessions from the Big Powers. Also, it was hoped that NAM and India in particular, would be able to stay clear of Cold War entanglement and conflicts. In the process, Nehru reveled in occupying the centre-stage of global politics with his high flown idealistic moral posturing. India gradually started losing international relevance in USA and the Western group of advanced industrialized countries as India's moral hectoring grew and India began adopting double standards in the Cold War standards.

The end of the Cold War and the new international realities that emerged forced India to recognize that non-alignment without political, economic and military muscle was not a workable concept and that if India was to actualize its latent great power potential, it had to shed its ideological obsession with non-alignment and join the international power game in the spirit of the REALISM school of political thought.

This was a total turnaround from the Nehruvian Doctrine of Non-Alignment and obviously had to be taken by a Prime Minister from outside the fold of the Nehru-Gandhi political dynasty. The man of the moment for this bold reversal of Indian foreign policy was P V Narasimha Rao. Subsequently, the BJP Govt under Vajpayee enlarged and added new horizons to India's foreign policy including the defining momentof the 1998 nuclear weapons tests. This has catapulted India into the Big Power league and has made Indian foreign policy trends so initiated as irreversible. So much so that the current Congress Government despite the Nehruvian Foreign Minister (since sacked over the Volcker Report) and Leftists pressure has found it prudent to stay the course set by the BJP Govt.

India today is being widely accepted as an emerging key global player and figuring in the strategic calculus of USA, Russia, China and the EU as a force to reckon with It has achieved this only after discarding the archaic concept of Non-Alignment that it obsessively followed for four decades. Indians of the current generation who would be moving India to its rightful future would naturally question India's losses as a result of the Non-Alignment Doctrine of India's foreign policy?

The answers in brief of India's losses are as follows:

National Security: It suffered as threat perceptions were de-emphasized and defence preparedness was ignored. It led to India's military debacle against China in 1962. It also severely impeded the evolution of independent India's appropriate strategic culture with the obsessive commitment to Pacifism and peace even at the cost of national security interests.

Political Influence: It stood confined to NAM countries as political penetration into global political groupings and strategic partnerships was a taboo as per non-alignment precepts and these partnerships were not open to India bound down by such precepts.

Economic Losses : India was self-prevented from integrating itself into a globalized economy and reaping the benefits of FDI, income generation and jobs generation. Socialistic pattern of economies was the hallmark of NAM countries. The result was poor rates of economic growth and stagnant economies which India could ill-afford for poverty-alleviation for its large population.

Nuclear Weapons as Currency of Power: BJP Foreign Minister was right in pointing out that a "moralistic nuclear policy" (which again was a spin-off from non-alignment moralism) paid no dividends to India. India's defining moment to catapult into the Big League was delayed for a quarter of a century with all the attendant losses.

India's Non-Alignment Doctrine as a foreign policy precept, therefore, has been a monumental failure. It was more idealistic than visionary and lacked the vital content of any foreign policy, namely, realism and realpolitik to secure India's national security interests. It was a poignant failure for Nehru that at the most critical moment of his political career as Prime Minister, the 1962 Sino-Indian Conflict his NAM colleagues failed to come out in his favor the Chinese line; a factor that hastened his death in 1964. So much for non-alignment.

INDIA'S FOREIGN POLICY-50 YEARS OF ACHIEVEMENT

The foundations of India's foreign policy were laid during the freedom movement when our leaders, even when fighting for independence, were engaged with the great causes of the time. The principles of India's foreign policy, that emerged then, have stood the test of time: a belief in friendly relations with all countries of the world, the resolution of conflicts by peaceful means, the sovereign equality of all states, independence of thought and action as manifested in the principles of Non-alignment, and equity in the conduct of international relations.

Under the leadership of Jawaharlal Nehru, India was the founder member of the Non-aligned Movement. India has played an active role in strengthening the Movement and making it an effective voice in representing the collective aspirations and interests o the developing countries on such vital issues as development, peace and stability. India hosted the 7th NAM Summit in New Delhi in 1983. In recent years, after the end of the Cold War, our foreign policy has been focused on strengthening the Movement by redefining its priorities in keeping with the changing times.

India has also been in the forefront of the world community in the struggle against colonialism. Indeed, the Independence of India itself played the role of a catalyst in removing the vestiges of colonialism in other parts of the developing world, particularly in Africa. India was also the first country to raise the question of racial discrimination in South Africa in 1946. It was at India's initiative that the AFRICA (Action for Resistance to Invasion, Colonialism and Apartheid) Fund was set up at the 8th NAM Summit in Harare in 1986. India was the Chairman of the AFRICA Fund Committee, which wound up in 1993.

A notable feature of Indian foreign policy has been its strong advocacy of general and complete disarmament, with nuclear disarmament being accorded the highest priority. Towards this end, India has taken several initiatives within the United Nations and outside. In 1988, India presented to the 3rd Session of the UN General Assembly devoted to Disarmament an Action Plan for Ushering in a Nuclear Weapons Free and Non-Violent World Order.

In order to highlight international concern about the unprecedented nuclear arms race, India was also a member of the Six-Nation Five-Continent joint Initiative in the 1980s. But while India has, and will, remain committed to nuclear disarmament, to be achieved in a time-bound framework, it has consistently and in a principled manner opposed such discriminatory treaties as the Nuclear non-Proliferation Treaty (NPT) and Comprehensive Nuclear Test Ban Treaty (CTBT) and has refused to give up its nuclear options until all countries in the world including nuclear weapon states embrace the idea of nuclear disarmament in a phased manner.

As a founder member of the United Nations, India has been firmly committed to the purposes and principles of the United Nations and has made significant contributions to its various activities, including peace-keeping operations. India has been a participant in all its peace-keeping operations including those in Korea, Egypt and Congo in earlier years and in Somalia, Angola and Rwanda in recent years. India has also played an active role in the deliberations of the United Nations on the creation of a more equitable international economic order. It has been an active member of the Group of 77, and later the core group of the G-15 nations. Other issues, such as environmentally sustainable development and the promotion and protection of human rights, have also been an important focus of India's foreign policy in international forums. Commensurate with national interests and security, the improvement of bilateral relations is an important component of any foreign policy, and India has succeeded in establishing a network of mutually beneficial relations with all countries of the world.

In particular, the improvement of relations with our neighbors has always been one of the pillars of India's foreign policy. India played an historic and unique role in the liberation of Bangladesh which emerged as a sovereign nation in 1971. Through the implementation of the 1964 and 1974 Agreements, the issues of the stateless people of Indian origin in Sri Lanka were resolved. In 1988, India helped preserve the integrity of Maldives by coming to the assistance of that country and preventing an attempted take over by armed mercenaries. The Indian government has taken recent initiatives to further strengthen ties with our neighbors, which have won international appreciation. These initiatives are based on five clear principles: First, with neighbors like Bangladesh, Bhutan, Maldives, Nepal and Sri Lanka, India does not ask for reciprocity but gives all that it can in good faith and trust. Secondly, no South Asian country should allow its territory to be used against the interests of another country of the region. Thirdly, none will interfere in the internal affairs of another. Fourthly, all South Asian countries must respect each other's territorial integrity and sovereignty. And finally, they should settle all their disputes through peaceful bilateral negotiations.

These tenets have paid rich dividends. A landmark Treaty has been signed with Bangladesh on the sharing of waters of the Ganga. With Bhutan and Nepal, major projects of economic collaboration have been advanced. Our relations with Sri Lanka have shown steady improvement. With Pakistan, India ha consistently pursued a policy seeking to improve relations under the framework of the Simla Agreement signed in 1972 which provided for the resolution of outstanding issues peacefully and bilaterally and for establishing durable peace in the Sub-continent. Bilateral discussions with Pakistan have resumed recently and India would continue efforts to have good neighborly relations with Pakistan. An important achievement of India's foreign policy has been the strengthening of regional co-operation. India is an active member of the South Asian Association for Regional Cooperation (SAARC) which was launched in December 1985. With India's full support, SAARC has recently taken significant steps in accelerating the pace of economic co-operation. The South Asian Preferential Trade Arrangement (SAPTA) became operational in December 1995. At the 9th SAARC Summit in Male in May 1997, which was chaired by India, a historical decision has also been taken to strive for a South

Asian Free Trade Area (SAFTA) latest by the year 2001 AD. The emergence of the Indian Ocean Rim Association for Regional Co-operation (IOR-ARC) in March 1997, as a major instrument of cooperation in the larger region, has also had the active support of India.

India's foreign policy has always regarded the concept of neighborhood as one of widening concentric circles, around a central axis of historical and cultural commonalties. From this point of view, it has always given due priority to the development of relations with South East Asia. In 1947, India organized the Asian Relations Conference. It chaired the International Control Commission in 1954 and was a major player in the organization of the Bandung Conference in 1955. Today, India is implementing a 'Look East' policy which is underpinned by important economic considerations. Some significant steps in the pursuance of this policy have been taken with the admission of India as a full dialogue partner of ASEAN and a member of the ASEAN Regional Forum, in 1996.

An attribute of a dynamic foreign policy is the ability to respond to changing developments. The emergence of the Central Asian Republics in the aftermath of the break up of the Soviet Union was one such recent development, and India, given the strategic and economic importance of this region, has been quick to strengthen its bilateral relations with each of these Republics. The shift in recent years by the countries of Central and East Europe to political pluralism and market-oriented structures has also seen India trying to build upon existing business and institutional linkages so as to further strengthen the traditional ties of friendship with the countries of this region.

The countries of the Gulf have a political and strategic importance for India. The region is a major market for Indian exports. Three million Indians are employed in these countries. The strengthening of ties with this region, therefore, has been a priority of India's foreign policy.

With China the aim of Indian foreign policy has been of developing a relationship of friendship, cooperation and good neighborliness, exploiting the potential for favorable growth wherever it exists, even as we seek to find a fair, reasonable and mutually acceptable solution to the outstanding border issue. Towards this aim, a series of high level visits have been exchanged, bilateral trade and economic cooperation is growing, and an Agreement on Confidence Building Measures, as part of a wider dialogue on security, has been signed.

India & the US-A Dialogue between Two Great Democracies

India values its bilateral relations with the US. As democracies, both countries have many shared ideals. Relations have also continued to grow with the 15 countries of the European Union, and with Japan. These countries are important economic partners of India, especially in the wake of our economic reforms. However, in pursuing bilateral relations, we have sought to preserve the independence of our viewpoint and protect our national interests from the pressures of conformity.

Our relations with Russia have grown over the years to constitute an important foreign policy priority for both countries. There is a recognition in both counties to the strategic dimension of our multifaceted ties. The considerable goodwill for India in Russia has been further cemented in recent years.

Economic diplomacy has been a key component of India's foreign policy. Apart from long established Divisions in the Ministry to deal with economic issues, an Investment Publicity Unit (IPU) was specifically set up in 1990 with a view to disseminating economic information and coordinating the economic and commercial activities of Indian Missions abroad in the light of the recent economic reforms underway in the country.

One aspect of economic diplomacy has been the promotion of South-South Cooperation. The Indian Economic and Technical Cooperation (ITEC) Program was established in 1964. Today it extends to 110 countries in Asia, East Europe, Africa and Latin America and facilitates the training of as many as 1000 foreign candidates in Indian institutions each year.

As many as 20 million people of Indian origin live and work abroad and constitute an important link with the mother country.

An important role of India's foreign policy has been to ensure their welfare and well being within the framework of the laws of the country where they live.

The strength of any foreign policy depends also on the professional abilities of those who implement it, both at Headquarters and in the field. With a view to ensuring this, the Foreign Service Institute was established to undertake specialist training for entrants into the Indian Foreign Service, and conduct several other specialist courses for Indian and foreign diplomats.

It is difficult to enumerate the achievements of a country's foreign policy in exactly quantifiable terms. With this as a qualification, it would be a fair assessment to make that Indian foreign policy has sought to preserve, with conviction and consistency, the principles that were enunciated by the founding fathers of the Republic, both in the development of bilateral relations, and in international forums, where our views have won recognition and respect. A significant factor underlying this achievement has been the consensus, cutting across political divides, within the country, on what the basic aims and objectives of Indian foreign policy should be.

7

Nehru Views on Economy

ECONOMIC POLICY REGIME

The rapid economic development strategy of post-Independent India had been one of self-reliant industrialisation under centralised investment planning. It had emphasised basic and heavy industries and adopted public sector as a major instrument in the institutional framework of a mixed economy where private ownership of means of production was permitted in a democratic political environment. The elements of path dependence of this strategy can be traced in the past to the identification of the causes of India's economic underdevelopment in the British colonial policy with laissez faire and free trade (Nayyar 1997).

Under this strategy, the activist state, acting on behalf of the society, assumed heavy responsibility of not only initiating economic development, which the private sector was deemed unwilling or unable to undertake but also shaping the entire pattern of investment (Second Five Year Plan 1956-61, pp. 21-24). The direct involvement of the state in economic development resulted not only in the heavily regulated markets and private economic activities in a functioning market economy but also in a significant extension of the public sector into diverse economic activities going well beyond the traditional economic rationale provided by market failures (Minhas 1991).

The strategy of self-reliant industrialisation that has been characterised as "economic nationalism" by Nayyar resulted in restrictive trade policy regime which had same elements as of the Nurksian strategy of import-substitution-driven industrialisation. Keeping the exchange rate overvalued, which discriminated against exports, and using tariffs and quotas on imports as instruments to contain the resulting excess demand for foreign exchange. Import requirements of basic and heavy industry-oriented industrialisation put further pressure on balance of payments and resulted in progressively more restrictive controls on imports of commodities and capital and perpetual shortage of foreign exchange in the face of non-expanding exports. In order to enable the activist state to guide the course of development toward socially desirable directions, domestic industrial policy reserved strategic industries like iron and steel, machine tools, heavy machinery and minerals for exclusive development in the public sector (Industrial Policy Resolution 1956).

This extended the boundary of the public sector activities beyond those justified by the perceived market failures, namely, electricity, telecommunications, rail - road - and air transport network and other public utilities.

Private industrial activity was sought to be guided toward socially desirable activities under the Industries (Development and Regulation) Act 1951. The important policy instruments used for this purpose included industrial licensing, controls over capital issues, price and distribution controls, and restrictions on foreign collaborations as well as imports of technology.

The activist state needed to transfer financial resources from private savers to itself in order to finance its own expanded activities as also to finance private sector activities in the priority sector. Initially, indirect taxes (excise and customs) were used as instruments to mobilise resources while allocation of private investment was sought to be controlled through industrial licensing. Later commercial banks were nationalised in 1969 to acquire control over private savings in the form of bank deposits.

The instruments of administered interest rates and progressive hike in cash reserve ratio and statutory liquidity ratios were used to transfer the private savings to the government. These were re-channelled through publicly owned term-lending institutions to finance investments in public sector enterprises and government approved private corporate investments. Apart from keeping the administered interest rate artificially low in order to induce private investment, the activist state enacted labour legislations to protect the interest of the industrial workers.

CONSEQUENCES OF THE EARLIER POLICIES

The evolution of post-Independence economic policy discussed above had three basic features: autarchic trade policy, extension of public sector, and direct, discretionary and quantitative controls on the private sector.

These features interacted in the institutional environment of functioning markets and private ownership of means of production to generate perverse incentives that constricted the operation of the market forces and private economic agents and resulted in a low rate of economic growth of 3.5 per cent per annum despite the doubling of the rates of domestic savings and investment over the thirty year period 1950-80.

Public sector units were expected to operate efficiently and generate resources for further investment. Instead, they were saddled with multiplicity of often-conflicting objectives, they had to accept politically driven inappropriate administered prices for their products and services, and were subjected to bureaucratic and political interference, which made their efficient operation difficult. They also faced the 'soft-budget constraint' with neither penalty for losses nor rewards for efficient functioning. Poor performance of public sector units had multiplier effects through inefficient, low quality and often irregular and fluctuating supplies of infrastructure services and universal intermediate inputs (like iron and steel and financial services), which partly contributed to the inefficiencies of the private sector units.

At the macro level, they became a drain on the exchequer through their recurring losses instead of generating resources for investment. Direct, discretionary, mostly quantitative controls on international trade and domestic investment and economic activities were not only inefficient micro economically but also generated perverse incentives (Bhagawati and Desai 1970, Bhagawati and Srinivasan 1975, and Joshi and Little 1994). Progressively restrictive trade regime insulated the domestic producers of import-competing products from international competition with often fair amount of 'water' in high tariffs.

The quantitative controls on domestic investment sought to micro-manage the private enterprises at the upper end of the investment scale by restricting their freedom with respect to output-mix, scale of operation and choice of technology thereby constricting their adjustment to changes in functioning markets. On the other hand, these controls unintentionally offered incentives to divert resources to directly unproductive rent-seeking activities aimed at pre-empting entry of potential competitors. The resulting non-competitive markets did not offer incentives for improving productivity or quality. Thus, the private industrial units had neither the freedom to adjust to market signals nor incentives generated by competition to improve efficiency. They did not lead to 'planned' allocation of private investment either.

At the same time, complex structure of differential indirect tax rates as also administered interest rates and labour legislation led to distortions in relative product and factor prices and resulted in not only inefficient allocation but also misallocation of resources out of line with relative scarcities of capital and labour.

Indian government used the public sector dominated financial system as an instrument of public finance with a complex set of regulations on fixed deposit and lending rates, and channelled credit to the government and priority sectors at below market rates. All these amounted to tax on financial intermediation, which not only reduced the allocative efficiency of intermediation but also resulted in the loss of efficiency and lower real growth of economy.

These regulations made maximisation of working capital and cash-credit loans and project financing as the primary objectives of banks and financial institutions. Monitoring debtors and recovering loans got low priority encouraged by budgetary support. As a result lending occurred with inadequate project appraisal and favoured companies established in line with government dogmas and loan amounts did not have any relation with perceived risks and expected returns. In addition, there was no uniform system of accounting practices, no provisioning for non-performing assets and valuation of securities held in the bank.

SHIFTS IN THE DEVELOPMENT STRATEGY

Trade policy deregulation started slowly in the 1970s under the compulsions of the oil price hikes and the breakdown of the Bretton Woods system of fixed exchange rates gathered some pace in the 1980s supplemented by hesitant relaxation in domestic industrial licensing. The result was the emergence of the Indian economy out of the low growth equilibrium. The growth rate of aggregate GDP that got stuck around 3.5 per cent per annum for thirty years till 1980-81 rose to 5.7 per cent per annum in the decade of the 1980s. However, this coincided with unsustainable fiscal and external deficits leading to the macroeconomic crisis of 1990. The combined external (balance of payments) and internal (fiscal) crisis provided the necessity as well as opportunity to correct the inefficiencies in the public policy framework that was directly responsible for India's inferior economic performance. The result was a strong dose of macroeconomic stabilisation as also microeconomic structural adjustment-oriented policy reforms.

During the last decade of economic reforms, important changes have taken place in the liberalisation and rationalisation of (a) import and export trade controls, (b) domestic and foreign investment, (c) tax structure and (d) public sector and financial sector activities including infrastructure.

Some of these steps have been irreversible while others are reversible. These reforms are being carried out in the environment of coalition politics at the centre. The apparent macroeconomic outcome indeed is impressive: a further rise in the aggregate growth rate in the post reform period to an average of over 6 per cent per annum.

International comparisons show that India has been among the fastest growing economies in the world. However, this average picture, impressive though it is, hides certain disturbing paradoxical features at the beginning of the millennium, namely, slow down in growth rate since 1997-98, re-emergence of large fiscal deficits, excessive accumulation of food and foreign exchange reserves, current account going in to surplus during 2001-02 and April - November 2002, slowdown in private foreign investment, public sector commercial banks are holding more government securities than they are required to hold, interest rates are falling, and despite current agricultural drought inflation is not a problem.

This constellation does not indicate a healthy state of affairs of the economy after a decade long reforms and clearly requires to be understood and explained. In the context of understanding the Indian policy reforms, the present study seeks to

1. Analyse the motivations underlying the wide ranging policy reforms in 1991 which appeared socio-politically infeasible earlier;
2. Take stock of the implementation of the reforms undertaken so far with reference to their (mostly) slow pace;
3. Undertake detailed discussion of two specific interconnected areas with wide ranging repercussions, namely, public sector and labour market reforms which have constrained the potential benefits of trade liberalisation so far and which are likely to pose very serious constraints on future growth.

Both the issues have been on the reform agenda since 1991. Both involve institutional reforms in comparison with mostly procedural reforms that have been carried out so far. Consensus building in a situation of coalitional politics at the centre and some states, and where different political parties might be ruling at the centre and states in a federal structure is a challenging task for both the issues. Most important the benefits from trade liberalisation are going to be undercut by the continued inefficiencies of the public sector and rigidities in the labour market.

In terms of scope, the discussion of public sector reforms would take us into considering important and critical components of the reform process, namely, financial sector reforms critical in the context of capital account convertibility, reforms in the area of provision of infrastructure services with clear cut externalities, disinvestments and privatisation of public sector commercial enterprises which remain shackled with liberalisation applicable only to private sector units, and finally reforms of the taxation system with rationalisation of rate structure and reduction of transaction costs associated with compliance.

Public sector has also become a dominant employer in the organised segment of the Indian labour market. Elaborate and protective labour legislation applies to all the public sector units and only large private units. With private units finding legal and extra legal ways of getting around the labour legislation and with gross over-manning of public sector establishments, efficiency gains from privatisation critically depend on right sizing the public sector units to which all trade unions and left parties are staunchly opposed.

This is where the two areas selected for detailed discussion get connected. Needless to add, labour market reforms are otherwise critical for efficiency gains that would accrue with rationalisation of distorted price structure, which would bring resource allocation in line with relative resource scarcities. Mobility of both capital and labour is an indispensable condition for efficiency gains.

INDEPENDENT ECONOMY POLICY OF NEHRU

The problem, as Nehru told the AICC in January 1947, was "to prepare a concrete picture of what should take" the place of the political and economic system established by the British. He started a nation wide campaign in favour of land reforms, industrialisation, planning and adoption of a model of economic growth which could make India self-reliant.

Countering the mischievous propaganda that planning meant regimentation and the rise of totalitarianism, he declared that planning meant the most rational use of available resources to achieve certain nationally accepted goals which could bring about an improvement in the standards of living of the people and strengthen political independence of the country. It did not mean the negation of freedom of the people.

He cleared many a confusion about what planning meant. He was appalled at the ignorance of even those who were involved with planning.

> *I would say that most of the people have no conception of what planning means. With all respect to those who use the word planning frequently enough even members of the Planning Department and the like-I would say that most of them have not the remotest conception of what planning means. Each person moving about in a little circle is not planning. Planning is a conception of the whole and developing each aspect of that whole in relation to other parts. You cannot plan separately, you cannot plan departmentally, you cannot plan in any way unless you grasp that planning means an all-round development of national economy and national life. You must bear the whole picture in mind and then you have to consider the basic things first on which the rest of the superstructure may be built. We shout a lot about our industries. In India they started mostly with jute, cotton textiles and the likes. They did some good and a lot of harm. But they are more or less auxiliaries, superficial industries, dependent on other countries for machinery, etc. You cannot industrialise a country by these superficial industries.*

The requirement was primacy to basic and heavy industries and infrastructural facilities like power which alone could lay down the foundations of a self-reliant economy. Nehru reiterated: "Let us have as great a measure of self-sufficiency as possible. If we are not self-sufficient, we are dependent on other countries, maybe for food, maybe for other things. If we are dependent we may get into conflicts while we may avoid them if we have a large measure of self-sufficiency.... Self-sufficiency does not mean cutting the international trade which will increase but not in the basic things that we require."

Replying to those who wanted to divert India from the path of economic development to achieve self-reliance because they asserted that India was a country of spiritualism and non-material values and the emphasis on the development of material production would destroy these long-cherished values, Nehru retorted: "For a hungry man or a hungry woman truth has little meaning. He wants food. For a hungry man, God has no meaning. He wants food. And India is a hungry, starving country and to talk of truth and God and even of many of the fine things of life to the millions who are starving is a mockery. We have to find food for them, clothing, housing, education, health and so on-all the absolute necessaries of life that every man should possess. When we have done that we can philosophise and think of God." In this endeavour to build a new India, the Soviet Union was a natural ally and India could learn much by cooperating with the USSR. Even months before the achievement of political independence formally, Nehru, while addressing the Soviet delegation to the 34th session of the Indian Science Congress, held in January 1947, said:

> *You are our neighbours and as neighbours we must take interest in each other; we must know each other and develop closer contacts with each other.*
>
> *But apart from being neighbours, you have been pioneers in many fields and you have transformed the vast tracts of your country before our eyes with a speed that has astonished humanity. Inevitably, when we want to produce great changes in India, we want to learn from your example. We want to know what you have done and how you have done it. Among the many things that you have done is this tremendous flowering of science in the Soviet Union and the application of that science to the betterment of human beings who live in those vast territories.*
>
> *It is our purpose also to better the lot of the millions who live in India and we want to utilise science to that end and want to learn from you what you have to teach in that respect.*

Internally, Nehru was of the view that there was no hope for the transformation of the Indian economy into a modern one without planning and without active State intervention. The role of the State in the economy was perfectly justified "because, after all, State is the expression of society." Ever since the days of Adam Smith the whole conception of the role of State had undergone a big change. It was no longer confined to protection of the citizens from external dangers and internal turmoil and the provision of certain communal services like roads, health and medical facilities, educational and training institutions.

The extent of State intervention might be a matter of detail and of argument. "But it is obvious that the State will intervene more increasingly in the future because life has become complex. You must have planned authority otherwise there will be chaos. It is quite impossible for the State not to interfere in the trade and commerce. It has interfered in the past and it will interfere more and more in the future."

In India planning and the active intervention by the State in economy were indispensable. The "key industries must inevitably be controlled very closely by the State." "Talking of industry as it is in India today sometimes seems to be a misnomer. Most of our so called industrialists are hardly industrialists. They are in reality financiers; that is not industrialisation. They are buying up industries here and there but there is hardly any industry as such. The prime need in India is industrial power. Without power we can achieve little. It is power that we want and there are big schemes to be operated: unless we have planning, we cannot achieve anything." The increasing skewness in the distribution of incomes and wealth in the country also necessitated the State intervention if the future social turmoils were to be avoided and harmony to be maintained. During the war this skewness had sharply increased and fiscal policies had failed to make any appreciable impact on the situation. Obviously, this happened because a handful of people could amass wealth and incomes by resorting to illegitimate methods and indulging in black marketing. "There is something wrong in this and the thing must be brought under human nature control. Maybe it is a fault of human nature; if so, human nature must be controlled. The spirit of the twentieth century demanded that the profit motive should go and give place to planned distribution. It is not good to have such enormous discrepancies between individuals in India. How it has happened I do not know; I cannot understand it by any mathematical calculation."

Nehru was among the few top leaders of the Congress, who comprehended the mechanism of colonial exploitation of India and its changing features since the middle of the nineteenth century. He was determined that the economy of Independent India must be out of the colonial shackles. He put his foot down on the question of giving or maintaining any kind of safeguards to British commercial and industrial interests in Independent India. He categorically stated that "no Indian Government can possibly approve of putting up with any form of safeguard or any kind of protection for anybody."

The interests of Indian nationals would be given primacy over those of foreign nationals. The latter would have to operate within the framework of rules and regulations and priorities laid down by the Government of India. The British private enterprise would not enjoy any position of superiority and preference. The aim of Independent India would be "to make India as little dependent on external agencies in the economic sphere as possible and also to make her as self-sufficient as possible.

Independent India of his conception was to follow a different road while developing its economy than that followed hitherto by other countries of the world, except the Soviet Union. "I want India to be an advanced country and develop her trade, not in an aggressive spirit or by creating any vested interests in other countries, but in a cooperative spirit. I dislike imperialism, political or economic. I do not want my own country to indulge in economic aggression because I think that leads to conflicts and war with other countries. In order to avoid such conflicts I want India to develop on more cooperative lines." At the same time, he categorically stated: "I do not want India to be a suppliant country." In a significant communication to Asaf Ali who was for sometime India's ambassador to the USA, Nehru wrote:

> *The United States are a great power and we want to be friendly with them for many reasons. Nevertheless I should like it to be made clear that we do not propose to be subservient to anybody and we do not welcome any kind of patronage. Our approach, while being exceedingly friendly, may become tough if necessity arises, both in regard to political and economic matters. We hold plenty of good cards in our hands and there is no need whatever for us to appear as suppliants before any country.*

Till then India did not have any significant official level contacts with the Soviet Union and Nehru wanted that this situation must be remedied. In a message to the people of the Soviet Union on January 12, 1947, he stated: "It is inevitable that free India should develop friendly relations in cultural and other matters with the people of the Soviet Union. If there is no other compulsion, there is the compulsion of geography and our being neighbours. But there are other reasons also, for we have much to learn from them." He felt that both countries had interest in and responsibility for maintaining world peace. Their mutual friendship would be useful for world peace.

World peace, however, could not be brought in so long as nations were not free and human beings in large parts of the world were denied security and opportunity in economic matters. Urgent steps must be taken to solve the problems of poverty and backwardness of the people "or else crisis and disaster might overwhelm us. We havc, therefore, to think in terms of the common man and fashion our political, social and economic structure so that the burdens that have crushed him may be removed, and he may have full opportunity for growth."

There were misgivings and misconceptions in the minds of Indian big businessmen about the policies of the government of Independent India and most of these arose out of ignorance. It fell on Nehru to enlighten its members and he tried to do it in his inaugural address to the annual session of the Federation of Indian Chambers of Commerce and Industry (FICCI) in March 1947. He explained:

> *Planning means having some conception of the goal we are striving for, of the kind of society we are aiming at, trying to work up towards that end harmoniously and peacefully with as few upsets as possible, laying down targets so that on all sectors we may advance simultaneously. If we advance on one sector and do not advance on others, even that one sector will come to a stop, and we will face bottlenecks and difficulties.*

The policy of the government was oriented towards encouraging industrialisation so that India's manpower was most rationally and fully utilised, no one who wanted and was capable of adding to the national output was denied the opportunity to do so and in this industrialisation there was no essential conflict between cottage industries and large-scale industries.

As the large-scale industries will not be in a position to absorb the vast manpower of India for a long period of time, the development of both types of industries could be adjusted which also necessitated planning. Then, there was another consideration for resorting to planning.

> *It should be remembered that economic factors do not recognise the limitations of boundaries. If we have the Damodar valley scheme, it will affect at least two provinces-Bengal and Bihar. It is not a Bengal scheme or a Bihar scheme. If we have a river commission for the Ganga valley, it will affect three provinces.... If we plan for the whole of India, the only right way to plan is to bring up the industrially backward parts so that there may be a balanced economy in all parts of India, not that a part of India should be industrialised and a part remain agricultural. That will be bad for India from every point of view, not only for the respective parts but for all. It is acknowledged from the defence point of view that industry should be spread out. Of course, nobody is going to force down something against the will of a province; a province will have to agree to and carry out that plan, but if the conception of a plan is to become provincial, it will become ineffective.*

According to him, the main problem of India was to increase its national output, which was increasing at a minimal rate. But, this did not mean that the problem of distribution would be neglected and it was wrong to say that "distribution would look after itself; in future, if there is no proper distribution and no proper social justice, there are going to be conflicts on an enormous scale. Therefore distribution must be taken in hand and considered as a highly important factor. Nevertheless, I do say that the production is the first thing today."

Nehru had a solid reason for giving primacy to production over distribution and it had much to do with his conception of building a self-reliant economy for India. The resources for such an operation had to be largely raised from internal sources and the task of capital accumulation would become easier if the production increased at a faster rate to yield a higher rate of savings and capital accumulation.

In this context it is difficult to agree with Prof. S. Gopal that "the enthusiasm was now tempered by the responsibilities of office. Radical theories of distribution gave place to an emphasis on production, and he no longer regarded nationalization as a talismatic concept." In fact, it was sound economics that informed Nehru's stand. Frankly speaking, on the eve of Independence, there were very few industries which could have qualified themselves for nationalization on the basis of a realistic analysis of their situation. The largest industries, namely, cotton textiles, jute and sugar had already entered their phase of sickness. Their nationalization could have complicated the situation rather than helping economic growth. Both cotton textile mills and jute mills were in the grip of an unprecedented crisis for a lack of raw materials because most of the areas which has been supplying raw cotton and raw jute had gone to Pakistan.

Prof. Gopal has ignored Nehru's appeal to industrialists, while inaugurating the annual session of All India Manufacturers' Conference on April 14, 1947. He told them that he was in favour of rapid industrialization of the country but this should be oriented towards bettering the standards of living of the people at large and not towards enriching only a handful of industrialists. "Raising the standard of living of the masses must be the first priority in any scheme of industrial advancement and not a subsidiary benefit that may follow from industrial reconstruction."

Referring to nationalization, he pointed out that it "should, of course, be discussed in a practical way and not in a theoretical sense.... At the present moment we have to consider what is the best way to get over the present economic difficulty and not indulge in schemes which may obstruct and delay progress during a very vital period of our existence."

Soon after Independence, the AICC met in New Delhi in November 1947 and appointed the Economic Programme Committee, headed by Jawaharlal

Nehru. Members of the Committee included Maulana Abul Kalam Azad, Jayaprakash Narayan, N.G. Ranga, Gulzari Lal Nanda, J.C. Kumarappa, Achyut Patwardhan and Shankar Rao Deo. The Committee, in turn, constituted four sub-committees to deal with the problems of agriculture, small-scale and cottage industries, large-scale industries and organization of distribution network.

The committee was asked to draw up the economic programme of the Congress so that the next task after the achievement of political independence, that is, "the establishment of real democracy in the country and a society based on social justice and equality" could be accomplished. The AICC talked of extending democracy from the political to the social and economic spheres. It made a significant statement that "Democracy in the modern age necessitates planned central direction as well as decentralisation of political and economic power, in so far as this is compatible with the safety of the State, with efficient production and the cultural programme of the community as a whole.... In so far as it is possible, national and regional economic self-sufficiency in the essentials of life should be aimed at. In the case of industries, which in their nature must be run on a large-scale and on centralised basis, they should belong to the community, and that they should be so organised that workers become not only co-sharers in the profits but are also increasingly associated with the management and administration of the industry. Land, with its mineral resources, and all other means of production as well as distribution and exchange must belong to and regulated by the community in its own interest."

The Economic Programme Committee defined the aims and objectives of the Economic Programme of the Congress which were to include, among others, (a) a quick and progressive rise in the standard of living of the people to achieve a national minimum standard within a reasonable period, (b) full employment, (c) maximum utilisation of material and manpower resources of the country, (d) equitable distribution of the existing income and wealth and prevention of the growth of disparities in the course of industrial development and the fixation of a ceiling of incomes, not exceeding forty times the national minimum and in the course of time the upper limit to be brought down to twenty times the national minimum, and (e) decentralisation so far as it was possible in the context of country's internal and external security, and national and regional self-sufficiency along with a proper balance between rural and urban economy.

It proposed a radical restructuring of agrarian relations and the establishment of direct relations between cultivators and the State. "Land should be held for use and as a source of employment." The Committee wanted imposition of a ceiling on landholdings, replacement of the existing land revenue system by progressive taxation of agricultural income and promotion of cooperatives.

It wanted coordinated development of village and cottage industries with large-scale industries, a strong and ever-expanding public sector, acquisition of excessive margins of profits, stable and friendly industrial relations and abolition of managing agency system.

It recommended establishment of a permanent Planning Commission which should work for a quick and progressive rise in standard of living, full employment, increase in production through maximum utilisation of resources, reduction in the distribution of incomes and widest diffusion of opportunities. In December 1947, the then Congress president, Dr. Rajendra Prasad, appointed an Agrarian Reforms Committee under the chairmanship of Dr. J.C. Kumarappa. It went into the agrarian situation, prevailing in the country after the abolition of intermediaries like zamindars, jagirdars, and talukdars. It was of the opinion that there could be a lasting improvement in agricultural production and efficiency only after comprehensive reforms in the land system. It was generally against subletting of land and recommended protection of non-owner cultivators. Any cultivator who cultivated a holding for six years continuously must get occupancy rights automatically. The future pattern of the agrarian economy must rest on four pillars, namely, (a) it should provide an opportunity for development of farmer's personality, (b) there should be no scope for exploitation of one class by another, (c) there should be maximum efficiency, and (d) it should be practicable.

Among other recommendations were assurance of a reasonable income to farmers through stabilisation of prices, crop insurance, appointment of agrarian reforms commissioners, regulated markets, multipurpose cooperative societies, scaling down of rural debts, provision of alternative sources of rural credit and protection of agricultural labourers.

A look at these recommendations reveals that they were just elaborations of the recommendations of the NPC and its subcommittees. They bore the imprint of Nehru's thinking and influence.

Nehru had to wage a strong battle to establish Planning Commission. In the second half of 1949, Nehru invited Dr. Solomon Trone, an American, who had considerable knowledge of planning in the Soviet Union to have a look at the Indian economy and recommend how its planned development could be organised.

Dr. Trone submitted a detailed report, recommending strongly the immediate establishment of the Planning Commission which should be an autonomous body, entrusted with the task of formulation and execution of a plan. Referring to the Soviet model of economic growth, the emphasis was placed on the establishment of capital goods industries in the beginning. Steel plants, machine-tool industry, engineering and heavy electrical industry were to be given priority.

Nehru welcomed these recommendations while the top bureaucracy resisted their implementation. The latter was in favour of setting up a Council of Economic Administration, comprising secretaries of economic ministries of the Government of India with responsibility to coordinate the activities, concerning economic development. A proposal to this effect was made by N. Gopalaswamy Ayyangar, a cabinet colleague of Nehru, who did not have any connections with the Congress or the National Movement. As if to placate Nehru and the Congress, a suggestion was appended that only when it was known that the people could have confidence in developmental schemes originating from an outside agency of experts, largely non-official, the government could consider setting up a Planning Commission.

Nehru could not take this lying down. It seemed, he was being outmanouvred by a group of bureaucrats and his struggle for planned development of the country for more than fifteen years was going to be in vain. He asserted that the failure of India on economic front was not due to any lack of effort but to a lack of appreciation of a particular situation and of data to judge it. This problem could not be solved without having an organised effort at planning. He was convinced that there was no lack of resources in the country, the main problem was to mobilise them and channelise them into various developmental activities according to a scale of priorities determined with a view to achieve certain clear-cut objectives.

All this meant having a plan and a planning body. He wrote to his cabinet colleague, John Mathai, on September 13, 1949: Indian capitalism had "proved totally inadequate to face things as they are today in the country. They have no vision, no grit, no capacity to do anything big. The only alternative is to try to put forward some big thing ourselves and rope in not only these classes but the people as a whole. Otherwise we remain stagnant and at the most ward off catastrophe."

He underlined the dangers of dealing with the problems separately and in isolation from the main task of country's overall socio-economic transformation. What was needed was an integrated approach and its formulation by a planning body. It was sad that the provinces of the country were thinking and working out their schemes of development in isolation from one another and this was not a happy situation.

An effective planning machinery could have coordinated their activities and directed by keeping in view the national perspective. These concerns found an echo in his letter to John Mathai, one of the staunchest opponents of planning in his cabinet, on September 29, 1949: "We may make mistakes and pay for them, but surely the greatest mistake is not to view the whole scheme of things in its entirety, realistically and objectively, and to decide on clear objectives and plans.

If once this is done, the next step of complete coordination follows much more easily and only by coordinated effort can real results be achieved." Mathai did not relent in his opposition to Nehru's efforts at setting up a Planning Commission, which, he thought, would reduce the importance of capitalist class and make it subservient to the State. Nehru did aggravate Mathai's fears when he wrote to him on February 16,1950 that a Planning Commission was needed to "balance the various social forces at work in India, and pay more attention to what might be called the vital forces which will ultimately lead to progress." Three months later, Nehru told Mathai that he was responsible to the masses who had trusted him and put him in the position of leadership and had commitment to Mahatma Gandhi's teachings. Gandhi had provided him his sheltering care all these years. He was unlike Mathai and others who had always served the government of the day irrespective of its complexion. It was difficult for Nehru to betray the trust of the people.

In the meantime (January 1950) the Congress Working Committee adopted a resolution calling for the establishment of a Planning Commission. Nehru told his opponents in the Cabinet that he was bound by the mandate of the Congress Working Committee and they could decide their course of action. This led to the resignation by John Mathai and the Cabinet approved the proposal to establish Planning Commission with Nehru as its chairman to enable it to get its recommendations cleared by the government without difficulty. In April 1950 a conference of chief ministers and PCC presidents took place in Delhi "to formulate an economic programme for the country and to devise the best methods to implement the programme."

To achieve a social order in which there would be justice— social, economic and political-"it is necessary to formulate not only a short-term but also a long-term plan, initially to cover a period of five years?"

The resolution at the Conference stated:

While the long-term plan will necessarily have to be well integrated and all-inclusive and will require a clear demarcation of the phases through which it should be worked out by the country and the people, for the purpose of the immediate programme, attention will have to be determined to indicate the order in which action for the fulfilment of the programme can most effectively be taken.

For the implementation of such a programme, emphasis should be laid on the rousing of mass enthusiasm and consciousness which alone can make it a people's programme. It will also be necessary to create such institutions as cooperatives in agriculture and industries and Panchayats, and to arrange for the training of local leadership to man the institutions. In the background of our limited resources, economic planning presupposes a period of austerity on the part of the people. In order to secure voluntary self-denial on a nationwide scale for the purpose of a programme of planned regional development, efforts should be made to create a sense of equality of sacrifice among all sections of the community.

It wanted fast recovery of the economy from the damages of the Second World War and the Partition of the country. It called for the creation of conditions for maintaining a stable and fair price level and for launching a more comprehensive planning with a view to "(a) promoting a balanced economy in agriculture, large-scale and basic industries, village industries and social services; (b) rationalizing production in agriculture and industry and taking steps for the establishment and administration of a just and decentralised cooperative economy; (c) bringing a definite rise in the standard of living of the people as a result of planned economy which guarantees a fair remuneration to those who participate in the creation of wealth." It said the rate of capital formation should be raised and local projects should be linked to local investible surplus. Besides there was need to promote multi-purpose cooperatives throughout the country.

The Delhi Congress of 1951 declared: "The Congress stands for the progressive extension of the public sector" and "The private sector should function in close accord with the public sector in the fulfilment of common national objectives "and also "Labour should be able to participate in the day to day working of industrial undertakings and in the handling of the general problems of each industry." It recommended the formation of village production councils charged with responsibility of developing and increasing production and should serve as link between the people and the agencies of the State. The Congress wanted incentives for organising small uneconomic holdings into cooperative farms. It emphasised the reorganisation of the whole system of production and distribution with the object of achieving the ends of social justice. The existing disparities in standards of living in rural and urban areas, backward and advanced regions and between different economic strata of the population were to be progressively narrowed down, and a ceiling was to be imposed on incomes and taxation and other economic policies were to be reoriented towards this. There was need to meet the requirements of planned development of the economy on the basis of internal mobilisation of capital. The First Five Year Plan was formulated by taking into account the ongoing projects for the rehabilitation of the ravaged economy. Though it was in the right direction, it did not lay down a clear-cut ideological framework and model for self-reliant economic growth. However its various constituent elements were embodied in the Plan. For example, Nehru told the Parliament, while speaking on the First Plan, that he had "no doubt at all that without the development of major industry we cannot raise the level of existence in this country. In fact, I go even a step further and say, we cannot remain a free country without heavy industries, for they are essential for our defence." He stressed the urgency to remove inequalities because they were inimical to the smooth running and success of political democracy, and adult suffrage would become meaningless.

> *He beseeched the Parliament to look at the Plan from a broader angle and not merely with a critical eye. We must remember that it is the first attempt of its kind to bring the whole picture of India—agricultural, industrial, social, and economic—into one framework of thinking. That is a very important thing. Even if it is wrong in parts, it is a tremendous achievement. It has made the whole country 'planning conscious'. It has made us realise mentally and emotionally that we are a united nation. We tend to go off at a tangent and think along narrow provincial, communal, religious or caste lines. We have no emotional awareness of the unity of our country. Our Plan has challenged us to think in terms of the good of the nation as a whole apart from the separate problems which we have to face in respect of our villages, districts or provinces. Therefore, the mere act of framing this plan and of having produced this report is something for which we can congratulate ourselves.*
>
> *We might remember that when we talked about planning two or three years ago, powerful voices were raised against it. It was said that planning should confine itself just to helping industry by tariffs, by subsidies, and so on. It should not interfere with the economy in any other way. While the essence of planning is some kind of controlled economy, our present plan only talks about a public and a private sector. Now, the private sector must function within controls in numerous ways. It must be controlled in regard to the dividends and the profits that it makes, but that is not enough. We have to control the strategic points of the economy of the country, for example banking and insurance... so as to fit them in more and more within the purview and sphere of a controlled economy.*

He promised that the Second Plan would be an improvement on the first. It would be more effective and far-reaching. Its model and philosophy would be clearly spelt out.

These views of Nehru were given an important place in the resolution on Five Year Plan, adopted at the Hyderabad Congress in January 1953. It called upon the people to give their cooperation and assistance for the success of the Plan. The same year in July, the AICC at Agra stressed three important points, namely, the speedy completion of land reforms, change in social structure to induce economic progress and the urgency to mobilise as much savings as possible to increase investments. All through the period of the First Five Year Plan, both Nehru and the Congress talked of a welfare society or social, economic and political justice and the equality of opportunity as the goal of economic development. They rejected capitalism and called for institutional changes to end the relations of production, which were exploitative. They, however, did not talk of socialism as their goal or objective. Nehru, as usual, campaigned in favour of socialism and wanted the Congress to accept it as goal, but, till this happened, he had to go by the accepted position of the Congress. Speaking at a meeting of the National Development Council on November 9, 1954 he said:

> *Take private enterprise. It is undoubtedly useful so far as our country is concerned; we wish to encourage it, but the dominance it exercised throughout the world, during a certain period, is no more. It is out of date in that sense. For a planner, it has no secondary place. A system which is based purely on the acquisitive instinct of society is immoral. That does not mean we are going away with private enterprise. I think there is much scope for it, and we must give it freedom and encouragement to develop. But we have to realise that the days of the acquisitive element in society are passing; other factors are coming in. Even in the highly capitalistic countries the social element is increasing at a tremendous pace. We have also to think on these lines and get out of the static habit of thinking. We have to be clear about the broad picture we are aiming at.*
>
> *The picture I have in mind is definitely and absolutely a socialistic picture of society. I am not using the word in a dogmatic sense at all. I mean largely that the means of production should be socially owned and controlled for the benefit of society as a whole.*

All through his tenure as president of the Indian National Congress during the 1950s, Nehru had one constant refrain in his speeches, that is, self-reliance. "We must seek to build up our strength on ourselves and not by dependence on others. Dependence in one direction leads to dependence in another. Nations, it is said, by themselves are made. By self-reliance, we shall command respect and we shall make our country more and more our own, of each one of us. For building a self-reliant economy people have to work hard and make great sacrifices.

They have to remain ever vigilant to avoid waste and reserve to increase the investible resources. This attitude would give strength to the country. "Our strength will come not from building up arms or entering into a competition in armaments, but from the development of our country and the well-being of our people." Retrospectively, the first general elections of 1952, held on the basis of universal adult suffrage, proved that Nehru's economic policies were well received by the people. He was greatly enthused.

He directed the Planning Commission to go ahead with the task of preparing the Second Five Year Plan. The Planning Commission invited experts from the Soviet Union and other socialist countries for discussions and interactions. Prof. P.C. Mahalanobis was to prepare the basic framework of the Second Plan which was to lay down the foundations of India's independent economy. As Nehru described later there was, at the meetings of the Commission, 'electricity in the air'. Nehru emphasised the need for a bolder approach in the Second Plan preparation. Nehru also realised that the time had come for declaring socialism as the primary goal of the country because "welfarism", "egalitarianism", "socio-economic justice", "equality of opportunism", etc. were too vague to rouse the enthusiasm of the people and they did not convey the message that India was trying to build a socio-structure which would be alternative to capitalism. The mere rejection of capitalism was not enough, the shape of what was going to come in its place was no less important.

INDIAN ECONOMIC PLANNING SYSTEM IN NEHRU PERIOD

In a planned economy, major economic decisions such as what and how much is to be produced, when and where it is to be produced and to whom it is to be allocated will be determined by a central authority such as the State, through the Planning Commission.

And the Government will have the powers of implementation. Before the Plan is drawn up, a detailed survey of all available resources – physical resources, financial resources and human resources – has to be made. For example, in the former Soviet Russia, after the Revolution in 1917, there was War Communism between 1918 – 1921. And there was New Economic Policy (NEP) from 1921 to 1924. And from 1924, the Government made a detailed survey of all available resources and only in 1928, it implemented its First Five Year Plan.

After the survey of resources, the objectives of planning will be determined. For example, one of the long term objectives of Soviet Planning was that Soviet Russia should catch up with the production levels of the leading capitalist nation of the world, namely U.S.A., in steel, coal and electricity. Keeping in mind, the objectives of the Five Year Plan, the physical targets will be fixed. And ways and means of mobilising financial resources will be explored.

The Plan will also spell out the details in which the fruits of planning will be distributed in a fair and just manner. The nature of planning is determined by the type of economic system – capitalism, socialism, mixed economy - in which it is practised.

There will be partial planning in a capitalist economy, (e.g., U.K.) but a socialist economy is a totally planned economy (e.g., Former Soviet Russia). In a mixed economy like India, both public sector and private sector play important roles in economic planning. Usually, the period of a Plan is five years. The Plan has to be drawn in advance. It is done by the Planning Commission in India. A plan will be of a definite size and it will fix the targets for the Plan period and it will also indicate the ways by which the financial resources are to be mobilized for the Plan.

The first step in drawing up a Plan is to determine a growth target for an economy over the Plan period. The planners then divide the economy into a number of sectors such as agriculture, industry and service sector.

The planners will fix the physical targets for the sectors and also decide how much investment must be made in each sector to achieve the targets. Then they will decide the right type of investment projects and production techniques. As the UDCs are poor, labour-intensive techniques will expand employment opportunities. But some heavy industries like steel have to be capital – intensive. The success or failure of a Plan depends upon the choices that are made.

Types of Planning

1. *Centralized Planning* : In a socialist economy (eg. Former Soviet Russia), there was centralized planning; it was planning by direction. In a socialist state, most of the means of production are owned by the State. All basic economic decisions such as whether priority is to be given for industrialization or for development of agriculture ; if it is decided to give importance to industrialisation, whether to give importance to basic and heavy industries or for consumer goods industries will be made by the central authority.
2. *Planning by Inducement* : In a democracy, Planning is done by inducement. For example, ours is a mixed economy where there is a public sector and a private sector. The government has to persuade the industries in the private sector to fulfil the goals of the Plan through inducements such as tax concessions and by providing incentives.
3. *Indicative planning* – In this type of planning, the government invites representatives of industry, and business and discuss with them in

advance what it proposes to do in the Plan under question and indicates to them its priorities and goals. Then the Plan is formulated after detailed discussions with varied interests. Planning in France is a good example of indicative planning. After we embraced liberalization and privatization policies in 1991, even Indian planning, in a way, has become indicative planning.

Economic plans can also be divided into midterm plans, shorterm plans and perspective plans. Our Five Year Plans are in fact, midterm plans. Short term plans are Annual Plans. During the period of implementation, Five Year Plans operated by dividing them into Annual Plans. Perspective Plans are long term plans and the period ranges from 20 to 25 years. The Five Year Plans are formulated by taking into account the long term objectives of the Perspective Plan.

Rolling Plan : Unlike the Five Year Plan with fixed targets, in the case of the rolling plan, at the end of each year, targets will be fixed by adding one more year to the Plan. That is, without fixed targets for all the five years, depending upon the performance of the Plan in the current year, targets will be fixed for one more year. Like this, it will go on a continuous basis. That is the idea behind the rolling plan.

A great advantage of centralized planning is that plans can be implemented with great speed and targets and goals can be achieved. For example, by means of planning, former Soviet Russia transformed its economy, which was predominantly agricultural into a predominantly industrial nation, within a short span of 12 years.

But a demerit of centralized planning is that as the State enjoys a considerable degree of monopoly, in the absence of competition, it is rather difficult to test the productive efficiency of state owned units.

Under planning by inducement (democratic planning), though there is a good deal of freedom for people, because of the procedures and delays associated with the democratic process and because of Parliamentary democracy, there will be a lot of delay in the implementation of programmes and economic growth will be slow.

Evolution and Objectives of Planning in India

The National Planning Commission was set up in India in 1950. A major function of the Planning Commission was to "formulate a plan for the most effective and balanced utilization of the country's resources". The Planning Commission formulated the First Five Year Plan for the period (1951–56). Since then, we completed nine Five Year Plans and we are now in the midst of Tenth Five Year Plan (2002–2007).

ECONOMIC PLANNING PROCESS

Meaning and Need for Planning

The 20th century was an era of planning. Almost every country had some sort of planning. In socialist countries, planning is almost a religion. Even in countries like the U.S.A. and the U.K. with a capitalistic system, they have partial planning.

The 19th century State was a *Laissez faire* state. It followed a policy of non – intervention in economic affairs. But the modern State is a Welfare State. The two World Wars, the Great Depression of 1930s and the success of planning in former Soviet Russia have underlined the need for planning. Planning is a gift of former Soviet Russia to the world. For, it was the first country to practise economic planning on a national scale. According to Lionel Robbins, "strictly speaking, all economic life involves planning.... To plan is to act with a purpose, to choose and choice is the essence of economic activity". In the words of Barbara Wootten, "Planning may be defined as the conscious and deliberate choice of economic priorities by some public authorities".

Many economists today agree that planning is an organized, conscious and continuous attempt to select the basic available alternatives to achieve specific goals. Planning involves the economizing of scarce resources. Most of the underdeveloped countries of the world became independent only fifty or sixty years back and most of them were poor at that time. So it became the main business of the Governments of the newly emergent nations to provide food, clothing and shelter to their people. For that, first of all, they had to increase their national income. Since most of them were agricultural countries, they had to evolve some programmes for agricultural development. Not only that, they had to industrialize their economies. And they had to provide more jobs to their people. That means, they had to do something for expanding employment opportunities. Further, as most of them were wedded to some kind of socialism, they had to reduce inequalities of income and wealth. All these things, the poor countries attempted to do by means of economic planning.

Laissez faire policy is a luxury for modern governments. So they have economic plans. In the developed nations of the world, they plan for economic stability. But in the underdeveloped nations, they plan for economic growth and development. Another main reason for the emergence of planning in underdeveloped countries is the failure of the market mechanism. The capitalist economy is basically a market economy and price mechanism works through the market system. The price system is a basic institution of capitalism. The allocation of resources and distribution of rewards are done through the price system. All decisions of the businessmen, farmers, industrialists and so on are guided by the profit motive. If the market is perfect, price system is good. But if there is monopoly and other types of imperfect competition, the market system fails. And it calls for government intervention by way of planning.

INDIAN ECONOMY IN THE FUTURE

What is in store for the Indian economy in the years to come? To be specific: what will be the pace of its growth? Besides, will it be wise to entrust the commanding heights of the economy to the private sector and relegate the state to a secondary position? Lastly, is it true to say that the Nehru-Indira era was disastrous to India's economy and the present momentum has been generated by the reforms under Washington consensus-based globalization?

These questions have been very convincingly answered in a not long ago released paper "Why India Can Grow at 7 per cent a Year or More: Projections and Reflections," by Prof. Dani Rodrik of the Harvard University and Arvind Subramanian of the IMF.

The performance of the Indian economy during the initial decades after Independence was so low that it invited jeers. And it was ridiculed as the "Hindu" rate of growth. Saner people did regard it as disappointingly low but not as disastrous in view of the kind of the problems inherited by the Nehru government. The British had partitioned the country and its economy had to bear its consequences. In addition, during the British rule the economy had developed in a lopsided manner. Capital goods sector was very unequal to the task of country's transformation into a modem industrialised economy. The forces of regionalism, casteism and communalism were ever ready to fragment the country. Moreover, the country faced invasion from China and conflicts over Kashmir and, later, Bangladesh. Western powers did their best to create troubles for India. Their stand on Kashmir and the liberation of Goa illustrated this. If one keeps all this in mind, one cannot dismiss the average yearly rate of 1.7 per cent at which the economy developed as calamitous. Since 1980, the rate of economic growth has been accelerating and during the next two decades it averaged as 3.8 per cent per annum. Only China and East Asian countries surpassed this rate of growth. Here one must remember that Indian growth rate was not subject to violent fluctuations. In fact, it was more stable than the behaviour of the growth rate in China and East Asian countries. Last, as Dani Rodrik and Arvind Subramanian underline, "the contribution of growth of total factor productivity to overall labour productivity growth was the highest in India about 60 per cent -a performance that was only surpassed by China. Indian per capita income growth has therefore been extensive motored by productivity and hence sustainable in the future, rather than based on deferred gratification, which runs into the limits imposed by diminishing returns to capital."

Now, let us turn our attention to the first quarter of the present century. Rodrik and Subramanian are of the view that during this period total factor productivity is likely to grow by 2.5 per cent per annum. Because of the changes 'in the demographic structure, dependency ratio is likely to decline from 0.62 in 2000 to 0.48 in 2025. This will lead to a rise in private and aggregate savings from 2.5 per cent to 3.9 per cent of GDP and will boost the rate of domestic investment. The rate of growth of capital stock will increase from 6 per cent to 8.3 per cent annum. During the next twenty years, working population will increase at 1.9 per cent per annum. Even if the level of education and the participation of labour in productive activities remain unchanged, the growth of labour will contribute another 1.3 per cent to the overall economic growth rate. And aggregate growth rate will come to 6.7 per cent and per capita growth rate to 5.3 per cent. Increasing total factor productivity, growing stock of skilled human capital and strong institutional base will be major factors in boosting the average growth rate of the Indian economy.

India will, however, have to worry about three things in particular. First, as the two authors have pointed out, growing regional disparities have to be tackled urgently. They have noted: "One disturbing trend in the last two decades of rapid growth has been the growing disparity in economic performance between two groups of states. Instead of convergence among the states, we see divergence... with peninsular India growing more rapidly than the hinterland BIMARU states. Moreover, in the future, this trend could widen as existing advantages are reinforced by new technologies. A related disparity that the future threatens is between skilled (typically urban) and semi-and low- skilled labour (typically rural) within and across states." Second, continuing dependence on the monsoon is worrying. Since almost one quarter of GDP comes from agriculture, any big shortfall in the monsoon rains or irregularity in their pattern may lead to big fluctuations in the overall economic growth rate. Last, fiscal situation continues to cause worries because neither deficits have been brought down nor have public debts been curtailed. The efforts of the government to raise adequate resources have not succeeded.

The authors have taken to task those who been attacking, day in and day out, Nehru's economic policies. What they have said needs to be carefully pondered over and its essence grasped. To quote: "In the conventional view of the Indian development process, there was a long and dark period the period of controls and import substitution followed by the burst of sunlight and reforms since 1991. The boom in the IT sector first awakened observers to the facts that the dark age was not all dark; important cumulative elements (the fundamentals) were being built up that yielded rewards with a lag; and triggers that sparked the IT boom. In this case, the fundamentals were the pools of skilled human capital built up through the technology, management, and research institutes sort of import-substitution effort in skilled human capital that were integral to the Nehruvian vision.

"Nevertheless the Nehruvian economic legacy went beyond the technical institutions. It included the meta-institutions of democracy: the rule of law, free press, and technocratic bureaucracy that recent research shows are crucial to economic development. To be sure, these meta-institutions have been buffeted and weakened over time by the vicissitudes of vested interests, time, and politics. It is also true that the potential created by these institutions went unexploited through decades of misguided throttling of private economic activity.... The house that Nehru and others painstakingly built before and after independence, wobbles and all, is now poised to seize the newly created opportunities."

The authors have cautioned India that it must avoid the mistakes made by Latin America in the 1990s by going in for economic liberalization and privatization without giving adequate consideration to the existing conditions in the country and the likely consequences for the people at large. It must see whether the existing institutions are in a position to support them. "Economic growth is best sustained by keeping the private sector excited about investing in the local economy. This requires a pragmatic list of policies toward the private sector that combine carrots with sticks, incentives for dynamic efficiency with market disciplines. The knee-jerk reaction of many economists to move as quickly and as broadly as possible in areas such as privatization (especially in the infrastructure sectors), labour market reform, and capital-account liberalization has to be tempered with serious empirical analysis and an appropriate concern for social and distributional impacts. The habitual pragmatism and gradualism of Indian policymaking, dictated by the need to manage pluralism and diversity the organizing principle of the "idea of India" is here more of an asset than a liability."

Bibliography

Ahmad, Imtiaz: *State and Foreign Policy: India's Role in South Asia*, New Delhi, Vikas, 1993.

Ahmed, Waheed: *Quaid-I-Azam Muhammed Ali Jinnah : Speeches Indian Legislative Assembly 1935-1947*, Quaid-i-Azam Accademy, 1991.

Ambedkar, B. R.: *Annihilation of Caste: An Undelivered Speech*, Arnold Publishers, New Delhi, 1990.

Anand, Som. *Lahore: Portrait of a Lost City*. Lahore: Vanguard Books, 1998.

Anthony, J. Parel : *Hind Swaraj or Indian Home Rule*, Cambridge University Press, 1925.

Asghar Ali.: *Mandal Commission Controversy*, Ajanta Publications, Delhi, 1991.

Ashton, S.R.: *British Policy Towards the Indian States, 1905-1939*, London: Curzon, 1982.

Balan, K. : *Mahatma Gandhi and Jawaharlal Nehru : The Two Stalwarts Who Shaped India*, Delhi, Authorspress, 2002.

Barill, C.: *Social and Political Ideas of B.R. Ambedkar*, Aalekh Publishers, Jaipur, 1977.

Bhattacharya, Sabyasachi : *Vande Mataram : The Biography of a Song*, New Delhi, Penguin, 2003.

Bose, Sipra: *Social Mobility Among Untouchables*, Cohesion and Conflict in Modern India, New Delhi, 1978.

Bourai, Himanshu : *Gandhi and Modern Indian Liberals*, Delhi, Abhijeet Pub., 2004.

Chakrabarti, Santosh : *Studies in Tagore : Critical Essays*, New Delhi, Atlantic, 2004.

Chaudhary, M.: *Partition and the Curse of Rehabilitation*, Calcutta, Bengal Rehabilitation Organization, 1964.

Dan Nabudere: *The Political Economy of Imperialism*, London, 1977.

Dash, Nibedita : *Life and Thoughts of Gandhi and Nehru*, New Delhi, Dominant, 2004.

Dhawan, S.K. : *Discovery of Indira Gandhi : A Select Chronology*, Wave Pub., Delhi, 1986.

Dubois, Abbe: *Hindu Manners, Customs and Ceremonies*, AES, New Delhi, 1983.

Frankel, Francine: *India's Political Economy, 1947-1977: The Gradual Revolution*, Princeton, Princeton University Press, 1978.

Ganesan, L.: *Relevance of Reservation*, Valentina Publications, Madras, 1991.

Gaur, Mahendra : *Indian Political Parties Annual*, Delhi, Kalpaz Pub., 2006.

Ghosh, Ila : *Rgvedic Rsikas : Life and Philosophy*, Eastern Book Linkers, Delhi, 2007.

Ghosh, Suresh Chandra: *Education Policy in India since Warren Hastings*, Calcutta, Naya Prokash, 1989.

Gopal, S. : *Selected Works of Jawaharlal Nehru*, New Delhi, 1994.

Hasan, Mushirul: *India's Partition: Process, Strategy and Mobilization*, New Delhi, Oxford UP, 1993.

Jha, Prem Shankar: *India: A Political Economy of Stagnation*, Bombay, Oxford University Press, 1980.

Joan V.: *Conquest of Violence; The Gandhian Philosophy of Conflict*, University of California Press, Berkeley, 1965.

Kamble, J. R.: *Rise and Awakening of Depressed Classes in India*, National Publishers, New Delhi, 1979.

Karve, Irawati: *Hindu Society: An Interpretation*, Sangam Press, Poona, 1961.

Kaushik, Asha : *Globalization, Democracy and Culture : Situating Gandhian Alternatives*, Jaipur, Pointer, 2002.

Kripalani, Krishna : *All Men are Brothers*, Navjivan Publishing House, 1937.

Mahar, Michael J.: *The Untouchables in Contemporary India*, University of Arizona Press, Arizona, 1972.

Maheshwari, Shriram: *Rural Development in India: A Public Policy Approach*, New Delhi, Sage, 1995.

Maheshwari, Shriram: *Rural Development in India: A Public Policy Approach*, New Delhi, Sage, 1995.

Meyer, Mark J.: *Religion as Social Vision: The Movement Against Untouchability in 20th Century in Punjab*, University of California Press, Berkeley, 1982.

Michel, A. A.: *The Indus Rivers: A Study of the Effects of Partition*, New Haven, Yale UP, 1967.

Mishra, Anil Dutta : *Challenges of 21 Century : Gandhian Alternatives*, New Delhi, Mittal Pub., 2003.

Murthi, R.K. : *Discovery of Nehru*, Indian Pub., Delhi, 1993.

Narula, Sanjay : *Indian Politics*, New Delhi, Murari Lal and Sons, 2007.

Nevile, P.: *Lahore: A Sentimental Journey*, New Delhi, Penguin, 1993.

Noorani, A.G. : *Indian Political Trials : 1775-1947*, New Delhi, Oxford University Press, 2005.

Prasad, Lal Bahadur : *Indian Political System and Law*, New Delhi, Shree, 2005.

Pruthi, R.K. : *Indian Political Thought*, New Delhi, Mohit Pub., 2007.

Ravikant and Saint, Tarun K.: *Translating Partition*, New Delhi, Katha, 2001.

Ray, B.N. : *Gandhigiri : Satyagraha After Hundred Years*, New Delhi, Kaveri Books, 2008.

Saksena, N.S.: *India: Towards Anarchy, 1967-1992*, New Delhi, Abhinav, 1993.

Salim, Ahmad: *Lahore 1947*, New Delhi, India Research Press, 2001.

Sankar Ghose: *Congress Presidential Speeches*, New Delhi, 1975.

Sarkar, J.: *Caste, Occupation and Change*, B. R. Publishing Co., Delhi, 1984.

Sarvepalli Gopal: *Jawaharlal Nehru: An Anthology*, Delhi, 1980.

Trivedi, P.R. : *Concise Encyclopaedia of India*, Indian Pub., Delhi, 1998.

Yasin, Mohammad : *Indian Politics : Processes, Issues and Trends*, New Delhi, Kanishka, 2004.

Index

I

L

M

N

O

P

R

S

T

U

W

❑❑❑